Writing Successful Undergraduate Disse[r]tations in Games Development and Computer Science

Writing a dissertation in the final year at university can be a highly daunting task for any student, but particularly if the degree is practically oriented and implementation based. This book provides an accessible, concise guide to producing a dissertation in computer science, software engineering, or games development degrees, with research projects typically involving design, implementation, testing, and evaluation.

Drawing on the authors' extensive knowledge and experience of supervising dissertation students, the book offers a step-by-step guide to the key areas of writing a dissertation alongside real-life examples. Chapters cover:

- Producing literature reviews.
- Formulating research questions.
- Understanding epistemologies.
- Selecting methodologies and research methods.
- Software development life cycle methodologies.
- Evaluation, statistical analysis, and formulating conclusions.

Working methodically through the different stages of writing a dissertation, this is an essential comprehensive guide for all students producing any form of dissertation in computer science, software engineering, or games development.

Thomas Hainey is Programme Leader of Computer Games Development at the University of the West of Scotland, UK.

Gavin Baxter is a lecturer in Computer Games Development at the University of the West of Scotland, UK.

Writing Successful Undergraduate Dissertations in Games Development and Computer Science

Thomas Hainey and
Gavin Baxter

Routledge
Taylor & Francis Group

LONDON AND NEW YORK

Cover image: © Getty Images

First published 2023
by Routledge
4 Park Square, Milton Park, Abingdon, Oxon OX14 4RN

and by Routledge
605 Third Avenue, New York, NY 10158

Routledge is an imprint of the Taylor & Francis Group, an informa business

British Library Cataloguing-in-Publication Data
A catalogue record for this book is available from the British Library

Library of Congress Cataloging-in-Publication Data
Names: Hainey, Thomas, author. | Baxter, Gavin, author.
Title: Writing successful undergraduate dissertations in games
development and computer science / Thomas Hainey and Gavin Baxter.
Description: First Edition. | New York : Routledge, 2023. |
Includes bibliographical references and index.
Identifiers: LCCN 2022023968 | ISBN 9780367517076 (Hardback) |
ISBN 9780367517083 (Paperback) | ISBN 9781003054887 (eBook)
Subjects: LCSH: Dissertations, Academic--United States--Authorship. |
Dissertations, Academic--Research--Methodology. | Computer
science--Study and teaching (Higher) | Computer
games--Programming. | Computer games--Design. | Application
software--Development.
Classification: LCC LB2369 .H26 2023 | DDC 808.06/
6378--dc23/eng/20220902
LC record available at https://lccn.loc.gov/2022023968

ISBN: 978-0-367-51707-6 (hbk)
ISBN: 978-0-367-51708-3 (pbk)
ISBN: 978-1-003-05488-7 (ebk)

DOI: 10.4324/9781003054887

Typeset in Bembo
by MPS Limited, Dehradun

Contents

Acknowledgements

Combined acknowledgements

We would like to thank all of the alumni, colleagues, and contributors who made this book possible and as informative as it is. Special thanks to:
 Alan Williams, Julie Black, Sabbir Ahmend Chowdhury, and Dr. Jan Elizabeth Smith.

Thomas Hainey

To the memory of my mother Anne Hainey who died during the production of this book and the memory of my father Thomas Hainey. May you both sleep peacefully. I would also like to thank Jim Aitken for his support. Finally I would also like to acknowledge my colleague Dr. Gavin Baxter for his efforts, patience, and friendship over the years and also the students who inspired me to write this book.

Gavin Baxter

I would like to dedicate this book my mother Maureen Baxter and to the memory of my father Gordon Baxter. I would also like to acknowledge my research colleague, Dr Thomas Hainey, for his friendship throughout the years and for helping to make the writing of this book a very worthwhile and knowledgeable experience.

How to Use This Book

This book is written to guide honours students to write successful dissertations in games development and computer science. We impart our knowledge and experience of supervising hundreds of dissertation students in the last decade to assist you (the student) on your dissertation path and academic journey.

We will take you through every part of an honours dissertation we can think of. This book is something of a how-to guide, with some specifics, and it also shares ideas and pointers when specificity is impossible. We have tried to strike a balance between answering all your questions while also being thought-provoking enough to provide ideas for your own unique dissertation. If you are stuck, there will hopefully be a section in our book to guide you and put you on track so you are never confused or out of ideas.

This book is your essential guide to writing a successful dissertation project in your field in a methodical, easily understandable manner, and all you have to do is read it to generate countless ideas to help you move forward to unlock your graduate capabilities, fulfil your potential, and achieve your dreams.

Dissertation examples

This book uses real-life practical dissertation examples from Table 0.1. The excerpts and examples are kindly used with permission from the authors. Throughout the book, the dissertation will be referenced with '*Dissertation*' and the appropriate letter.

Table 0.1 Dissertation key

Reference	Title	Author
A	Development of a 3D platform game to evaluate game aesthetics and level design typologies to support the game dynamics of fun, challenge, and reward.	Kenneth Yorke (Games Development Graduate)
B	Development of an Entity Relationship Editor and Schema Generator. •	Thomas Hainey (Software Engineer Graduate)
C	Reviewing Artificial Intelligence in the context of games development: an analysis of its application within racing games.	Kamil Witonski (Games Development Graduate)
D	Analysing the effects of progression in RPGs.	Alasdair Hendry (Games Development Graduate)
E	Effects of Narrative on Player Immersion, Motivation and Engagement.	Michael O'Neil (Games Technology Graduate)
F	Development of a Requirements Framework for a Serious Game to Teach Rudimentary Programming Concepts in Higher Education.	Thomas Hainey (Computer Science Graduate)
G	Development of a 3D Platform Game to Evaluate Game Aesthetics and Level Design Typologies to Support the Game Dynamics of Fun, Challenge and Reward.	Julie Black (Games Development Graduate)
H	Investigating the level design principles that are required to develop a truly convincing survival horror game.	Michalis Antonis (Games Development Graduate)
I	Using Blogs for Organisational Learning: A Case Study in an ICT Division.	Gavin Baxter (Computer Science Graduate)
J	Does MySQL stand up against more powerful DBMSs in relation to a company's needs?	Stuart Graham (Software Engineer)
K	Using games-based learning to teach requirements collection and analysis at tertiary education level.	Thomas Hainey (Computer Science Graduate)

USEFUL TIPS (UT)

We have placed useful tips throughout this book that will be highlighted and summarised using the abbreviation key: **UT**. We will summarise these in the final chapter.

1 Introduction to Dissertations

In this chapter you will learn:

- What a dissertation is.
- Why writing one is a challenge.
- Why academic writing and dissertations are important.
- Why dissertations in games development and computer science are different.
- Preparation is key.
- Some techniques of committing yourself to paper.
- About finding your voice.

Stephen King, bestselling author and master of horror, alludes to writing being a process. When asked "*how does he write?*," he invariably answers – "*one word at a time.*" Dissertations and horror novels are no different in that respect, and for games development and computer science, students can be associated with horror!

Are you a typical games development or computer science student in your last year of university? Have you met all relevant criteria to graduate with your bachelor's degree, and are you progressing to honours level? Congratulations, and well done on getting this far! Now there is a gargantuan and unfamiliar task before you: a major piece of individual research and development to be written up in a dissertation!

An honours degree in higher education (HE) in Scotland requires 480 credits, with 120 credits coming from level 7, 8, 9 and 10 of the Scottish Credit and Qualification Framework (SCQF) (SQA, 2020). What sets it apart from an ordinary degree is that it includes a research element, which can come in the guise of a dissertation in the final year. In Scotland, this dissertation can account for nearly a third of the available credits. In England, Wales, and Northern Ireland, an honours degree is part of the three years associated with undertaking a bachelor's degree and must be completed at level 6 of the

DOI: 10.4324/9781003054887-1

Framework for Higher Education Qualifications (FHEQ) (QAA, 2014). This again includes a large independent research and development project. In the USA, the structure is fairly similar, where a thesis or project is required beyond the normal bachelor's degree. In Australia, an honours degree requires the production of a high-quality research thesis. We know that we are using the words '*thesis*' and '*dissertation*' interchangeably, and we will discuss this distinction shortly. We could continue to dissect the educational structure of every individual country, but we would most likely conclude that an honours (Hons) classification requires research, reporting, implementation, and evaluation, all presented in a dissertation. No matter where you hide on this planet, if you want an honours degree, you will have to write.

Whether this idea makes you feel good, bad, or indifferent, we want to reassure you that we have written this book to share all of our secrets for writing a successful dissertation in games development and computer science; these secrets include essential pointers and easily understandable examples. This is a journey of deep learning and opportunity, an exciting, gratifying challenge well within your capabilities. Everything up until this point has prepared you to tackle this new problem, and we have written this book to help you succeed.

What is a dissertation?

The *Concise Oxford Dictionary of Current English* defines a dissertation as "*a detailed discourse on a subject especially one submitted in partial fulfilment of the requirements of a degree or diploma.*" The derivation of the word from Latin origins comes from the word '*disserto*' meaning to "*discuss, discourse, argue or negotiate*" (Latin Dictionary, 2022). The Royal Literary Fund (2020) distinguishes the differences from an essay, exploring exactly what the word '*debate*' implies; that is, you will examine not only a subject but also the different points of view on that subject. They also present a definition that encompasses scholarly mastery of a subject, implying that comprehensive knowledge must be raised to a superior level.

This means knowing your selected subject and demonstrating investigative, critical analytical skills, integrity, specialisation, and objectivity. Objectivity means to detach from the research and material collected, critically and logically evaluating pros and cons, and then reporting these findings in an impersonal, balanced, unemotional manner without letting passion for your subject override better judgment.

You likely have heard about three pieces of academic work during your education. It is important to clarify what we mean by these (since they are easily confused) but also to make you aware that some of these definitions overlap and are used interchangeably, depending on the source and country. These are: '*essay*', '*dissertation*', and '*thesis*'. AllAssigmentHelpUK (2016) provides a useful distinction:

- An '*essay*' is usually considered to be a smaller piece of work presenting a personal view of the writer, exploring a stance or argument about a subject with 1500–2500 words.
- A '*dissertation*' is "*is a written work that helps in advancing a fresh point of view resulting from research. It is usually a requirement for an advanced educational degree.*" Greetham (2019) highlights the most obvious difference between an essay and a dissertation as one of size. Essays can range from 2000–3000 words and a dissertation from 8000–12000 words requiring extensive analysis and critical evaluation of a greater volume of material.
- A '*thesis*' is usually longer than a dissertation and generally refers to an advanced degree by research, such as a doctorate, but can be relatively small in a scientific subject.

The terms '*dissertation*' and '*thesis*' are used in different ways depending on where you are in the world (Paltridge and Starfield, 2007). In the UK, the term '*dissertation*' is generally for honours or masters level, and the term '*thesis*' is for a PhD, whereas in the USA, a '*thesis*' is for masters or honours level and '*dissertation*' is for a PhD. Generally, '*thesis*' and '*dissertation*' can be used interchangeably (Paltridge, 2002).

Why is writing a dissertation challenging?

Dissertation students are considered to be the upper end of the academic elite who have proven themselves worthy of progressing into the honours system. Paltridge and Starfield (2007) compiled the following general expectations of dissertation assessment, which we have adapted:

- demonstrating an appropriate understanding of the literature (previous research) surrounding the subject area.
- synthesising and critically evaluating the material.
- formulating a concise, clear, comprehensive, investigative plan of a subject area.
- objectively selecting and appropriately utilising research methodologies, methods, and techniques.
- interpreting and presenting results.

- deriving conclusions, recommendations, and future directions with reference to the initial research questions, methodological framework, literature review, and results.
- establishing a high standard or presentation and literary quality.

A dissertation is far more than just writing another report and handing it in on time. It is an in-depth process requiring commitment, research skills, critical analysis, evaluation, synthesising, excellent communication skills, writing skills, selection of an interesting subject, and the ability to continuously think autonomously and independently. Dissertations can be perceived as stressful since they require thought and planning; in addition, they can be an obsession until you finish, and, in some cases, after you finish. They require self-motivation, discipline, and the formation of good habits and the ability to take constructive criticism without taking it personally as a positive opportunity to grow.

Why academic writing and dissertations are important

We encourage you to see writing as an excellent opportunity to enhance your skill set, which is always necessary in these disciplines, by learning new technologies, engines, coding practices, or languages. Academic writing is a major requirement of university undergraduate and post-graduate courses (Winstanley, 2009). It may be that you decide to progress up the academic ladder, to master's or PhD level to enhance employability, and academic writing and dissertation writing skills will follow you to the next step. A master's dissertation is about twice the complexity of a bachelor's dissertation, and a PhD is about three times the size and complexity of a masters, so academic writing is imperative if you choose this route. Regardless, this skill will serve you in all walks of life, such as producing professional reports in a company, working in an academic job, or writing letters, CVs, or professional emails in everyday life.

Research can be fairly addictive, and we recommend that you take this opportunity to research an area you find interesting, make it your own and produce a dissertation you are proud of. Move beyond a stereotypical developer/programmer role and tackle academic writing. It can be exciting, rewarding, and challenging and is never a waste of time; you are honing your academic, research, critical analysis, problem-solving, evaluation, impartial reporting, and synthesising skills. Fortunately, in games development and computer science, you will also be developing implementation and design skills simultaneously – it is a win–win situation!

To be an expert in a subject requires taking responsibility for your own learning and moving beyond simply memorising and following instructions to becoming a fully autonomous, free-thinking individual. Now we actually cannot remember when this happened to us – we were simply subjected to the educational system until we began thinking for ourselves and taking charge of our own learning. It will happen to you too! It means being assertive, respectful, inquisitive, diplomatic, and politely insistent when standing up for what you think. The truth of the matter is this: if you are not willing to take command of your learning and responsibility for your life and advancement – no one else will.

Universities provide the ability to earn a degree in a formal structure with support and the benefit of accessible expertise. This support means that a supervisor/mentor advises you, providing formative feedback throughout the entire process. To illustrate becoming an expert, we will use the cognitive domain of Bloom's taxonomy (Bloom et al., 1956; Anderson and Krathwohl, 2001) of educational objectives for illustration. The taxonomy provides a set of comprehensive classifications for learners' cognitive process, allowing classification of learning objectives. It is often presented in a pyramid with higher-order thinking skills located at the top. Mastery of the lower levels is necessary before mastery of the top levels can be achieved. Up until now, you have possibly only been active in the knowledge, comprehension, and application levels. Now that you are organically progressing, you will pass to the analysis level and beyond.

Why dissertations in games development and computer science are different

These types of dissertations are very different from science, education, social science, or business-related dissertations for the following reasons:

1   Computer science is multidisciplinary, encompassing very technical aspects with projects drawing on social science–related research and cross-curricular subject matter. It is not just experiments and mathematical reporting, but also software and gameplay testing and evaluation involving participants.
2   Students are fixated with design and implementation of software or a game. Your entire degree up to this point has consisted of worrying about the implementation, game working, or program compiling. The successful delivery of the implementation is paramount, with documentation perhaps being a secondary concern and something that is even reverse engineered to this point.

Now, dissertations, scholastic mastery, and academic skills are debatably just as important as development and implementation, or even more so. Implementation can now become an instrument of testing and evaluation to check your theories or hypotheses. In these disciplines, you require knowledge of research methodologies, methods, statistical analysis techniques, and how to perform literature reviews, but you also have to think about the methodologies, methods, and tools that are discipline specific. These include: software/game development lifecycle methodologies, design methodologies, user interface design and software or game components design, implementation tools, games engines, integrated development environments (IDEs), development platforms, version control, software testing techniques, and evaluation.

Why preparation is key

When about to undertake a large project, it can be easy to become overwhelmed. Writing a dissertation requires the same approach as anything else in life. Whether dieting, studying a martial art, or learning to play the piano, it takes consistency, practice, and discipline. Everything in life, whether academic, professional, or a hobby, is accomplished with small, incremental, transformational steps. If we take the piano-playing example: one day, you are playing scales and simple melodies, but you dedicate one hour a day to practice, and years later, you can play grade 8 Bach without really remembering how. Learning is incremental, gradual, iterative, and transformational; it is a process and an outcome. You can also outline and execute a plan of attack within the timeframe. This can be a document or a Gantt chart to plan when to complete individual sections. This is particularly important here because we know that, in a project like this, the implementation takes far longer than you originally anticipate. Modularity and breaking the whole thing into manageable components instantly make it seem more plausible and less stressful (Greetham, 2019). Here are our tips to get started:

1   Select an area you want to research that will sustain your interest and engagement.
2   Select an academic supervisor (mentor) in your school. Approach a suitable supervisor, someone with whom you have rapport, and have a discussion about the research interest. Try not to go empty handed, and have a plan to increase your chances. Try not to be offended if they say no; they may be at

maximum capacity, or they may refer you to a more suitable academic. Hopefully, they will have some research they want performed, or perhaps they have sent out a list of projects, and one catches your eye. Ideally, this relationship can be symbiotic, where you benefit from mentoring guidance and perform some work for them.

3   Start a project proposal (discussed in the next chapter) to outline the project, synthesise the ideas, and establish the marking scheme.

4   Start a detailed plan for completing the project on time with the main constituent parts.

Committing yourself to paper

Academic writing is all about practice. This skill must be refined. Here are a few pointers for committing yourself to paper:

1   Starting early is beneficial for drafting a quality dissertation. It is a skill tailored by trial and error, which is time consuming but the only way to ensure transformational learning takes place. As Jodi Picoult says: "*You can always edit a bad page, You can't edit a blank page.*"

2   Have the goal of showing something to your supervisor. Even if it is a small, well-written section − it is still progress! You could show some development or have an agenda and take notes. Generally, we find that students prefer to show development progress to shy away from the writing part. We recommend you face your fears and write small sections each week in tandem.

3   A dissertation is about demonstrating how you think and the overall process. Define everything in your title, and have an insatiable lust for knowledge. For example, a dissertation on *computer game mechanics* and *level design* to enhance *player satisfaction* should define the italicised terms, catalogue any empirical evidence, investigate whether they are effective, and find any existing examples).

4   Practice reading and processing academic papers efficiently by reading abstracts and conclusions to see if they are relevant. You can use Table 1.1 to produce a repository of relevant papers quickly and efficiently without reading the whole paper.

5   When collecting literature sources (books, journals, grey literature), it is good practice to summarise relevant parts. Reading does not

Table 1.1 Relevant paper questions template

Questions	Answers
What is the source? Journal, conference, book, edited book, website, YouTube, other?	
What is the quote, definition, or point?	
Is it primary, secondary or both?	
Is it qualitative, quantitative, or mixed method?	
What methodology is used?	
Is it empirical or discussion based?	
Are there participants? How many?	
What are the research questions?	
What are the results?	
What are the limitations?	
What analysis techniques are used?	
Is there a control group?	
Full reference in referencing style:	

necessarily relate to absorbing, processing, recording, or committing yourself to paper, and it is easy to procrastinate for a long time by *"reading around the literature,"* but remember, ten thousand words do not magically appear. To digest and process what you read, you must actively engage with the text (Chang and Ku, 2015, University of Melbourne, 2010). This engagement can be hard, but we recommend citing the definition or point in a paper, complete with reference, and write any salient points in your own words. This step ensures that you do not just passively read the text and forget, but instead, organise it in your own words, understand it, and record it. There is nothing worse than remembering something you want to reference, forgetting where it is from, and having to find it.

6   Typing notes into a document/spreadsheet or even by hand is a useful way to process the information; experienced researchers sometimes use referencing software. Computing students generally prefer soft copies of papers; very few actually print papers to read them. Even if that is the case, selecting the relevant section from a paper, noting the citation, adding the source to the reference section, and re-iterating the findings in your own words is common practice. This practice enables efficient engagement with the literature and starts to compile your dissertation. Even though you may not use all of the sources, it is never a wasted effort. You are compiling an electronic dossier of information you can use in the future. While performing this activity, you are searching, identifying, processing, engaging, understanding, and recording. Figure 1.1 outlines the process of disciplined paper recording.

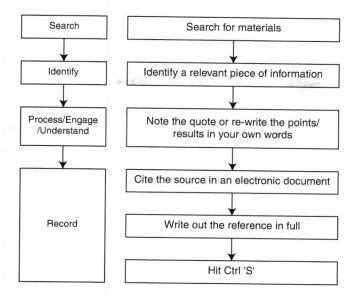

Figure 1.1 Recording relevant papers in a disciplined fashion.

Finding your voice

Many writing styles exist, and this small section is designed to provide perspective and be a confidence booster. There are more than 7 billion people in this world, and their opinions are no more important than yours, so we must get into the spirit of debating. At this level, you can be critical, disagree, not take things at face value, and debate points (in a diplomatic manner) as part of your academic growth/development. Remember that you are an intelligent academic who can accomplish anything with effort, determination, and hard work, and your opinion matters.

Summary

This chapter has introduced you to dissertations and why they are an extremely worthwhile undertaking. We have provided a small system for keeping track of all of your sources to begin your literature review and start your dissertation journey. Writing a dissertation in games development and computer science takes specialised knowledge in these fields, as well as development and implementation. The rest of the book will be dedicated to specific dissertation sections, which are easily accessible and helpful on your journey.

References

AllAssigmentHelpUK (2016) *Difference between an Essay, Dissertation and Thesis.* Available at: https://www.allassignmenthelp.co.uk/blog/difference-between-an-essay-dissertation-and-thesis/ (Accessed: 20 February 2020).

Anderson, L.W. and Krathwohl, D.R. (Eds.) (2001) *A Taxonomy for Learning, Teaching, and Assessing: A Revision of Bloom's Taxonomy of Educational Objectives.* New York: Addison Wesley Longman.

Bloom, B.S., Engelhart, M.D., Furst, E.J., Hill, W.H. and Krathwohl, D.R. (1956) *Taxonomy of Educational Objectives: The Classification of Educational Goals. Handbook I: Cognitive Domain..* New York: David McKay Company.

Chang, W-C. and Ku, Y-M. (2015) 'The effects of note-taking skills instruction on elementary students' reading', *The Journal of Educational Research*, 108(4), pp. 278–291. doi: 10.1080/00220671.2014.886175

Greetham, B. (2019) *How to Write Your Undergraduate Dissertation.* 3rd edn. London: Red Globe Press.

Latin Dictionary (2022) *Latin-English Dictionary.* Available at: https://www.online-latin-dictionary.com/latin-english-dictionary.php?parola=disserto (Accessed: 24 February 2022).

Paltridge, P. and Starfield, S. (2007) *Thesis and Dissertation Writing in a Second Language: A Handbook for Supervisors.* London: Routledge.

Paltridge, P. (2002) 'Thesis and dissertation writing: An examination of published advice and actual practice', *English for Specific Purposes*, 21(2), pp. 125–143. doi: 10.1016/S0889-4906(00)00025-9

QAA (The Quality Assurance Agency for Higher Education) (2014) *The Frameworks for Higher Education Qualification of UK Degree-Awarding Bodies.* Available at: https://www.qaa.ac.uk/quality-code/qualifications-and-credit-frameworks (Accessed: 2 March 2020).

Royal Literary Fund (2020) *What Is a Dissertation? How Is It Different from an Essay?* Available at: https://www.rlf.org.uk/resources/what-is-a-dissertation-how-is-it-different-from-an-essay/ (Accessed: 20 February 2020).

SQA (Scottish Qualifications Authority) (2020) *Scottish Credit and Qualifications Framework (SCQF).* Available at: https://www.sqa.org.uk/sqa/71387.html (Accessed: 2 March 2020).

The Concise Oxford Dictionary of Current English (1990) 8th edn. Oxford, England: Clarendon Press; New York, USA: Oxford University Pres.

University of Melbourne (2010) Helpsheet Reading Skills. Available at: https://www.jmu.edu/valleyscholars/files/studyreadingskills.pdf (Accessed: 24 February 2022).

Winstanley, C. (2009) *Writing a Dissertation for Dummies.* Chichester, West Sussex, England: John Wiley & Sons, Ltd.

2   Academic Rigour

In this chapter you will learn:

* The importance of using credible sources.
* The difference between reliable and questionable academic sources.
* How to identify reliable academic sources.
* How to complete a project specification.
* How to choose your project supervisor.

To a degree, when commencing an honours dissertation, students sometimes appear to be uncertain about the term '*academic rigour.*' In lectures on this topic, students are often encouraged to use credible academic sources, especially in relation to writing their literature reviews. This uncertainty may be because some students may lack any experience with academic research and do not originate from an academic background. In addition, they may have a lack of insight or experience in how to distinguish between a credible academic source and less reliable ones. One of the fundamental aims of reiterating to students the importance of applying credible academic sources to coincide with their writing is to substantiate the points they are addressing within their dissertations. In this chapter, the importance of using and identifying reliable academic sources is discussed, with examples provided. How to search for academic sources is also reviewed. This chapter also addresses how to complete an honours project specification, in addition to discussing how to choose a project supervisor and moderator for guidance and support.

Academic rigour explored

Why is writing an academically rigorous dissertation something that is expected of you during your honour's year? For example, you may well be thinking that as a computer science or games development student, surely

DOI: 10.4324/9781003054887-2

all that matters is the final output – the game or software application. Academic rigour is important because it defines the mindset and approach adopted toward writing the dissertation. This concept is meant to challenge you cognitively and prompt you to reflect on your discipline. Furthermore, it allows you to digest academic concepts associated with your subject area and illustrate that you have understood them within your chosen topic. This can be new educational territory. It is therefore important to instil the notion of academic rigour toward the very outset of the writing process. This goal can be achieved via a series of lectures when covering the topic of how to conduct a literature review. Alternatively, a solid pedagogical approach is to inform students through example about the differences between credible and noncredible sources, as well as where to locate them and their institutional resources.

Distinguishing between reliable and questionable academic sources

When performing your literature review, it is inevitable that you will have to define various concepts associated with software or game design. For example, terminology such as '*games immersion*', '*agile development*', or defining a '*serious game*' or '*responsive web design*' requires a credible source from either a book, journal paper, or a plausible online source, such as an acknowledged industry report. It is expected that when undertaking your literature review, you will gradually become familiar with where to locate your sources. Once you have undertaken your literature review and collected the sources you need to substantiate the points you will address, it is important to assess the validity of these sources.

Google search

Performing a search of the term '*games immersion*' on *Google* generates a multitude of hits, and it may be tempting to select the first available option. Intead, you must evaluate the credibility of the source to use, consider what it is you are trying to communicate, and assess how the source you intend to use best validates your point.

Your search, for example, may uncover "The Game Developer" website. This is an acknowledged games industry source, and it remains credible, providing regular industry updates and explorative articles from people who work within the industry. These articles can be theoretical or practical, ranging from topics associated with game flow, immersion, and level design. It is useful for you to become familiar with the important recognised sources within your industry area.

Wikipedia

Wikipedia is an invaluable knowledge repository for a wide range of subjects. Wikipedia is a recommended starting point for initially digesting and understanding terminology in your discipline area. Wikipedia is also beneficial for providing an audit trail toward locating additional sources, which can be found in the reference section of the Wikipedia article.

Though Wikipedia is a good resource for providing an overview of terminology, remembered that it is a community-driven site. This means that a definition you find on a page one day may be altered on the following day – so bear this in mind. The resource section toward the end of a page on Wikipedia is very useful for following leads to other sources.

Grey literature

Many students will predominately search what is often referred to as the '*grey literature*'. Though there appears to be no unanimous definition surrounding the term '*grey literature*', it is often associated with publications or outputs produced by organisational bodies or companies outside normal academic channels. If, for example, you were including an organisation's annual published research, or a government report related to the current state of the creative industries, this would be an illustration of the grey literature. Including aspects of the grey literature in your dissertation is useful because you can often find interesting facts, statistics, and synopses of the current state of an industry that you would not ordinarily locate in an academic journal paper or book. For example, the House of Commons Scottish Affairs Committee report on the video games industry in Scotland (2011) is a good example of grey literature. These types of reports can provide you with the state-of-the-art of the industry discipline and are highly beneficial toward providing background information and setting the scene or context of your industry area. For example, you may want to quote some facts and figures about the state of the mobile games sector in the UK or the rise of 5G if you are pursuing a computer-networking degree.

When citing these reports, it is not necessarily expected that you must read them from cover to cover. Instead, you can extract the salient facts from the report that best suit the purpose. It is also important to check their credibility in terms of who the author and publisher is. Sometimes a useful thing to do is to check how many times other people have cited or referenced the source. Table 2.1 shows useful bodies in games and computer science.

Table 2.1 Useful representative bodies of the games and computer science industries

Representative body	Website address
UKie (The Association for UK Interactive Entertainment)	https://ukie.org.uk/ (Accessed: 09 January 2022)
TIGA (The Independent Game Developers Association)	https://tiga.org/ (Accessed: 09 January 2022)
IGDA (International Games Developers Association)	https://www.idga.org/ (Accessed: 09 January 2022)
IEEE (The Institute of Electrical and Electronics Engineers)	https://www.ieee.org/ (Accessed: 09 January 2022)
ACM (Association for Computing Machinery)	https://www.acm.org/ (Accessed 09 January 2022)
W3C (World Wide Web Consortium)	https://www.w3.org/ (Accessed: 09 January 2022)
WHATWG (Web Hypertext Application Technology Working Group)	https://whatwg.org/ (Accessed 09 January 2022)

Making use of your library

A useful resource students often overlook in undertaking more technical dissertations is the university library. In addition to being able to locate books and articles through your library's online catalogues and academic journal subscription services, your university library can also provide other useful services. For instance, your library should have an appointed subject librarian who can recommend sources and resources for you and assist you toward locating them. If there is a specific article, book, or journal paper that you cannot access online due to your library not having it, then you can order it via an inter-library loan system.

A useful piece of advice when commencing your degree at university – and this applies for students of any academic discipline – is to become familiar with your university's library and its resources. There will be plenty of online guides to assist you with any queries that you might have about locating sources.

Students in creative disciplines often perceive the university library as a waste of time. For games design and computer science students, the library is seen as unnecessary when there is a surplus of educational *YouTube* videos out there. Blog posts from developers say how it is. There are easily accessible web pages providing posts about subject areas and various perspectives of the industry and developments surrounding it. Combined with the use of the grey literature, the use of books from your library can help solve any exploratory issues in the early stages of your dissertation writing. They are also very beneficial for finding definitions that will aid you in the writing of your literature review.

Locating books

Searching for books is generally straightforward. Just go to the library, find a book, take it from the shelf, and add it to your library account. It would, however, be useful to take the time to find out where the books in your subject area are located in your library. As previously mentioned, your subject librarian should be able to help you with this. **UT:** Go to the library, introduce yourself to the subject librarian, and ask about available resources.

Ordinarily, most students will use their library's online catalogue when searching for books.

A basic search for material related to *'game design'* or *'software development'* can return multiple copies of books and sources – some that are only available online, but often, most are available in the library itself. Searches can also be conducted by author if you cannot remember the exact title of the book you are seeking.

It is worthwhile to make use of your library's interlibrary loan service, which allows you to request papers and books from other academic libraries, as well as academic journals the library might not subscribe to.

In terms of locating journal papers from online academic databases, you will find that your library, per subject discipline area, has a subscription to relevant academic literature. For computer science and games-related subjects, academic journals such as the IEEE, ACM, SpringerLink, and ScienceDirect are useful. Once you have found where to search for academic papers via your library's website, you will need to log in with your student ID to access what you are after. Also be conscious of the fact that you may be only able to access some articles on-campus as opposed to off-campus, depending upon the library's subscription deal with the academic publisher. When undertaking general searches, the search terms returned are usually highlighted in yellow to indicate their relevancy to the search. You can browse the abstracts of the articles to assess whether they are of relevance to your research area. Unlocked PDFs indicate that you can download and save an article.

Using the academic databases is highly recommended because you can find a wealth of material within them. **UT:** Start to get to know your academic journals and the literature surrounding your discipline.

It is important to use credible academic sources and maintain good academic standards. This is necessary from the start as you will need to cite and refer to relevant academic sources when completing your honours project specification.

Completing your honours specification

The honours project specification, which is really a research proposal, often baffles students prior to completing it. This process demands important consideration because undertaking a project that you are passionate about will, and should, result in a good submission. You should also select your supervisor as soon as possible. One reason for doing so is that it is sensible to choose a dissertation topic that aligns with your supervisor's interests. This is not always mandatory, but your supervisor can assist you by sharing their knowledge in that specific research area.

We will now review some relevant section of the proposal/specification.

The project title

The project title itself can cause difficulty because focusing a subject(s) and expressing it using a short title requires a great deal of thought and focus. Some examples of honours project titles might include the following:

- Reviewing web accessibility issues in the context of responsive web design.
- An evaluation of technology stacks toward app development: a front-end and back-end perspective.
- Games AI: a state of the art of pathfinding strategies.
- A comparison of C# and C++ programming languages towards learning the fundamentals of coding.

A concise dissertation title helps to maintain concentration on the chosen topic. Too many elements contained in the title can lead to deviation from the core subject area and too much concentration in other areas, spreading yourself too thinly across many topics.

The mandatory details

The overview of your project is part of any proposal and provides a good opportunity to solidify your thinking and ideas about the subject area you want to focus on. This overview also allows consideration of the underpinning research design and ethical aspects that may impact on your research. Your project specification also allows you to reflect on the technology you will adopt and use in the development of your game, piece of software, app, or website and to assess its suitability in this respect.

Project outline example

We will now scrutinise a submitted computer-game project specification in terms of how it has been presented and written, as well as the overall clarity regarding its overall research design and focus.

Outline of project

This project aims to determine the impact that difficulty and challenge has on a player's emotions, as well as assessing how this affects the immersion within the gameplay. This will involve the creation of a 3D platforming game with contrasting levels of difficulty and an optional adaptive difficulty feature, which will tailor the game's difficulty in real time based on the player's performance. Testing will be used to evaluate participants' reactions to each of the different difficulties and how these reactions affect their enjoyment and immersion in the game. Participants will be selected from the game development group, with participant information sheets and consent forms provided. The evaluation will be undertaken via the use of Google Forms and the results disseminated in the dissertation.

The game to be developed will be a 3D collect-a-thon platformer about a sausage-obsessed talking dog named Crazy and his quest to stop the evil President Pig from taking control of the town. The gameplay mostly consists of collecting items, playing through mini-games, and platforming through the worlds. These aspects of the game are intended, through its design and features, to help accentuatd the aspects of challenge, difficulty, and immersion within the gameplay. Adhering to an agile development methodology, the game will be created using Unity Engine 2019 and programmed in C#. The game will contain multiple themed levels teeming with collectables, such as Sausages, Golden Bones and Collars. The music will be royalty-free music from the Unity asset store, which will be acknowledged throughout, in addition to 3D models purchased from the Unity asset store.

For version control and source control, GitHub will be used. This repository will be set to private since the project will use paid

---

unity asset store assets that cannot be re-distributed. For the purposes of project management, Trello will be used. This allows the bigger tasks to be split into smaller more manageable tasks and helps the project to stay on track.

White Box testing will be conducted regularly to ensure that the game is continuing to progress in the correct direction. One testing session every 2–3 months would be preferable for undertaking Black Box testing with game development students who have consented to participate in the research.

What can be seen is that the outline of this project specification is quite focused and that the aim of the project is stated clearly from the outset. Clarity is important so that no ambiguity exists about what the project intends to concentrate on and the aim is clear. It is also important to try and state the intention of your research focus within the opening sentence of your specification. In doing so, the reader can grasp very readily what it is you intend to do.

The main aim of the project is clearly stated:

"This project aims to determine the impact that difficulty and challenge has on a player's emotions as well as assessing how this affects the immersion within the gameplay."

When you post the main aim, mention how the overall project aim(s) will be achieved.

When completing a project specification in games development or computer science, we recommend you concentrate on

- The focus of the project and what it is going to involve.
- Whehter the project is relevant to your chosen subject area and why it is worth doing.
- The software you are going to use and why (e.g., game engine of choice, back or front-end stack, visual studio, programming language of choice).
- How you are going to test or evaluate your implementation.
- Whether there will be any ethical implications involved associated with the study.
- The timescales of the project and whether they are manageable and achievable.

Choosing your project supervisor

Based on our supervisory experience, we have provided some tips to guide you on how to identify members of academic staff for honours supervision and moderation:

Tip 1: Try to discuss the idea as early as possible.
Seek advice early from a member of staff to discuss the feasibility of your research idea. Assess whether your dissertation idea aligns with their research interests.

Tip 2: Browse staff members' research pages.
Search the research pages of potential supervisors. You may identify research topics and find commonality.

Tip 3: Submit an early draft proposal.
Send a working draft of your proposal to your identified supervisor for constructive feedback.

The role of the project supervisor

We have briefly outlined the role of a project supervisor:

- They provide guidance and support throughout the entirety of the dissertation process.
- You meet with them at mutually designated times to discuss progress, receive feedback, and plan the sequential stages.
- They review drafts of chapters and various sections of the dissertation at certain stages of the research.
- They provide an element of pastoral care should you be experiencing any external issues out with your studies and point you in the right direction for help.

It is important that you keep up to date with the progress of your dissertation and inform your supervisor if you are experiencing any problems or difficulties.

It is always important to remember that your project supervisor is there to help and support you and that the feedback you receive will always be constructive. There is, however, scope for negotiation regarding how you proceed. This is when you must work well with your project supervisor to mutually agree how you will take the project forward.

Compromises can be made, and the concepts of flexibility and adaptability are paramount. Produce the work, and constructive feedback should follow. Remember that your project supervisor is on your side, working with you and not against you.

Summary

This chapter has emphasised the importance of using robust academic sources when writing your dissertation. Becoming familiar with material associated with your research topic will allow you to assess the academic credibility of what you want to do and commence your project specification. There are many academic sources you can use to help you, and these have been outlined in this chapter.

- Choosing a project supervisor to guide you during the dissertation process is important. Your supervisor is there to support you throughout your research project, so remember to seek their advice when you have a question.
- You may also have to ask an academic to act as a moderator.
- Using credible academic sources for your dissertation will help to substantiate the facts and arguments you want to present in your literature review.
- Adhering to academic rigour helps enhance the reliability of your dissertation and its findings.
- Try to make use of all academic sources at your disposal. If you are unsure what to use, then check with your project supervisor.
- Knowing what a credible source is and is not takes time to identify. Becoming more familiar with sources associated with your subject area will help you to overcome this learning barrier.
- Remember that you can use numerous sources in various formats; these include online journals, reports, e-books, or hard copy, or even industry standard blogs or websites.

Reference

Scottish Affairs Committee. (2011, January 19) *Second Report Video Games Industry in Scotland*. Available at: https://publications.parliament.uk/pa/cm201011/cmselect/cmscotaf/500/500i.pdf (Accessed: 15 January 2022).

3   Citations, Referencing, and Hierarchy of Academic Sources

In this chapter, you will learn about:

- Academic writing and the style of academic writing when referring to scholarly studies.
- Citing credible sources within a dissertation and gaining an understanding why the use of references is important.
- How to reference various academic sources in a dissertation.
- The concept of plagiarism and how to avoid it.

What is referencing?

Academic referencing is a skill that takes some time to perfect. The time needed is understandable since computer science and games students are predominantly focused on the practical side of their degrees as opposed to the '*softer*' side, such as report writing. At university, more is expected of you regarding how you approach written work. This is especially true when this work is designed to be academic in focus. As a student, in HE, you are not expected to copy or transcribe facts or lists but rather evaluate facts or substantiate the points you have made by citing and referencing the identified sources (Williams and Carroll, 2009). Referencing is very important, and various definitions of referencing exist, though a comprehensive one is provided by Pears and Shields (2019, p.1):

> " ... *referencing is the process of acknowledging the sources you have used in writing your essay, assignment or piece of work. It allows the reader to access your source documents as quickly and easily as possible in order to verify, if necessary, the validity of your arguments and the evidence on which they are based.*"

DOI: 10.4324/9781003054887-3

In the context of a dissertation, referencing is highly relevant because you must be able to support the points you are making in your writing, disseminate knowledge, and acknowledge the work of other authors (Neville, 2010).

Though the concept of referencing within dissertation writing might seem self-explanatory, when do you use it and how does it work? The following conditions apply to academic referencing. Keep them in mind when working on dissertation writing. Referencing occurs when you:

> EITHER quote someone else directly OR paraphrase someone else's work, i.e., put it into your own words.

We will now describe how referencing works in academic or dissertation writing. When someone quotes or paraphrases another source, they add (UWS library, 2021):

> 1   A citation in the text.
> 2   The reference for the item concerned – usually at the end of the work.

The information contained within an academic reference varies from source to source, but the following commonalities are included:

> 1   The name of the author.
> 2   Date of publication of the work.
> 3   Title of the work.
> 4   Publication details or details of how the source can be accessed.

Relationship between citing and referencing

To reemphasise, referencing, in the academic sense, can be succinctly summarised as "*acknowledging one's debt to other people's ideas or opinions …*" (Kargbo, 2010, p. 222). Undergraduate students who have no experience in academic writing may well understand its value in the context of intellectual property (IP) rights. If you have created a piece of software, a website, or developed a game, and if someone were to modify or adapt it slightly, it is important that you are acknowledged as the original creator. It is similar if you are acknowledging someone's written work or their ideas and not passing them off as your own. Though the concept of referencing remains the same in principle, the confusion surrounding its adoption and use can be exacerbated by the fact that different citation styles are used for referencing academic sources.

Despite this variety, the main ethos of citing in your dissertation will be associated with the concept of in-text citations. This refers to when you have quoted someone's work or if you have mentioned someone's ideas or a particular concept in the main body of your dissertation. Citations that you make within the text should be fully referenced in your reference section.

Citations in your dissertation

When including a citation in the main body of your dissertation, you are attributing acknowledgement to someone else's work or ideas. This applies whether you are quoting a source directly or paraphrasing someone's views, theories, or general opinions. Citations in the main body of a work are known as in-text citations. Note that there are various styles of how to cite sources. This chapter will demonstrate the most common styles used by our students, namely: the Harvard referencing style and the APA referencing style. Key citation examples will be illustrated and explained, though, and we will focus on salient examples based on our supervisory experience.

Harvard referencing style

The Harvard citation style uses parentheses. The author's surname, the resource year, and, if applicable, the page number(s) are enclosed in parentheses. These citations can be embedded mid-sentence or toward the end of the sentence. The citations must be accompanied by a list of references toward the end, set out in alphabetical order by author surname. Table 3.1 shows some basic examples of Harvard reference citations:

Table 3.1 Basic examples of Harvard citations

Example	Description
In recent research exploring virtual reality use in HE **(Author Name, year of publication)** …	Use author surname and year of publication if referring to the entirety of the study.
According to **Author Name, (year of publication, page number from source)** states that *"virtual reality has great pedagogical potential … "*	Place the year and page number in parentheses after the author if using a direct quotation.

Regardless of the citation style adopted, it is important to remember the concept of in-text citations. They are used to provide details of an author's work, such as a research study or findings from a study. **UT:** The main rule of thumb is whenever you are referring to someone else's work, whether you are summarising or paraphrasing their ideas, you must cite the author, authors, or work concerned.

Applying direct quotations

A common quandary is when and how best to use quotations. When writing literature reviews, a common mistake is to overuse direct citations and to cite an author's work too often, at times using the same author in multiple paragraphs. Try to avoid this reuse where possible since it indicates that you have been unable to locate varied sources. Direct quotes are useful to apply toward the background and literature sections when defining specific terminology associated with your research topic.

Here are some examples in the context of defining what a game is:

- *"Games are a complex social phenomenon that eludes holistic categorization"* (Calleja, 2011, p.7).
  OR
- *"**GAMES** are a type of play activity, conducted in the context of a pretended reality, in which the participant(s) try to achieve at least one arbitrary, nontrivial goal by acting in accordance with rules"* (Adams, 2014, p.2).

When quoting an author's work directly, you enclose the quote in quotation marks and refer to the author's surname, the year of publication, and the page number where the quote appears. For example, if quoting from a book, the inclusion of a page number allows the reader to locate the original source and page from where you have quoted.

Citing multiple authors

When citing an academic work, it can become confusing if the paper or study being referenced has been written by more than one author. For example, it is not uncommon for journal or conference papers to include multiple authors' names, i.e., they are co-authored by several individuals. Citing multiple authors is relatively straightforward, as illustrated in Table 3.2.

Table 3.2 Citations examples for number of authors

Number of authors	In-text citation examples
I.	Author Name (Year of Publication).
II.	Author A and Author B (Year of Publication).
III.	Author A, Author B, and Author C (Year of Publication).
IV. (or more)	Primary Author *et al.,* (Year of Publication).

In Table 3.2, note the use of "et al.," which refers to the Latin term "et alia," meaning "and others"; it is included when you are citing more than one author.

Citing multiple authors and sources

It may be necessary to cite multiple authors or sources in your literature review. This is useful when you want to substantiate and strongly emphasis a particular point based on the literature you have read or when summarising similar viewpoints from multiple authors. Examples of in-text citations are:

A research study investigating virtual reality use in HE by **Author Name et al., (Year of Publication) ...**
Author Name et al., (Year of Publication) argue that virtual reality adoption has potential pedagogical benefits ...
Various research studies (**Author Name, Year of Publication; Author Name, Year of Publication**) investigating virtual reality use have indicated ...

Citing sources published in same year by same author

When citing a particular author's work, you may have to cite two or more publications from that author published in the same year. You might also come across a scenario where two authors with the same surname have published works in the same year. Should this situation arise, you can use the "a", "b", "c" format to distinguish between the various authors and their works. For example, this could be achieved in the following way:

> An initial study by **Author Name (Year of Publication a)** found that augmented reality was a useful pedagogical approach towards teaching computer programming. This was further confirmed in a follow-up study by **Author Name (Year of Publication b),** which indicated that … .

When you are compiling your reference, 'a' and 'b' would be alphabetical.

Citing sources with no date

Sometimes a source that you would like to reference may have no specific date of authorship or publication. This issue could present itself in the form of a report or website you have found during a search on *Google Scholar* or another search engine. This lack of date can be rectified in the following way:

> In a recent survey about virtual reality use in HE **(Author Name and Author Name, no date or n.d.)**.
> Serious games are clearly popular … **(Serious Games Review, no date or n.d.)**.

You add the author(s) surname or the source you are referring to and 'no date' or 'n.d.'.

How to paraphrase

You often will need to convey someone's writing in your own words, as opposed to using direct quotations. Expressing someone's else's thoughts or ideas in your own words is done through paraphrasing. Paraphrasing allows you illustrate that you have understood the central points that an author has been articulating in their work. When paraphrasing, you do not alter the central meaning that the author was trying to convey. It is crucial that you can reiterate in your own words what you have read and display your overall general knowledge and understanding of that work. Here is an example of paraphrasing:

> *It has been argued by* Hainey (2016) *the application of digital games in education is becoming more prevalent in different educational contexts that include Primary Education (PE), Secondary Education (SE) and Higher Education (HE).*

When paraphrasing a particular source or an author's views, you can include the page number in your citation to allow the reader to directly locate the main argument that you have paraphrased from that work.

Social media and the internet

It is common for students in the creative disciplines to use sources other than books, academic conferences, or journal papers. The internet has a wealth of useful information and material that may only obtained from a website, an online blog, or an online report. The main format for providing a citation for a website is:

- The author's name (e.g., if it is an online blog entry or article on a website).
- If there is no date of publication associated with an online article or blog post, you would state no date in brackets – e.g., (n.d. or no date).
- Year of publication or when the site was published or last updated.
- The URL (uniform resource locator) of the webpage.
- The date when the page was accessed (indicating that it was accessible at that specific time).

For example, when including an in-text citation of an article from the W3C's Web Accessibility Initiative (WAI) page, '*Essential Components of Web Accessibility*' you would express this along the following lines:

> There are various fundamental elements associated with web site design that must be included by a web designer to adhere to the web accessibility standards of the web (Henry and Duffy, 2018).

If you wanted to be more specific and direct the reader to the exact section of the website, you could cite the web page in the following way:

> There are various fundamental elements associated with web site design that must be considered by a web designer to adhere to the web accessibility standards of the web (Henry and Duffy, 2018, **Introduction**).

You would stipulate the year of the source as being 2018 since this was the last time that the web page was updated at the time of writing this book. This information can always usually be located at the foot of the web page. It is also important to note that on certain websites, permission is at times granted for you to use images in the context of academic writing if the work is for educational purposes only. Should this prove not to be the case, then you will need to seek permission from the author or website concerned.

Online blogs

Another online medium that you can make use of and refer to, especially in the context of games development, are blogs. It is important to remember although blogs can be a useful source of information, providing insights into topics and industries, they are, at the end of the day, people's opinions. Sometimes an author's perspective on a blog post is not always substantiated by fact. Game Developer: https://www.gamedeveloper.com/blogs, for example, is a website that contains articles and blogs often written by game developers in the industry. When citing a blog post within the main body, you include the author's surname and the year of publication of the post. This will sometimes include the date when the blog post was published online, if it has been made available. In the following example, you could set out an in-text blog citation along the following lines:

> In an online blog post published on **Game Developer, Brycer (2009)** discusses three core fundamentals that a game developer requires to produce a successful game.
> **You would reference the source in the following way:**
> Bycer, J. (2020, December 9) *The Not so Secrets to Success in the Game Industry*. Available at: https://www.gamedeveloper.com/disciplines/the-not-so-secrets-to-success-in-the-game-industry (Accessed: 11 December 2020).

Computer games and software

Another common source that game students often cite and refer to are references to games that have influenced the design of the ones they are going to create. The in-text citation when referring to a game would include the following:

> * The name of the game.
> * The game company or publisher.
> * Year of release.

For example, if you are going to develop a horror game, you might want to cite an influential horror genre that has influenced you, such as the *Resident Evil* franchise. Similarly, if you are going to develop a platformer game you might refer to the *Super Mario Bros.* franchise as an inspiration for your idea. Here are some examples:

> One of the most popular horror game franchises, **Resident Evil, (Capcom, 1996)** …
> In the context of platforming games, the original **Super Mario Bros. (Nintendo Co., Ltd, 1985)** was very popular among gamers when released on the NES (Nintendo Entertainment System) in the 1980s.

You would reference these citations via the following examples:
Reference to game: Capcom Co., Ltd (1996) *Resident Evil* [Video game]. Capcom Co., Ltd.
Reference to game: Nintendo Co., Ltd. (1985) *Super Mario Bros.* [Video game]. Nintendo Co., Ltd.

When citing and referencing a computer software program or application, you would adopt the following approach:

GitHub (GitHub, Inc. 2008) is an online version control platform that is useful for version control and sharing code collaboratively. **Reference to software:** GitHub, Inc. (2008, February 8) *GitHub* [Computer programme]. Available at: https://github.com/ (Accessed: 17 February 2022).

Illustrations or images

A common source cited by games students are images of games or game characters. Also, students who are engaged in computer science or web development dissertations include images of software development or testing methodologies in their design and implementation sections. For an image in general, something aesthetic, such as a piece of artwork, you can include the name of the artist or photographer and the year the drawing or photograph was taken. For an online diagram or model, you refer to the online source where it has originated and include the creator's name (if applicable) and year when it was published online.

UT – It is important that you acknowledge the source of any images you include in your dissertation that are from online sources.

If you were going to provide an online image depicting how *Super Mario* has evolved graphically as a character, then you would cite the name of the website where the image came from and the year where the website was last updated. If the image was included as part of an online blog or article, then you would cite the author's surname and year of publication of the blog piece or article.

You may wish to include an image of the evolution of *Super Mario* from a website, in which case you would label the image and reference the source:

Label: Figure * shows the evolution of the Super Mario character (Hackett and Glatz, no date).
Reference to website: Hackett, L. and Glatz, K. (no date) *SuperLuigiBros: Welcome to Super LuigiBros: Mario & Luigi Mega Fan Site. The Evolution of Mario – A History of how Mario has Evolved from the 80's to Modern Day.* Available at: https://www.gamedeveloper.com/disciplines/the-not-so-secrets-to-success-in-the-game-industry (Accessed 12 December 2020).

If the image of *Sonic the Hedgehog* had come from a blog post or online article, you would therefore include the name of the author and date of online publication. You would also label the image in the following way:

Label: Figure * showing the evolution of Sonic the Hedgehog (green man gaming, 2020).
Reference: green man gaming (2020, January 17) *The Evolution of Sonic the Hedgehog.* Available at:https://www.greenmangaming.com/blog/the-evolution-of-sonic-the-hedgehog/ (Accessed 17 February 2022).

If you were going to cite a software development lifecycle methodology diagram from a website, you would cite in a similar way to the previous examples. If there is no author's name on the website with no date of publication (i.e., an online blog post or article), you would then cite the company name and current updated status of the website. So, in this case, you would label the figure with a citation and reference it in the following manner:

Label: Figure *: Agile Software Development Lifecycle (SDLC) **(JavaTpoint, 2011–2021).**

Reference: JavaTpoint (2011–2021) *Agile Software Development Lifecycle (SDLC)*. Available at: https://www.javatpoint.com/agile-sdlc (Accessed 17 February 2022).

If you were to cite this source in the main body of the text, it would be the following:

The agile methodology is a highly iterative and sequential approach toward software development **(JavaTpoint, 2011–2021)**.

Online reports

A useful and often invaluable source to use in the background and literature section are online reports. Industry-based reports are often a highly beneficial resource of information when investigating the 'state-of-the-art' of a particular sector, for example, the mobile games industry or developments in mobile data networks. Usually, reports published online can be cited by author or by the company that undertook the research, including the year when the research was conducted. We will now examine the following example relating to a report associated with investigating the animation industry in Scotland. The report was commissioned by Creative Scotland, and the research was performed by BOP Consulting. The in-text citation for this report would read as follows:

The animation sector in Scotland continues to steadily grow **(BOP Consulting, 2017)** …

According to evidence from a report produced by **BOP Consulting, (2017)** that animation sector in Scotland continues to increase at a steady rate …

The reference would be the following:

BOP Consulting (2017) *Review of the Scottish Animation Sector*. Available at: https://www.creativescotland.com/__data/assets/pdf_file/0008/38861/Animation-Sector-Review-Final-Report.pdf (Accessed 12 December 2020).

APA style

UT: The citation and reference style that you use will be dependent upon your academic discipline in addition to the style that is advocated by your academic institution. Another commonly used citation and reference style is the APA (American Psychological Association). In-text citations in the APA format are like Harvard except when citing more than one author. When citing sources with more than one author, all surnames should be used for the first citation. After this, further in-text citations for the same authors can use the *et al.* format. Here is an example:

> **First citation:** Author A, Author B, and Author C (year of publication).
> **Ensuing citations:** Primary Author *et al.* (year of publication).

In the main body of the text, the APA style joins authors' names with 'and' but uses the ampersand – '&' symbol – when the citation is placed within parenthesis. For example:

> Asynchronous online learning has greater pedagogical benefits than synchronous online learning (Author A, Author B & Author C, year of publication).

Referencing with Harvard and APA

Table 3.3 shows the Harvard Referencing and APA system.

Table 3.3 Harvard and APA referencing system

Source	Harvard referencing example	APA referencing example
Journal Paper by one author (print version)	Baxter, G. (2015) 'Social Media in Organizations', In: *The International Encyclopedia of Digital Communication and Society*, First Edition. (eds. Mansell, R. and Hwa Ang, P.). John Wiley & Sons, Inc. doi: 10.1002/9781118290743. wbiedcs025	Hainey, T. (2016) *Moving digital games for learning forward.* On the Horizon. 24(1), 132–136. doi: https://doi.org/10.1108/OTH-08–2015-0037
Journal Paper by more than one author (print version)	Baxter, G.J. and Hainey, T. (2019) 'Student perceptions of virtual reality use in HE'. *Journal of Applied Research in Higher Education*, 12(3), pp. 413–424.	Baxter, G.J. & Hainey, T. (2019) *Student perceptions of virtual reality use in higher education.* Journal of Applied Research in Higher Education. 12(3), 413–424.

(Continued)

Table 3.3 (Continued)

Source	Harvard referencing example	APA referencing example
Journal Paper from online database (online version)	Baxter, G.J. and Hainey, T. (2019) 'Student perceptions of virtual reality use in HE', *Journal of Applied Research in Higher Education*, 12(3), pp. 413–424. doi: https://doi.org/10.1108/JARHE-06–2018-0106	Baxter, G.J. & Hainey, T. (2019). *Student perceptions of virtual reality use in higher education.* Journal of Applied Research in Higher Education. 12(3), 413–424. doi: https://doi.org/10.1108/JARHE-06–2018-0106
Book (print version)	Pears, R. and Shields, G. (2019) *Cite them right: the essential referencing guide.* 11th edn. London: Red Globe Press/Macmillan International Higher Education.	Pears, R. & Shields, G. (2019) *Cite them right: the essential referencing guide.* 11th edn. London: Red Globe Press/Macmillan International Higher Education.
Book (e-book version)	Pears, R. and Shields, G. (2019) *Cite them right: the essential referencing guide.* Available at: URL for the e-book would go here. (Accessed 12 February 2022).	Pears, R. & Shields, G. (2019) *Cite them right: the essential referencing guide.* Retrieved from URL: URL for the e-book would go here. (Accessed 12 February 2022).
Website	Web Accessibility Initiative (2018) *Essential Components of Web Accessibility.* Available at: https://www.w3.org/WAI/fundamentals/components/ (Accessed: 11 December 2020).	Web Accessibility Initiative (2018) *Essential Components of Web Accessibility.* Retrieved from URL: https://www.w3.org/WAI/fundamentals/components/ (Accessed: 11 December 2020).
Online Blogs	Bycer, J. (2020, 9 December) *The Not so Secrets to Success in the Game Industry.* Available at: https://www.gamedeveloper.com/disciplines/the-not-so-secrets-to-success-in-the-game-industry (Accessed 11 February 2022).	Bycer, J. (2020 9 December) *The Not so Secrets to Success in the Game Industry.* Retrieved from URL: https://www.gamedeveloper.com/disciplines/the-not-so-secrets-to-success-in-the-game-industry
Computer Games	Projekt Red (2021) *Cyberpunk 2077* [Video game]. Projekt Red.	*Cyberpunk 2077.* (2021) [Video game: PlayStation 5, Xbox Series X/S, 17+] CD Projekt Red.

(Continued)

Table 3.3 (Continued)

Source	Harvard referencing example	APA referencing example
Online Reports	BOP Consulting (2017) *Review of the Scottish Animation Sector.* Available at: https://www.creativescotland.com/__data/assets/pdf_file/0008/38861/Animation-Sector-Review-Final-Report.pdf (Accessed 12 December 2020).	BOP Consulting (2017). *Review of the Scottish Animation Sector.* Retrieved from URL: https://www.creativescotland.com/__data/assets/pdf_file/0008/38861/Animation-Sector-Review-Final-Report.pdf

Plagiarism

When writing any piece of coursework at university, it is important that you do not plagiarise or copy someone else's work and acknowledge it as your own. Plagiarism does not have to be deliberate; in fact, it can be accidental. Due diligence is encouraged in the context of HE because plagiarism is deemed a serious offence. If discovered, the student can face a plagiarism panel and potentially lose their university place. There are many definitions of the concept. *"Plagiarism means knowingly presenting the work or property of another person as one's own, without appropriate acknowledgment or referencing"* (Yeo, 2007, p. 200).

UT: Plagiarism is something you should avoid at all costs. Academically, and in relation to your degree qualification, it is not worth jeopardising everything that you have worked toward. Should you ever be in doubt about how to articulate something from an alternative source or author, then seek advice from your project supervisor who will be able to advise and guide you.

Summary

This chapter has outlined the importance of citing and referencing sources that you use in your dissertation. When referring to other people's work, regardless of source, it is important to cite and reference the exact source of the material you are using. Be mindful that plagiarism is to be avoided, and, if in doubt, then ask your project supervisor for guidance.

- Academic referencing can take time to understand and get right.
- Find out the preferred referencing style of your institution from your supervisor or university library.

- If you are referring to someone else work or ideas, always include a citation.
- Citations can take the form of direct or indirect citations.
- Try to use direct quotes sparingly, such as for a verbatim definition of a particular concept.
- Always reference external sources you have used, such as images, and make clear their source of origin.
- Above all, do not plagiarism someone else's work. If in doubt about anything, consult your supervisor.

References

Adams, E. (2014) *Fundamentals of Game Design*. 3rd edn. Berkeley, California: New Riders.

Baxter, G. (2015) 'Social Media in Organizations', In: *The International Encyclopedia of Digital Communication and Society*, 1st edn. (eds. Mansell, R. and Hwa Ang, P.). John Wiley & Sons, Inc. doi: 10.1002/9781118290743.wbiedcs025

Baxter, G. and Hainey, T. (2019) 'Student perceptions of virtual reality use in higher education'. *Journal of Applied Research in Higher Education*, 12(3), pp. 413–424. doi: 10.1108/JARHE-06-2018-0106

Bycer, J. (2020, 9 December) *The Not so Secrets to Success in the Game Industry Available* at: https://www.gamedeveloper.com/disciplines/the-not-so-secrets-to-success-in-the-game-industry (Accessed: 11 December 2020).

Calleja, G. (2011) *In-Game: From Immersion to Incorporation*. Massachusetts Institute of Technology.

Game Developer (no date) Available at: https://www.gamedeveloper.com/blogs (Accessed: 27 February 2022).

Hainey, T. (2016) 'Moving digital games for learning forward'. *On the Horizon*. 24(1), pp. 132–136. doi: 10.1108/OTH-08-2015-0037

Henry, S.L. and Duffy, M. (2018) *Essential Components of Web Accessibility*. Available at: https://www.w3.org/WAI/fundamentals/components/ (Accessed: 11 December 2020).

Kargbo, J.A. (2010) 'Undergraduate students' problems with citing references', *The Reference Librarian*, 51(3), pp. 222–236. doi: 10.1080/02763871003769673

Neville, C. (2010) *The complete guide to referencing and avoiding plagiarism*. 2nd edn. Open University Press.

Pears, R. and Shields, G. (2019) *Cite Them Right: The Essential Referencing Guide*. 9th edn. London: Red Globe Press / Macmillan International Higher Education.

University of the West of Scotland. (2021) *Brief Guide to Referencing at UWS*. Available at: https://uws-uk.libguides.com/referencing (Accessed: 13 December 2020).

Williams, K. and Carroll, J. (2009) *Referencing and Understanding Plagiarism*. Palgrave MacMillan.

Yeo, S. (2007) 'First-year university science and engineering students' understanding of plagiarism', *High Education Research & Development*, 26(2), pp. 199–216. doi: 10.1080/07294360701310813

Additional referencing guides

American Psychological Association Tutorials and Webinars (2022) Available at: https://apastyle.apa.org/instructional-aids/tutorials-webinars (Accessed: 26 February 2022).

Imperial College London (no date) *Citing & Referencing: Harvard Style*. Available at: https://www.imperial.ac.uk/media/imperial-college/administration-and-support-services/library/public/harvard.pdf (Accessed: 26 February 2022).

Purdue University *APA Formatting and Style Guide* (no date) 7th ed. Available at: https://owl.purdue.edu/owl/research_and_citation/apa_style/apa_formatting_and_style_guide/general_format.html (Accessed: 26 February 2022).

University of York (no date) *Referencing styles – a Practical Guide: Harvard Referencing Style*. Available at: https://subjectguides.york.ac.uk/referencing-style-guides/harvard (Accessed: 27 February 2022).

4 Research Ethics

In this chapter, you will learn:

- The importance of ethics in academic research.
- The key aspects of research ethics when undertaking a dissertation.
- The concepts of anonymity and confidentiality.
- The steps to take when applying for ethical approval in your university.

Why research ethics?

The concept of research ethics, and the term, may be alien to you, and the notion of research ethics can be a minefield. There are so many questions and scenarios to reflect upon that it can all become confusing. One such question posed often inevitably reverberates around the idea of why research needs to be ethical. The outlook from computer science students that are developing a piece of software often perpetuates the view that the inclusion of any form of ethical perspective is redundant. Ethics are associated with the rules of conduct in relation to what is acceptable and unacceptable behaviour (Clark, 2019). This, of course, applies to educational research, which often involves the participation of human subjects. Furthermore, most ethical principles affiliated with research today are associated with the Belmont Report (1979), which identifies guidelines related to respect for persons, beneficence, and justice.

Research ethics are fundamental when dealing with human subjects and matter in all types of research (Fujii, 2012). If the research process is not given due ethical consideration, it can potentially bring harm to participants when exploring sensitive issues that could also have psychological effects (Fujii, 2012). It is important to be conscious of the fact that various unforeseen ethical scenarios and problems can impact on all aspects of research, whether it is of a qualitative or quantitative nature (Guillemin and Gillam, 2004).

DOI: 10.4324/9781003054887-4

What quantifies a research study to be ethical?

For a research study to be deemed ethically driven, it is not only the manner of how the research is conducted that is important, but also the procedures and processes that the researcher has implemented to ensure the ethics. The researcher should consider several things prior to conducting a research study, and it may be that a games development or computer science-related dissertation can involve human participants. For example, during the evaluation stage, you may require participants to provide you with feedback about how your game or piece of software performed. This could take the form of a questionnaire or interview. If you are conducting a virtual reality related study, then you might also want to undertake some observational research. It is most likely that the participants involved in your research will be your peers, fellow students in your class, or students from other academic disciplines. Recruiting participants can sometimes be challenging, though your project supervisor can help you. It is therefore important to consider participant involvement from an early stage of the dissertation.

You must address several important ethical principles from an ethical standpoint prior to commencing your research. One such aspect is how to communicate the significance and relevance of the study to your potential participants and the reasons for their inclusion within it. This can be achieved through the creation and use of an ethics research statement and an informed consent form. In relation to informed consent, it has been considered that the salient preconditions for informed consent in a research study relate to the participant being given the right to understand what the research is about and to voluntarily decide whether to participate (McNamee, Olivier, and Wainwright, 2007). Furthermore, the requirements of anonymity, confidentiality, and privacy are also pivotal obligations of the research ethics research design that need to be communicated to the participant.

Ethical considerations for the dissertation

The purpose of the study will ultimately dictate whether human participation is required. For example, the dissertation could be one that is predominately literature based, such as reviewing the state-of-the-art of virtual reality use in HE. If the dissertation is practical, this potentially raises ethical questions related to the research methodology, research methods, and evaluation of the software to be developed. If this is the case, then several pertinent issues should be considered:

- The setting and context of the research determines aspects of accessibility to participants and whether there are special access requirements.
- Your sample size determines the scope of your study and is dictated by your research design.
- How will you recruit your participants (e.g., use of social media platforms such as LinkedIn)?
- How will you inform participants about the research aims and objectives? They have the right to make an informed decision to participate.
- To make an informed decision about whether to participate in the research, participants must be told about the purpose of the study, why they have been chosen, what is required of them, and how the results will be disseminated.
- Participant anonymity must be adhered to and ensured throughout the duration of a research study when dealing with participants. This can be achieved using an alphanumeric ID as an alias for the participant.
- Where and how will the data from the research be stored, and who will have access to it? The research team are the only ones who should have access to the data, and access should be password protected and encrypted.

Recruiting participants

When recruiting your participants, it is important to consider who will evaluate your software or game and why. You also have to consider your intended target audience.

Involving external organisations with your university can also be problematic since you may have to complete a disclosure form and arrange agreements with the company concerned. This process also at times exacerbates the potential issue of data privacy, confidentiality, and participant anonymity. For example, if you were undertaking a study to investigate the use of games-based learning in primary school education, you would need to complete a disclosure form for access.

It is usually best to avoid a blanket cold-calling approach toward recruiting potential participants. For example, this might involve an e-mail being disseminated by your project supervisor on your behalf to your peers who are undertaking modules in other years of your program, asking them to take part in your research. However, you can adopt alternative approaches toward recruiting participants:

- Using social media platforms such as *LinkedIn* to promote your research and invite potential participants to complete your online questionnaire.
- Making use of any online groups or channels (e.g., a *Discord* community group or one relevant to your discipline area) to inform potential participants about your research. This recruitment approach can provide you with constructive technical feedback relating to your implementation.
- Sharing details about your research and the questionnaire to complete on your university's VLE (i.e., within a module you are studying).

Informed consent

"Informed consent is the major ethical issue in conducting research" (Fouka and Mantzorou, 2011, p. 4). Informed consent relates to the process of obtaining permission from a subject to participate in research or a study of some kind (Parvizi et al., 2008). Three fundamental elements of criteria must be considered and ensured prior to requesting it. The subject or participant must be competent, sufficiently informed, and not coerced (Cocanour, 2017). Prior to being involved in a research study, participants must be able to understand what the research is about and why they are being asked to become involved. The information provided to them must be informative enough to allow them to make an informed decision, in addition to being able to understand any potential consequences that may arise from such a decision. It is important that the decision to participate is voluntary and not coerced. When informed consent has been achieved, it is also important to remember that the participant has the right to withdraw from the study at any point. Simply stated, *"right of withdrawal states that a subject may discontinue participation in a study at any time for any reason or no reason at all"* (Sachs, 2011, p. 17). It is important to ensure that research is fully explained to the participant, and a useful approach to achieving this goal is through the creation of an A4 document stating the aims and objectives of the research. We will now go through the main stages of such a document so that you can gauge the salient ethical points that must be considered.

1 Providing research details

State the subject area or title of the proposed research project in addition to your own details. These details might include your name, e-mail address, name of your school, and project supervisor.

2 Providing the participant with the choice of participation

You could emphasise:

- The fact that the participant is being invited to take part in the study.
- The importance of taking the time understand why the study is being undertaken.
- That no undue pressure is applied to be involved in the research and that is it up to the participant to decide whether to be involved.

Providing an overview of the research study gives participants a sense of comfort that they are not being coerced into the research, with the onus on them if they engage or not.

3 Clarifying the purpose of the study

It is important to clarify what the aim of the study is and the form that it will take. This could mean detailing the research methods that will be used and some of the topics that might be addressed. So, if you were going to adopt a mixed methods questionnaire approach, you could state something along the following:

- The questionnaire aim and whether it adopts a mixed methods approach using open and closed questions.
- Information about the various research themes that the questionnaire will explore.
- Explaining research concepts or theories participants might be aware of.

4 Justification for having been chosen

You also must provide an explanation to participants about why they have been chosen. There must be some form of relevancy to them that they can either relate to the study from personal experience or provide relevant data based upon their generalist views and opinions.

5 Transparency that participation is voluntary

This section reinforces the ethical concept of 'Right of Withdrawal', and this needs to be made clear to the participant prior to the study's commencement. They have the right to withdraw from your study at any time and without prior notice having been provided.

6 Informing the participant what they must do

The participant must understand what they are being asked to do. This must be explained to them, leaving no room for ambiguity. In doing so, this provides the participant with reassurance that they are happy to partake in the study. So, if the participant is being asked to complete a questionnaire, some initial background needs to be provided to them stating the nature of the questionnaire.

7 Ensuring participant anonymity and confidentiality

It is important to state how participant anonymity and confidentiality will be ensured. This will be foremost in the participant's mind and may have a direct bearing about whether they will participate. It is also important to mention how the research data will be stored and who will have access to it. The main thing to reaffirm here is that the real name of participants or organisations will not be disclosed.

8 How results will be disseminated

It is also imperative that you clarify how the results will be applied, such as how they will be disseminated, how this will be undertaken, and where they will be published. It is also important to stress that the research is being undertaken for noncommercial gain. In the context of a dissertation, the results will, of course, be published in it – for educational and academic purposes only. It might also be worthwhile to emphasise that all results will remain confidential and how this will be achieved.

9 Provide reassurances that research is credibly organised

Another relevant aspect to mention in your research ethics planning is who is organising the research and who is spearheading or supporting it. The participant must be made aware that you are from a reputable institution – in your case, this will be your academic institution. Though you are the principal investigator, you are being supported by your project supervisor, and through them, your academic institution. In addition, you are also representing your institution, so the research must be ethically sound.

10 *Peer assessment of the research study*

A useful piece of information to also include is to provide further reassurance to the participant that the research has been reviewed and approved by the project supervisor and the Ethics Review Board.

11 *Providing contact details*

You can provide a final summarisation of your contact details in case a participant would like to follow up and ask further questions about the study. Your contact details could include your name, e-mail address, and the name of your school or department.

Distinguishing between anonymity and confidentiality

The concepts of anonymity, confidentiality, and privacy are deemed to be important because they serve a fundamental purpose of safeguarding subjects from harm, in addition to protecting them from having any of their sensitive information disclosed (McNamee, Olivier, and Wainwright, 2007). Anonymity is defined as: "... *not true-naming participants or sites and not providing information that enables them to be identified*" (Kelly, 2009, p. 432).

The contextualisation aspect often associated with qualitative research means that ensuring participant anonymity is an important consideration. It can be argued that in the context of ethical research: "*an anonymous individual is capable of engaging others or providing information without identification*" (Novak, 2014, p. 37). When writing up your research findings, one method toward safeguarding a participant's anonymity is to use some form of alphanumeric identification. For example, in an interview transcript, you could say, "Participant A said the following" ... or "according to Participant B ...," thereby not disclosing the real identity of the participants. UT: The principal point is not to disclose the identity of the participant throughout the course of the research when you are presenting your results.

Closely aligned to the notion of anonymity is the term confidentiality. Confidentiality relates more to how the researcher intends to keep the data safe and secure. In the domain of research ethics, "*confidentiality was designed to prevent consequential harm associated with the compulsory disclosure of identifiable research data*" (Yu, 2008, p. 161). When combined with the aspect of anonymity, confidentiality has become fundamentally important when undertaking online research such as online questionnaires. Conducting research with online survey/questionnaire software means that the issues of confidentiality and anonymity are relevant. Consider how confidentiality will be maintained as problems could arise with any websites that you are using to store information, such as IP addresses that might be identifiable or the hacking of information stored on the website (Emery, 2014). Also clarify who has access to the data/information, such as the student and project supervisor.

Research ethics committee

Once you have completed your project proposal or outline and have had it approved, the next logical step is submitting your research ethics application if you intend to use participants. Your school or department should have its own research ethics committee (REC). The REC and ethical process itself is sometimes viewed as a potential hurdle to get over. Usually, your own academic school should have its own REC whose main aim is to review research proposed within their school that involves human participants to ensure that no harm comes to them. The REC's role is also to make certain that ethical standards are upheld in the research dissertation and that the name of the academic institution is not negatively compromised.

We present the following guidelines for your research ethics application:

1 Become familiar with the online application process

Familiarise yourself with the online application form you must complete and the relevant supplementary documentation (e.g., consent form, ethics research statement). Take the time to read the form because you need to understand what the REC are asking you. If you are unsure of anything, then discuss the issues with your supervisor.

2 Work through the form in stages

Do not rush the application process, and be aware that it can take a bit of time. It is best to get it right first time or as best you can. While there are no guarantees, you should work through the form in stages, saving what you have done. You can return to complete the form when you have reflected on some of the more important questions (e.g., anonymity and confidentiality).

3 *Complete the sections you can first*

To avoid procrastination, you can complete the initial sections of the online form that are straightforward, such as: your details, project title, and director of studies.

4 *Provide detail*

Use judgment and common sense to provide relevant detail in the relevant sections. Do not waffle, but make sure that you are expressing your research study in a way that a member of the REC can understand. Remember that the REC can be interdisciplinary, so be concise, relevant, yet informative.

5 *Consider what you are being asked*

It is important to think about the key questions in the application. These will be aspects relating to the purpose, justification, design, and methodology of the planned study. Questions relating to the justification of your intended sample size, how you will recruit participants, and how you will disseminate your results are equally fundamental. A good approach toward addressing these questions is to answer them on a Word document and then send them to your supervisor for review prior to committing your responses on the online form.

6 *Anonymity and confidentiality*

You will be asked how you will ensure participant anonymity and confidentiality. It is important that you understand the distinction and relationship between the two terms. You can seek clarity about these terms from your project supervisor, in addition to reading around the subject area. These ethical considerations will be of particular interest to the REC.

7 *Ensure supporting documentation completed*

At various sections, you will need to upload your supporting documentation, such as your participant consent form and research ethics statement. If you are undertaking questionnaires, you will need to provide the questionnaire. Run all these by your supervisor prior to uploading them with your application.

8 Treat the form as an academic assignment

When you are undertaking the ethics application process, it is important that you treat it like working on an academic assignment (Greaney et al., 2012). Take the time to proofread what you have written and check your grammar and punctuation prior to finally submitting your application. Again, check that you have included all your supporting documentation; failure to do so could delay the application process.

9 Be patient

The response from the REC could take anything from a week to potentially a month, so be patient. While waiting for a response from the REC, you can continue to work on other sections of your dissertation, such as the literature review. Do not remain dormant while waiting. If you don't get ethical approval, then you will need to alter the project to reflect this.

10 Make necessary amendments

The REC will make a decision based upon your application. If your application is accepted, you will receive a letter of approval by the REC. The other scenario is that you might have to make further revisions based on REC feedback. If you need to make revisions, take your time, consider what is being asked of you and why, and work through the changes with your supervisor. Once you are happy with the revisions, then you can resubmit.

Summary

Undertaking research that involves human participation will require you to obtain ethical approval to begin your empirical research. This applies to whether your research paradigm is qualitative, quantitative, or mixed methods. The incorporation of research ethics into your research design allows you to reflect upon: (1) how your study will be conducted; (2) why there is the need for human participation; (3) what will be expected of participants, and (4) how you will ensure that no associated risk or harm will be caused to them. It is important that you are transparent throughout the entirety of the research process and allow participation consent to be withdrawn at any point.

- **UT:** When involving human participants in your research study, you require ethical approval to commence your project.
- It is important that your subject area will not cause undue harm to participants or investigate sensitive issues causing unnecessary distress.
- You need to give prior thought to how you will recruit your participants and whether there will be any complications in doing so (e.g., the need to complete a disclosure application).
- Prior to starting your evaluation, it is important that you explain to potential participants why they are being involved and what is required from them.
- Participants can only engage in your study once they have consented to do so; hence, the process of informed consent.
- When writing your findings, you should ensure that participant anonymity is maintained and that subject details have not been disclosed in your dissertation.
- Confidentiality is also important as you must keep your research data secure and protected and clarify who has access to the data.

References

Cocanour, C.S. (2017) 'Informed consent – It's more than a signature on a piece of paper', *The American Journal of Surgery*, 214, pp. 993–997. doi: 10.1016/j.amjsurg. 2017.09.015

Clark, K.R. (2019) 'Ethics in research', *Radiologic Technology*, March/April 2019, 90(4), pp. 394–397.

Emery, K. (2014) 'So you want to do an online study: Ethics considerations and lessons learned', *Ethics & Behavior*, 24(4), pp. 293–303. doi: 10.1080/10508422. 2013.860031

Fouka, G. and Mantzorou, M. (2011) 'What are the major ethical issues in conducting research? Is there a conflict between the research ethics and the nature of nursing?', *Health Science Journal*, 5(1), pp. 3–14.

Fujii, L.A. (2012) 'Research ethics 101: Dilemmas and responsibilities'. *PS: Political Science & Politics*, 45(4), pp. 717–723. doi: 10.1017/S1049096512000819

Greaney, A.M., Sheehy, A., Heffernan, C., Murphy, J., Mhaolrúnaigh, S.N., Heffernan, E. and Brown, G. (2012) 'Research ethics application: A guide for the novice researcher', *British Journal of Nursing*, 21(1), pp. 38–43. doi: 10.12968/bjon.2012.21.1.38

Guillemin, M. and Gillam, L. (2004) 'Ethics, reflexivity, and "ethically important moments" in research', *Qualitative Inquiry*, 10(2), pp. 261–280. doi: 10.1177%2F1 077800403262360

Kelly, A. (2009) 'In defence of anonymity: Rejoining the criticism', *British Educational Research Journal*, 35(3), pp. 431–445. doi: 10.1080/01411920802044438

McNamee, M., Olivier, S. and Wainwright, P. (2007) *Research Ethics in Exercise, Health and Sport Sciences*. Oxon: Routledge.

Novak, A. (2014) 'Anonymity, confidentiality, privacy, and identity: The ties that bind and break in communication research', *Review of Communication*, 14(1), pp. 36–48. doi: 10.1080/15358593.2014.942351

Parvizi, J., Chakravarty, R., Og, B., and Rodriguez-Paez, A. (2008) 'Informed consent: Is it always necessary?' *Injury, Int. J. Care Injured*, 39, pp. 651–655. doi: 10.1016/j.injury.2008.02.010

Sachs, B. (2011) 'Going from principles to rules in research ethics', *Bioethics*, 25(1), pp. 9–20. doi: 10.1111/j.1467-8519.2009.01744.x

U.S. Department of Health & Human Services. The Belmont Report (1979) *Ethical Principles and Guidelines for the Protection of Human Subjects of Research*. Available at: https://www.hhs.gov/ohrp/regulations-and-policy/belmont-report/read-the-belmont-report/index.html (Accessed: 26 November 2020).

Yu, K. (2008) 'Confidentiality revisited', *Journal of Academic Ethics*, 6, pp. 161–172. doi: 10.1007/s10805-008-9061-0

5 Dissertation Structure in Games Development and Computer Science

In this chapter, you will learn about:

- Basic structure.
- How dissertation structures vary dependent on discipline.
- A suitable structure for games development and computer science.
- What should go in each section.
- Producing a table of contents.
- Producing a mind map of the structure.

It is a very good idea to consider the structure to act as a blueprint template to eventually fill in. This approach is advantageous because, first, it means you are less likely to miss things, and second, it indicates progress in terms of the amount of work you have to do and the amount you have done. Parts of a dissertation are presentational and can be added in sooner rather than later; it is a pity to have a presentation distract from a brilliantly written dissertation. When you hold the finished product in your hands, you should be able to flick through it and view it as a professionally published book. Determining the structure before commencing is beneficial; it allows effective planning and the formulation of a holistic view before launching into writing. You will be able to visualise this plan in your brain, answer questions on it, use it as a reference, and have intimate knowledge of it for years to come. Many dissertations have a relatively similar basic structure, which can vary slightly depending on discipline and focus. There are certain rules and guidelines to follow; however, at the end of the day, it is your dissertation, and as long as you can justify the structure, then that is all that matters. This chapter provides a dissertation structure guide in games development and computer science. Consider it and plan your content effectively.

DOI: 10.4324/9781003054887-5

Basic structure

Regardless of discipline, all dissertations have a reasonably similar basic structure where the primary goal is to keep your point/argument running throughout it, driving the content. The structure is:

- Abstract
- Introduction/Rationale
- Methodology
- Literature Review
- Findings
- Conclusions, Implications and Future Recommendations

How dissertation structures vary dependent on discipline

Every discipline, or even supervisor, has a preferred structure. However, a main source of potential contention between academics is where to place the literature review. Some academics believe that the methodology should come in a chapter before the literature review containing the research questions. Some believe that the literature review should be performed in the first instance to identify gaps, informing the research question(s) before construction. Some believe that that archival research should be performed with the purpose in mind and described in the methodology chapter, and the results presented in the literature review because archival research is really a literature review. We are of the opinion that the computer games and computer science literature is too vast to review without a specific goal in mind as a starting point. We recommend constructing an idea of interest to you and your supervisor and ascertaining whether the topic is workable. The methodology chapter and research questions (if any) will be presented first, and then the literature review looking at the main topic will follow. The structure should be an agreement between you and your supervisor.

A suitable structure for games development and computer science dissertations

In our combined experience of supervising hundreds of dissertation projects in games development and computer science related subjects, and also producing many dissertations at various levels ourselves, we have formulated the following suggested starting structure as a guide to be adapted as required by supervisors and students. Table 5.1 shows a proposed structure.

Table 5.1 Proposed structure for dissertations

Section number	Title of section
	Title page
	Project Specification/Proposal/Outline
	Declaration/Cover sheet
	Acknowledgements
	Table of Contents
	List of Figures
	List of Tables
	Glossary
	Abstract
1	Introduction
2	Research Methodology
3	Literature Review
4	Software Development Lifecycle Methodology
5	Software Design Methodology
6	Design
7	Implementation
8	Testing
9	Evaluation/Results
10	Discussion
11	Conclusions/Recommendations/Future Research Directions
	References
	Appendices

We will now provide a summary description of the content of the constituent parts to provide an idea of what to expect.

1 Title page

There will likely be a standard title page provided by your institution, generally consisting of:

- Emblem/logo of your institution,
- Degree programme/course title,
- Dissertation title,
- Your full name and identifying institutional number,
- Date submitted,
- Qualification,
- Academic team names.

2 *Project specification/proposal*

Any form of project specification, proposal, or outline should be included at the beginning or as an appendix. In our institution, this has a marking scheme to assess the final dissertation.

3 *Declaration/cover sheet*

The declaration is traditionally for you to sign an agreement that it is your own work presented. Here is an example:

Declaration

This dissertation is in partial fulfillment with the requirements for the degree of BSc Computer Games Development (Hons) in the University of the West of Scotland.

    I declare that this dissertation embodies the results of my own work and that it has been composed by myself. Following normal academic conventions, I have made due acknowledgement to the work of others.

Name: Thomas Hainey
Signature:
Date: 17//02/2022

A cover sheet may also be included if you submit a paper-based copy. This can be a submission requirement, or perhaps you just feel better submitting something physical rather than virtual. It may very well be that only a soft copy is necessary. In any event, after you have worked hard on a dissertation, people like to get a copy printed to keep and gaze upon.

An example cover has this basic structure:

Form to accompany dissertation

Surname: Gordon	
Forename: Tom	
ID: B0000000	
Course Code: COMP10000	

Course Description: BSc Computer Science
Project Supervisor: Dr. Thomas Baxter
Dissertation Title: Development of an Entity Relationship Editor and Schema Generator
Session: 2020/2021

4 Acknowledgements

A dissertation can be a monumental part of your degree, and you will have relied greatly on the support of other people (either academically or generally), such as: supervisor, lecturers, partner, parents, siblings, colleagues, friends, or even pets! This is an opportunity to thank anyone who supported you. It is important to keep it the right length and thank those who matter from your institution in particular and your personal life. You should look at the requirements of your school and institution and use the appropriate tone; remember that everything in a dissertation is scrutinised, so be careful. See the 14 examples provided at the following link: https://londonproofreaders.co.uk/dissertation-acknowledgements-examples/

5 Abstract

An abstract consists of about two to three hundred words summarising the entire dissertation quickly, allowing the reader to assess if it is relevant to them. It has a certain dynamic in our disciplines where a problem to be addressed is briefly outlined, a potential solution to that problem is described, and some overall optional results of implementation, testing, or evaluation is presented. An abstract for a research paper can have a formal pre-defined structure, such as: **purpose, design/ methodology/approach, findings, practical implications, originality.** The structure can mirror the contents of the overall work. Abstracts can be written at the start or end of the dissertation project, depending on preference. Here is an example:

Source: *Dissertation B*
Abstract
This paper presents the development of an Entity Relationship Editor that is capable of generating a relational database schema from the diagram. Current CASE tools, such as Rational Rose and Select

SSADM professional edition, have the problems of either being too complex or are not in the notation of the Unified Modelling Language. As well as presenting a thorough investigation of the functionality and behaviour of current CASE tools, the paper will identify criteria from these CASE tools to be considered in the development of the Entity Relationship Editor.

6 Introduction

The introduction can be split into three sections: the problem, proposed solution, and structure. The **problem** seems similar to the abstract, but it elaborates on the problem and provides some academic rigour, i.e., academic references to support the problem statement. If you find two or three references to support the problem that you are saying exists, then it starts to have a completely different look and structure from the abstract. Here is an example problem excerpt, with the citations in bold for to illustrate rigour:

Games for learning have been used in a number of areas, including business, computing, social issues, and health **(Boyle et al., 2016)**. There is, however, a lack of evidence in terms of games types/genres applied to groups for particular pedagogical content arising from problems associated with generalisability **(Hays, 2005)**.

This technique has two advantages: first, the structure will become notably different from the abstract, and second, setting up the rationale for the problem in the introduction will get you looking for evidence to back up your statements.

The proposed solution section outlines how you intend to '*address*' the research problem. Notice that we say '*address*' and not '*solve*' or '*ascertain*' rather than '*prove*'. In research, you are objectively reporting that you are attempting to contribute to solving a problem – so it is more accurate to say you are '*addressing the problem*' as you may not solve it. This may require developing a new game, piece of software, technique, framework, or model, and to evaluate success needs a research plan, which can be outlined briefly here. The structure section allows you to elaborate on the structure that follows, which is good for getting your word count up without too much effort and allows thought on subsequent sections.

Start on section two, and elaborate in a small paragraph on what each chapter will contain, remembering that you should be on chapter/section one at the moment.

7 *Methodology*

This is the first part where you can demonstrate your thought processes, objectivity, and meticulousness. You have many research methodologies and methods to choose from, and you can demonstrate that you have considered several of them for your project, and, more importantly, can objectively select the best one(s). Going through this process is highly illuminating, revealing, and educational since it allows you to reflect on and discover what kind of researcher you are by identifying the methodologies and methods for your project. We recommend the following useful sections:

- Defining what research is.
- Defining what a research methodology and methods are.
- Investigating the schools of research including quantitative, qualitative, and mixed.
- Investigating primary and secondary research methodologies.
- Investigating the hard and soft research dichotomies at different levels, including ontological, epistemological, and methodological level.
- Stating what particular kind of researcher you are.
- Reviewing the application, advantages, and disadvantages of the main research methodologies.

We suggest the following structure for this chapter:

1   What is research?
2   Methodology and methods
3   Schools of thought

    a   Quantitative
    b   Qualitative
    c   Mixed
    d   Primary
    e   Secondary

 f Hard – Positivist

 g Soft – Interpretivist

4 Main research methodologies

 a Experiment
 b Quasi-experiment
 c Correlational studies
 d Surveys, tests, and questionnaires
 e Case studies
 f Observational research
 g Longitudinal research
 h Archival research
 i Ethnography
 j Meta-analysis
 k Content analysis

5 Research questions
6 Methodologies selected to answer research questions

This may seem overkill, but it will become obvious fairly quickly what kind of researcher you are and what methodologies you will use as some of these are simply not practical in the context of an honour's dissertation. For example: longitudinal research is generally over many years, and you have one year. If you select a very common methodology, such as survey with the method of questionnaire, then it would be beneficial to add a section here on questionnaire development, construction, and potential deployment. Questionnaires are covered in *Chapter 22*.

8 Literature review

The main literature review provides the rationale for the project and identifies the gap in the academic literature being addressed. It is basically everything that you can find on your selected subject, or similar comparable subject area, and can account for a large number of marks. We discuss the literature review in *Chapter 8*, but for the moment, it is where you get the opportunity to explore your selected area, and this can be interesting and even addictive. Exploring a subject area can include:

- Looking at different definitions of your basic terms in your subject title. For example, if you are writing a dissertation with the following title: *"Using Story and Narrative in Serious Games to Teach History,"* you may wish to define the terms "story," "narrative," and "serious games."
- Looking at previous examples in the academic literature of computer games to teach history or any subject for that matter.
- Trying to find empirical examples of serious games utilising narrative and story as a tool or potential development frameworks utilising story and narrative to teach history.

The literature review is very organic and is a result of your investigative thought processes and what is discovered. The final polished chapter is a synthesis of the literature that you have found and is not regurgitation but interpretation. Obviously, it is impossible to find every relevant piece of information in the world, but you are trying to show that a fair amount of effort has been put into finding sources and synthesising them.

9 Software development and game development lifecycles

It is essential to utilise the tools for the discipline you are studying, and games development and computer science have many software development and game development lifecycles to use. It is another opportunity to show the reader the process of how you have made your decisions. This generally requires an objective review of available choices, weighing up the pros and cons and then selecting the best option. There are software development lifecycles that you can use from classical computer science and information systems literature and newer games development lifecycles from games companies, computer games literature, or the grey literature. We recommended this structure:

- Defining a software/games development lifecycle methodology.
- Establishing why a development methodology is necessary.
- For each methodology, provide a description, diagrammatic representation, advantages, and disadvantages.

  - Waterfall model
  - Incremental model

- Spiral model
- Rapid application development
- Agile method
- Blitz games studios (GDLC)
- Arnold Hendrick's
- Doppler interactive

- Justify the selection of the lifecycle.

10 Design methodology

This section involves selecting software design modelling techniques, such as the UML (Unified Modelling Language), Entity Relationship Modelling or SSADM (Structured Systems Analysis and Design Methodology) (Boghosian, 2000). Selecting a particular diagrammatic format to design a holistic view of your implementation can add an extra level of technical precision to your dissertation. This section may include:

- Selection of a design, modelling technique.
- Presentation of a holistic view of your software/game utilising this selected technique.

11 Design

For computer science, this may entail: high level objectives, a requirements specification, conceptual models, pseudocode, and structure diagrams. For a games dissertation, you may produce a games design document or technical design document. We cover all of these areas in depth later in the book. This section should be as professional and concise as possible, which seems to be easier for computer science students in our experience. Any supplementary information can be put into an appendix.

12 Implementation

The section should convey a sufficient amount of information about the software program or game developed without the reader actually running the software. A dissertation must stand on its own without the extra added elaboration of running the software. The majority of the readers will not have the time, but links to video demos can be included in this dissertation section for interested readers to view in their own time. A suitable structure could be:

- Basic functionality – basic functionality description, including screen shots.
- Advanced functionality – a description of interesting functionality that has been difficult to implement and possibly the focus of the dissertation, e.g., the mapping algorithm of *Dissertation B* or complicated AI implementation.
- A discussion of project management and version control.
- A showreel, link to a proof of concept, demonstration or prototype.

---

13 Testing

Testing is the process of trying out your software or game with the intent of finding errors. This entails objectively reviewing the software and games testing approaches available, making an objective justifiable selection, and providing testing evidence. We suggest the following adaptable structure:

- What is a software/games testing?
- Testing techniques

  - Functional testing
  - Structural testing
  - Error-oriented testing
  - Play testing
  - Alpha/Beta testing

- Test plan
- Test log
- Crash report/bug reports
- Improvements made

---

14 Evaluation/results

Evaluation can be confused and merged with testing; however, testing in a computer science context usually means running the implementation to make sure that it works properly in terms of functionality. Evaluation (probably more common in games dissertations) is trying out the implementation to ascertain if it performs its purpose. If that purpose is to provide a more immersive approach for teaching programming than traditional teaching approaches, then this is different from testing functionality and moving into the games user research domain. This could require a controlled experiment with evaluation instruments. We provide the following example section:

- Defining evaluation.
- Reviewing evaluation types (formative and summative) and selecting the best approach.
- Describing the procedure and format of how, where, and when the evaluation is performed. This may entail an experimental design or distributing a questionnaire.
- Description of instruments used, e.g., description of a questionnaire.
- Describing the participants demographics.
- Presenting results collected.
- Synthesis the interesting findings.

---

15 Discussion

The discussion allows you to highlight interesting, perhaps even surprising, findings. This allows you to show the reader (marker) that you can interpret the results beyond just basic reporting and make comparisons between your results and previous academic studies.

16 Conclusions, recommendations, and future research directions

Conclusions are the main findings of your project, and if you have research questions, you would reiterate them and answer them. You may possibly go back to the main title of your investigation and provide an overall answer/summary of the result. The dissertation has possibly started with a number of research questions on a particular topic and split into several different directions to investigate. The conclusion is where you bring it all back together in an objective, logical manner. This section can cause confusion if students want to focus on the software/game they have produced, but the conclusion should focus on the overall findings.

Recommendations that you make to the academic community or industry are based on the results of your investigation so others can use them.

Future directions can be a combination of how the general academic community can continue your investigation in some way and also how you are going to continue your work. It is beneficial to suggest a number of future research directions, even if you intend to never look at the research again since it signifies that you have been interested in the work and it is worth continuing. The last thing you want to do is give the impression that you will never look at it again and are glad it is over.

17 References

The reference to every citation goes in the appropriate format, generally in alphabetical or numerical order, depending on the referencing standard. This is not a bibliography, and it is highly important in the eyes of an academic. They instantly consult your reference section to see how many quality, up-to-date references you have. **UT:** Try to have well-recognised references that have stood the test of time and newer ones to make your dissertation unique and current.

18 Appendices

The appendices are where to put things that are too large, break the flow, and are part of the work to be included for completeness, including:

- Surveys details and questionnaires.
- More detailed games design documents.
- Large requirements specifications.
- List of literature review papers.
- Data sets.
- Qualitative results such as transcripts.
- Participant evaluation forms.
- Ethics forms.

Producing a table of contents

A table of contents can be easily generated in Word. It is worthwhile to draft a basic one to provide an overall vision of what the finished article will contain. We suggest a relatively formulaic template/guide that can be adapted for individual circumstances. While the majority applies to all, some parts are unique to each selected project/topic area. We suggest the following:

Abstract

1 Introduction

   1.1 Problem overview
   1.2 Proposed solution
   1.3 Dissertation structure

2 Research methodologies

   2.1 What is a methodology?
   2.2 What are methods?
   2.3 Quantitative
   2.4 Qualitative
   2.5 Hard and soft schools of information systems (IS)
   2.6 Mixed methods
   2.7 Main research methodologies
   2.8 Research questions
   2.9 Justification of selection of research methodologies

3 Literature review

   3.1 Defining key terms
   3.2 Appropriate academic examples
   3.3 Empirical evidence
   3.4 Summary and synthesis

4 Software/game development lifecycle methodologies

   4.1 What is a development methodology?
   4.2 Main development methodologies
   4.3 Selection of project development methodology

5 Design methodology

   5.1 What is a design methodology?
   5.2 SSADM
   5.3 UML
   5.4 EER
   5.5 Selection and justification

6 Design

   6.1 Overview
   6.2 Class diagrams

6.3 Level design
6.4 GDD

7 Implementation

7.1 Basic functionality
7.2 Advanced/interesting functionality
7.3 Version control
7.4 TDD
7.5 Show reel video demonstration

8 Software games testing methodology

8.1 What is software/games testing?
8.2 Functional testing
8.3 Structural testing
8.4 Error-oriented testing
8.5 Playtesting
8.6 Alpha/beta testing
8.7 Selection of testing methodology

9 Evaluation

9.1 What is evaluation?
9.2 Types of evaluation

9.2.1 Formative
9.2.2 Summative

9.3 Procedure
9.4 Materials
9.5 Results

10 Discussion

10.1 Discussion of overall results
10.2 Interesting points
10.3 Comparison with other studies

11 Conclusions

11.1 Main findings
11.2 Recommendations
11.3 Future research directions

References
Appendices

Producing a mind map of your dissertation structure

A mind map is useful for several reasons:

- It allows planning and demonstrates to the reader how the overall point flows through your work.
- It shows the purpose of each constituent section in relation to the overall objective.
- It shows how sections and chapters feed into, inform, and complement each other.

Figure 5.1 gives an example mind map from a dissertation looking at the application of computer games to teach programming concepts.

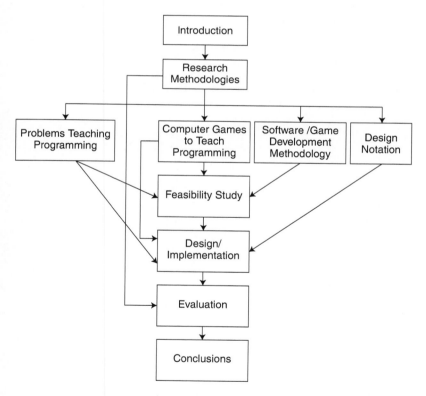

Figure 5.1 An example dissertation mind map.

Summary

This chapter has provided a basic adaptable structure for a dissertation in the disciplines of computer games and computer science. We have provided a brief description of each of the sections, with relevant examples for clarification. The chapter has also presented an adaptable table of contents for appropriate planning and an example mind map to illustrate the potential beneficial use of such an approach.

References

Boghosian, B. (2000) *Software Design Modeling Techniques and Tools.* Available at: http://www.continuum.org/~brentb/casetool.html (Accessed: 13 February 2022).

Boyle, E.A., Hainey, T., Connolly, T.M., Gray, G., Earp, J., Ott, M., Lim, T., Ninaus, M., Ribeiro, C. and Pereira, J. (2016) 'An update to the systematic literature review of empirical evidence of the impacts and outcomes of computer games and serious games', *Computers & Education*, 94, 178–192. doi: 10.1016/j.compedu.2015.11.003

Hays, R. (2005) The Effectiveness of Instructional Games: A Literature Review and Discussion. Tech Report Jul-Oct.

London Proofreaders (2018, December 11) *14 Dissertation Acknowledgments Examples.* Available at: https://londonproofreaders.co.uk/dissertation-acknowledgements-examples/ (Accessed: 13 February 2022).

6 Research Methodologies and Methods

In this chapter, you will learn about:

- The relationship between a research methodology and method.
- Different ontological and epistemological research perspectives and how they relate to qualitative and quantitative research.
- When best to adopt various research methods for mixed-methods research.

Research methodologies and methods

When undertaking your dissertation project, you will inevitably be asked what your research methodology is (probably by your supervisor). You may also be asked about your methodology when you have to do a project presentation. The concept of a research methodology will most likely be unfamiliar to you. To complicate matters further, you will also have to consider and explain your chosen research methods. Before elaborating on these terms, it is important to clarify that research methodologies and methods are dictated by your research focus and research question(s). This topic will be addressed in more detail in Chapter 7. This process involves determining what the aims and objectives of your research are and selecting an appropriate research methodology and methods to address your research questions.

What is a research methodology?

A research methodology is defined by Saunders, Lewis, and Thornhill (2019, p. 808) as:

DOI: 10.4324/9781003054887-6

"The theory of how research should be undertaken, including the theoretical and philosophical assumptions upon which research is based and the implications of these for the method or methods adopted."

Two main philosophical viewpoints dictate how academic research is performed. These philosophical outlooks are traditionally referred to as interpretivism and positivism (Ryan, 2018). These research perspectives are also sometimes called research paradigms (Burrell and Morgan, 1979). One philosophical position that these schools of thought differ on is the nature of reality. This is often referred to as the ontological position of the research (Willig, 2008, Collis and Hussey, 2014).

The interpretivist view of ontology argues that reality relates to the following traits:

- Individuals are social in nature.
- Knowledge is constructed through shared interaction among individuals.
- Reality is always changing, as is a person's subjective view of it.

In contrast, positivists regard reality as follows:

- Objective, not subjective.
- Everyone has the same view of reality, and subjective multiple realities do not exist.
- Rules and procedures impact the way an individual conducts their life.

Figure 6.1 provides the fundamental components of the interpretivist ontology.

Figure 6.2 provides the fundamental components relating to the positivist ontological position.

We present a simplified flowchart to decide ontological position in Figure 6.3.

Identifying your ontological position helps to solidify how you intend to obtain the data you require to answer your research questions.

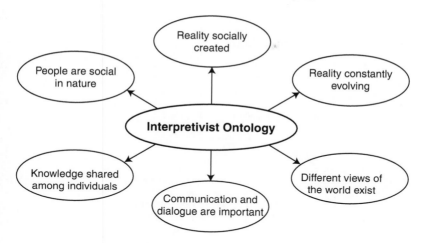

Figure 6.1 Interpretivist traits of reality.

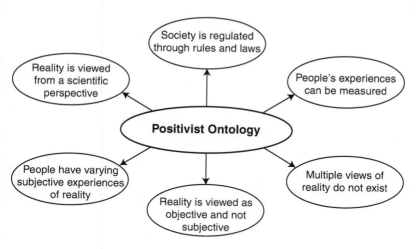

Figure 6.2 Positivist traits of reality.

Qualitative and quantitative research

Your research position or ontological view of reality will determine whether your research will be predominately qualitative or quantitative in focus. Yilmaz (2013, pp. 311–12) provides 1 definitions of these research terms to assist in explaining the differences.

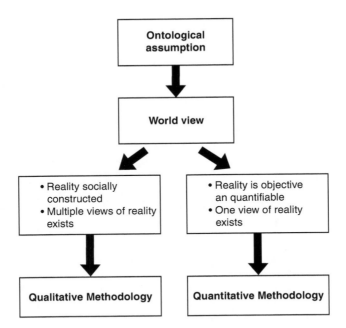

Figure 6.3 Simplified ontological position flowchart.

Qualitative research: " … *an emergent, inductive, interpretive and naturalistic approach to the study of people, cases, phenomena, social situations and processes in their natural settings in order to reveal in descriptive terms the meanings that people attach to their experiences of the world.*"

Quantitative research: " … *research that explains phenomena according to numerical data which are analysed by means of mathematically based methods, especially statistics.*"

The characteristics of qualitative and quantitative research are displayed in Figures 6.4 and 6.5 respectively.

Based on our supervisory experience, computer scientists predominantly adhere to quantitative research that involves testing and evaluating code, algorithms, AI, applications, or websites they have created. In contrast, game development students are adopting a more mixed-methods approach that combines elements of qualitative and quantitative

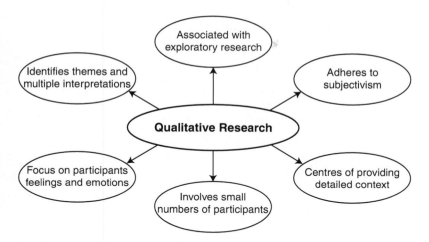

Figure 6.4 Characteristics of qualitative research.

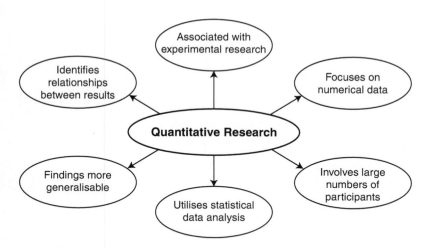

Figure 6.5 Characteristics of quantitative research.

research. This approach often involves the use of open and closed questions within the questionnaires used for evaluation purposes. The primary research methodologies undergraduate students often employ are: case study, survey, experimental and quasi-experimental. Table 6.1 shows

Table 6.1 Common research methodologies employed in games and computer science dissertations

Methodology	Features	Advantages	Disadvantages
Case Study	Studies a problem area in a real-life natural context. Case studies can be multiple or single.	Suitable for focusing upon specific job roles, project teams, or using new software in an organisation.	Assumption that single case studies cannot produce generalisations.
	Uses various research methods, both qualitative and quantitative.	Allows investigation of practical problems involving software use or technology.	Aspects of reliability of findings viewed as potential barriers to case study research.
	Often placed in a context defined by what is going to be studied in terms of subject area.	Provides qualitative contextual findings to coincide with quantitative data.	View that there can be an element of researcher bias with case study research.
Surveys	Used to collect data from large samples achieved using questionnaires.	Allows you to obtain a good response rate from a large audience.	If questionnaires are too long, then respondents may not complete them.
	Associated with the positivist methodology.	Can be used with the interpretivist paradigm.	Ethical issues may impact what questions you can and cannot ask.
	Researcher can utilise quantitative data for statistical analysis.	Using online survey software provides large response numbers.	Badly designed questionnaires can result in a high noncompletion rate.
Experiments	Direct manipulation of the independent variable within a controlled environment	Interesting factors can be isolated to draw conclusions on causality. The only real mechanism of proving cause and effect.	Ethical issues may be associated with the manipulation of variables.
	Can have a number of designs and a control including pre-test and post-test.	Far more effective at measuring change.	Requires far more effort and planning to set up.

(Continued)

Table 6.1 (Continued)

Methodology	Features	Advantages	Disadvantages
Quasi-experi-mental	Resembles experimental design without the randomisation.	Predictable relationships can be identified.	Causality cannot be fully confirmed.

benefits and drawbacks of these research methodologies (Flyvbjerg, 2006, Yin, 2009, Clark-Carter, 2010, Saunders, Lewis, and Thornhill, 2019).

There are many research methodologies, and to mention them all is beyond the scope of this chapter. A key consideration when choosing an methodology is time. For example, undertaking the qualitative methodology of ethnography would be incredibly time consuming and not practical since you only have so much time to complete your dissertation!

Epistemology and research methods

The research methods or data-gathering techniques you adopt to obtain the data for analysis will be informed by your epistemological stance. The concept of epistemological assumptions relates to the researcher's philosophical position concerning " ... *what constitutes valid knowledge in the context of the relationship of the researcher to that being researched*" (Collis and Hussey, 2014, p. 341). Figure 6.6 presents a simplified flowchart to determine epistemological stance.

Utilising mixed-methods research

We have observed that a common research approach adopted is a mixed-methods research design. The concept of mixed-methods research allows the researcher to obtain both quantitative and qualitative data. This is quite often achieved (in our experience) using the survey methodology and the questionnaire research method employing close-ended and open-ended questions. Close-ended questions are ones where respondents select a series of potential answers and are analysed quantitatively. Open-ended questions are where respondents are allowed to express their answers in writing so that their views and perceptions can be analysed qualitatively. Questionnaire design is discussed in Chapter 22.

It is important to consider how data is analysed when using mixed-methods research. The qualitative and quantitative data should be used to complement one another when interpreting and reporting your

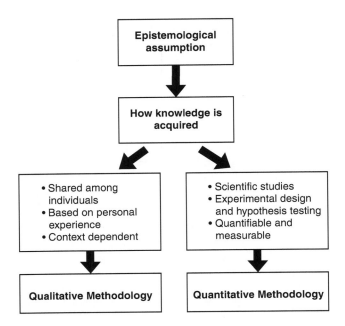

Figure 6.6 Simplified epistemological position flow chart.

research findings (Creswell, 2015). The primary assumption being that interpretation and presentation of qualitative and quantitative data provides a more substantiated understanding of a problem area or research question (Creswell, 2014, 2015).

Using research methods

The research methods used to collect the data to be analysed will be primarily dictated by your research questions. Your research methodology and design will also influence the research methods you choose for gathering your data for analysis. For example, a case study methodology is a flexible research design in the sense that it can accommodate and utilise a combination of qualitative and quantitative research methods (Yin, 2005). When choosing your research methods, it is important to consider which ones will be the most rigorous for helping you obtain the relevant data you require to address your research topic.

Questionnaires

Questionnaires can conform to a mixed-methods research design primarily due to the inclusion of open and closed questions. Both types of questions can provide you with scope for both qualitative and quantitative data analysis. Questionnaires are beneficial in a research study because they provide you with an opportunity to gain data from more respondents, allowing you to have greater scope for interpreting your findings.

Online questionnaires can be useful in the following ways when undertaking a large-scale evaluation of a game, app, or website:

- They can be easily circulated by e-mail.
- They can be easily edited and allow differing types of questions for statistical analysis.
- They can generate the descriptive analysis of your results for presentation purposes.
- Sending questionnaires electronically online provides you with a better opportunity of receiving an acceptable response rate to allow for statistical and thematic analysis of data.

Interviews

Three common types of interviews can be incorporated into a mixed-methods research study; they are (1) structured interviews; (2) semi-structured interviews, and (3) unstructured interviews. These are summarised in Table 6.2.

Interviews are an important and frequently used data collection method in case study research (Merriam, 2009; Yin, 2009). When selecting the choice of interview technique to adopt in a research study, Creswell (2007) states that it is important to choose the interview approach that will generate the most useful information to answer the research questions. Interviews are useful for providing some contextualisation to the quantitative findings produced from questionnaires. In contrast to quantitative data, interviews provide the researcher with an opportunity to interpret the views and opinions of participants. The use of interviews provides the researcher with scope to analyse and understand the meaning of participant views.

Table 6.2 Interview styles (adapted from Myers, 2009, p.123)

Types of interviews	Interview characteristics
Structured Interviews	• Questions prepared in advance of the interview occurring. • Follow a specific order and sequence. • Often conducted under time constraints.
Semi-structured Interviews	• Questions are devised in advance though less structured in sequence. • Allows for new themes to be explored beyond the main interview questions.
Unstructured Interviews	• No real predefined questions. • Provides complete freedom for interviewee to express their views during interview. • No restricted time scales.

Focus groups

Focus groups are another qualitative research method that can be used in conjunction with mixed-methods research design. Focus groups serve a different research purpose when compared to interviews. The primary difference is that interviews are traditionally conducted on a one-to-one basis, whereas focus groups involve group discussions. The dynamic nature of focus groups means that they encourage participants to share their experiences about a particular subject area (Krueger and Casey, 2009).

Researching in the "new norm"

The Coronavirus has had a massive impact on how research is conducted. The way research methods, such as interviews and focus groups, are utilised have changed to adhere to restrictions. Issues such as social distancing and the use of face coverings will inevitably affect how research is performed qualitatively (e.g., action or ethnographic research) and quantitively (e.g., experimental research designs). Despite this change, research will also continue to be conducted online, such as through questionnaires using *SurveyMonkey* and *Google Forms*. Interviews and focus groups can also be conducted online by using *Microsoft Teams and Zoom*. A major benefit is that a transcript can be automatically generated in some cases. A slight drawback of doing online interviews is that the notion of context and conducting the research in situ could be distorted and lost.

Summary

Your research methodology and methods will be dictated by your research philosophy. Undertaking an exploratory and social approach to your research will result in a predominately qualitative study. If your research focuses on experimental design, your research will be quantitative. There are various research methods you can use to answer your research questions. Based on our supervisory experience, we have addressed the ones we consider to be most used by games development and computer science students.

- Selecting an appropriate research methodology and the accompanying research methods to coincide with it is challenging since there are many to choose from.
- **UT:** Select the research approaches that are most applicable to addressing your research topic and questions.
- Ontological and epistemological assumptions will help to inform your research design and methods used to conduct your research.
- Mixed-methods research can conform to multiple designs and is beneficial for analysing and comparing qualitative and quantitative results from a study.

References

Burrell, G. and Morgan, G. (1979) *Sociological Paradigms and Organisational Analysis.* Aldershot: Ashgate Publishing Limited.

Clark-Carter, D. (2010) *Quantitative Psychological Research: The Complete Student's Companion.* 3rd edn. Hove: Psychology Press.

Collis, J. and Hussey, R. (2014) *Business Research: A Practical Guide for Undergraduate and Postgraduate Students.* 4th edn. Palgrave MacMillan Higher Education.

Creswell, J.W. (2015) *A Concise Introduction to Mixed Methods Research.* Thousand Oaks, California: SAGE Publications, Inc.

Creswell, J.W. (2014) *Research Design International Student Edition: Qualitative, Quantitative, and Mixed Methods Approaches.* 4th edn. Thousand Oaks, California: SAGE Publications, Inc.

Creswell, J.W. (2007) *Qualitative Inquiry & Research Design: Choosing Among Five Approaches.* 2nd edn. Thousand Oaks, California: Sage Publications, Inc.

Flyvbjerg, B. (2006) 'Five misunderstandings about Case-Study research', *Qualitative Inquiry*, 12(2), pp. 219–245. doi: 10.1177%2F1077800405284363

Krueger, R.A. and Casey, M.A. (2009). *Focus Groups: A Practical Guide for Applied Research.* 4th edn. Thousand Oaks, California: SAGE Publications, Inc.

Merriam, S.B. (2009) *Qualitative Research: A Guide to Design and Implementation. Revised and Expanded from Qualitative Research and Case Study Applications in Education.* San Francisco, California: Jossey-Bass.

Myers, M.D. (2009) *Qualitative Research in Business and Management*. London: SAGE Publications Ltd.

Ryan, G. (2018) 'Introduction to positivism, interpretivism and critical theory', *Nurse Researcher*, 25(4), pp. 41–49. doi: 10.7748/nr.2018.e1466

Saunders, M.N.K., Lewis, P. and Thornhill, A. (2019) *Research Methods for Business Students*. 8th edn. Harlow, United Kingdom; New York: Pearson.

Willig, C. (2008) *Introducing Qualitative Research in Psychology: Adventures in Theory and Method*. 2nd edn. Buckingham: Open University Press.

Yilmaz, K. (2013) 'Comparison of quantitative and qualitative research traditions: Epistemological, theoretical, and methodological differences', *European Journal of Education*, 48(2), pp. 311–325. doi: 10.1111/ejed.12014

Yin, R.K. (2009) *Case Study Research: Design and Methods*. 4th edn. Thousand Oaks, California: SAGE Inc.

Yin, R.K. (2005) 'Appendix: Doing Case Studies in Education', In: *Introducing the World of Education: A Case Study Reader*. (ed. Yin, R.K.). London: Sage Publications Ltd., pp. 379–398.

7 Formulating Research Questions

In this chapter, you will learn about:

- Identifying your primary research question(s) or overall research aim(s).
- The appropriate number of research questions for a dissertation.
- Distinguishing between research aims and objectives.
- The importance of the literature review and its impact upon formulating your research questions.
- Knowing when you have sufficiently addressed your research questions.

Choose a topic that interests you

Prior to commencing your dissertation or even your honours year, it is often useful to consider the following when choosing a potential topic:

- Consider an interesting topic you have encountered/studied during your degree programme that you find interesting and motivational.
- Make sure you want to study that topic in more detail.
- Make sure that it is interesting enough to keep you working enthusiastically for a full academic year.
- Make sure it is manageable within the time scales provided for your project.
- Make sure that it is a subject that you can practically do. In other words, if you suddenly decide that enhancing security to a banking system sounds good, are you going to have access to a bank system to implement this?

DOI: 10.4324/9781003054887-7

Keep your dissertation title focused

Here are some tips to highlight the main concepts and keep your dissertation title focussed:

- Your chosen subject area(s) should be clear in your title.
- Try to make it clear to the reader what the area of investigation covers.
- You could use a short and snappy title that requires later elaboration in the main body.
- You could also try a long title encompassing a number of subject areas, which will require drilling down later to establish the focus.

Here are some examples:

Example 1

Source: *Dissertation B*
Primary concepts of focus: drawing tool development, CASE tools, database systems, mapping of relational schema, extended entity relationship model.
Intended outcomes: Review current CASE tools, gather requirements, and implement a drawing tool to map a relational schema from an EER diagram.

Example 2

Source: *Dissertation C*
Primary concepts of focus: artificial intelligence (AI); games development; racing games.
Intended outcomes: Investigate what AI is as a concept, its theoretical underpinnings, why AI is relevant to games development; the impact AI has for making a game-engaging and immersive with specific reference to the racing game genre.

Example 3

Source: *Dissertation D*
Primary concepts of focus: progression; gameplay; RPGs.
Intended outcomes: Analyse and investigate how progression in video games affects immersion and enjoyment; assessing the various categories of progression in gameplay; evaluating the impact progression has on immersive gameplay.

We provide the following advice to help you achieve a balance when considering your title:

- Try to keep your title succinct.
- If it is complex, make sure the subject areas tie together and make sense.
- Ensure that the concepts outlined in your title are addressed in your dissertation.
- The inclusion of multiple terminology in your title means that you might be stretching the scope of your research topic too extensively.
- Keeping the title too short may not give you sufficient scope for exploration.
- Be realistic in what it is you want to achieve, and reflect this goal in your dissertation title.

Consider the wider implications of your research topic

One thing to consider when identifying the subject is to think about whether it may be applicable to further study and help you later should you want to undertake a postgraduate degree, such as an MSc or a PhD. You may also wish to select a subject area that could help you be more employable in a software development or games company and explore the latest trend, such as XR (extended reality). Choosing a hot topic that involves using a certain piece of technology or hardware may help you get a specific job.

Why is your subject area worthy of investigation?

Some questions to pose when contemplating the subject area are: Why is this topic worth doing? Why is it worthy of investigation? In covering this topic, what value would that be to the field of study? A useful approach to help you decide is to undertake a quick scoping preliminary review of the academic and grey literature or a quick feasibility study to quickly assess what is available already. This helps identify the state of the art, in addition to gaps in knowledge that might be worth pursuing.

Identifying your research questions

One of the main difficulties often encountered when embarking upon your first dissertation is its focus and the subsequent research question(s) identification. Research questions are important to have because they help guide and dictate the focus of the study. It is also important to consolidate your research question(s) at an early stage to determine the scope of your dissertation. Too many research questions can result in a study that is too wide ranging in scale and devoid of academic depth or rigour. Furthermore, the more research questions you have, the more challenging it is to answer them all in sufficient detail and accuracy.

When devising your research questions, it is useful to have one overriding problem area that informs the primary focus of the research though you can also include a series of sub questions that aid you towards achieving this goal. Here is an illustration:

Example title: Using virtual reality (VR) to support student perceived self-efficacy toward problem-based learning in teaching computer programming constructs.

   Sub-research questions:

1   What are the benefits and barriers of using VR for teaching and learning purposes in educational settings?
2   Does VR enhance student self-efficacy and problem-based learning skills in the delivery of programming subjects?
3   What framework(s) would be appropriate to evaluate VR use for teaching computer programming constructs?

The inclusion of sub-research questions adds individual research components that serve the purpose of addressing the primary research question.

Identification of research questions summary

* Research questions are useful for guiding and dictating the focus of the research.
* Too many research questions can result in a study that is too wide ranging in focus.
* UT: Choosing a subject area that is of interest to you will increase your level of motivation and engagement toward completing it.
* Consider why your research topic is worth doing.
* Reflect upon what the value that your research topic will bring to the field and yourself.

Distinguishing between research aims and objectives

An aspect that often causes confusion is distinguishing between the terminology of '*aims*' and '*objectives*'. It is important to explain these from the start; they should be included in the project specification. This allows you to clarify what is it you are doing and how you intend to achieve it by establishing the goals of the research to focus the scope and outline the main targets..

UT: A research aim states what you intend to do and focus upon, while a research objective states the steps you will adopt to achieve your research aim.

Stating your aims clearly and concisely will help to negate any ambiguity or confusion to the reader concerning the research aims. The following list of example research aims is followed by their corresponding research objectives.

Example research aims

* **Example 1:** The aim of this research is to assess whether the use of source control can support software development projects in large project team environments.
* **Example 2:** To assess the pedagogical effectiveness of virtual reality for teaching computer programming constructs to computer science undergraduates.
* **Example 3:** To help advance the research of serious games in supporting student engagement in the context of blended educational delivery.

- **Example 4:** The primary goal of this dissertation is to evaluate website accessibility features and assess their importance towards UI and UX design.

The research objectives should outline how you intend to address the aims of your study. Here is where you describe what research methods or approaches you are going to employ to answer your research aims. The following objectives correspond to the previous aims:

- **Example 1:** Undertake focus groups involving software developers to ascertain views about the use of version and source control when involved in large-scale software development projects..
- **Example 2:** Disseminate a questionnaire to undergraduate computer science students to evaluate their views concerning virtual reality use to teach computer programming constructs.
- **Example 3:** Perform user evaluation of an app to obtain participant views about user experience (UX) and responsive web design.
- **Example 4:** Running focus groups to gauge IT staff members opinions concerning the latest issues surrounding computer security and cryptography.

The importance of the literature review

The relevancy of the literature review in helping you to formulate your research questions will be addressed in more detail in Chapter 8. It is however worthwhile to emphasise its importance. Undertaking a thorough literature review, such as an early scoping review or an examination of the grey literature, can help you to identify your research questions at an early stage and solidify your research direction.

It is still reasonable to proceed when there is very little literature since this perhaps means that your chosen topic might be a new research area. Your literature review will also allow you to identify areas of interest and potential gaps in knowledge so that you can focus on relevant academic areas of your subject area. UT: Do the groundwork to ensure that there is sufficient academic literature to place your study into context.

When do know your research questions have been addressed?

You will know when you have addressed your research questions when you encounter the process of *data saturation*. Data saturation is when the qualitative or quantitative data you gather starts to become similar and does not contribute anything new to the research findings (Saunders, Lewis, and Thornhill, 2019). This result can be common in the process of dissertation writing that depends on the volume of participant responses. When respondents to questionnaires, interviews, or focus groups repeatedly say the same thing during a particular stage in your research, this is when you know that you have addressed your research questions. In this context, you are finding out as much as you can in the allotted time frame, and data saturation may never happen.

Summary

Deciding what you intend to do and how your research topic, aims, and objectives will help you achieve it is challenging. It is important to identify a subject area that is relevant to your degree discipline. Consider why is it applicable to your area and how what you are going to do potentially advances this subject. Undertaking prior research with the academic literature associated with your research topic will help you to solidify your research questions, aims, and objectives. Prior research thought and planning is crucial! Here are some summary tips:

- Choose a dissertation topic that interests you to motivate you and make it an enjoyable process.
- Choose one that is worthy of investigation and will advance a field.
- Make the dissertation process work for you as a stepping-stone by targeting what you want to do next, i.e., further study or employment.
- Keep the title of your dissertation short and succinct if you can since this will allow you to make the research more manageable.
- Be aware that a large title adds more scope for exploration but requires synthesising all the concepts together. If you choose a large title, then be sure you can cover the topic.
- Identify your research aims and outline the primary goals of the research project and the research objectives relating to how you intend to achieve these aims.
- Formulating your research questions early provides you with the opportunity to assess the feasibility of what you intend to do and how you are going to achieve the objectives.
- Undertaking a preliminary scoping literature search will help you to decide whether there is sufficient supporting academic material to ground your research questions and your overall write-up. If there is little literature found, then you could be on to a new topic!

Reference

Saunders, M.N.K., Lewis, P. and Thornhill, A. (2019) *Research Methods for Business Students*. 8th edn. Harlow, United Kingdom; New York: Pearson.

Further reading

Behrendt, J. (2021, 2 September) How to Formulate a Research Question. Asking the Right Questions Is the First Step. Available at: https://www.citavi.com/en/planned-accidents/articles/how-to-formulate-a-research-question (Accessed: 13 February 2022).

Lantsoght, E.O.L. (2018) 'Formulating Your Research Question', In: *The A-Z of the PhD Trajectory. Springer Texts in Education*. Springer, Cham. doi: 10.1007/978-3-319-77425-1_5

McCombes, S. (2019, 16 April) Developing Strong Research Questions | Criteria and Examples. Available at: https://www.scribbr.com/research-process/research-questions/ (Accessed: 13 February 2022).

Research,com (2021. 4 May) How to Write a Research Question: Types, Steps, and Examples. Available at: https://research.com/research/how-to-write-a-research-question (Accessed: 12 February 2022).

8 Performing a Literature Review

In this chapter, you will learn about:

- Beginning your literature review by locating credible sources underpinning your work.
- Different types of literature review.
- The structure of literature reviews and how to organise them and incorporate them into the overall layout of the dissertation.
- Identifying, extracting, and summarising main points from the literature.
- Knowing when you have finished your literature review.

What is a literature review?

Undertaking a literature review allows you to assess the literature in your chosen research area and to examine its current state of the art. Literature reviews are necessary to substantiate the research you are doing because they allow you to solidify your research questions and topic by identifying current research trends in your subject area, in addition to things that have yet to be explored. Performing a literature review can be perceived as a daunting task; however, it can be an enjoyable one.

The literature review will undoubtedly become familiar to you during your dissertation. Your project supervisor will often ask you how your literature review is progressing. The literature review is central to the dissertation in that it helps inform your research question and aims and influences how you will accomplish your research objectives. Furthermore, the literature review has additional roles to play in the dissertation process. It is important in the sense that it allows you to scrutinise and examine the state of the art of your chosen research area. It permits you to identify who is saying what in your chosen subject area, the academic debates surrounding the topic, to focus on the gaps in knowledge and to identify new avenues of research in your chosen topic. Literature reviews involve the application of research skills

DOI: 10.4324/9781003054887-8

that help identify relevant sources, review them, extract information, and synthesise the information that is pertinent to academically grounding your chosen research topic. The literature review is an activity that should begin at an early stage of your project, though the process should continue throughout the dissertation life cycle.

Literature reviews can be undertaken for various reasons. When undertaking one, it is important to have your primary research question in mind so you can remain focused when searching. The question helps to formulate sub-questions associated with the main research title. The focus of your research, in addition to research questions, can deviate or alter as you uncover new evidence or facts.

Table 8.1 provides an overview of the key strands of what constitutes a literature review.

Table 8.1 Definitions of a literature review

Key points	Definition	Author
• Identification of key research and theories. • Formulating research position through relevant sources. • Informs your research methodology.	*"The literature review is where you identify the theories and previous research which have influenced your choice of research topic and the methodology you are choosing to adopt."*	Ridley (2012, p. 3)
• Should not be viewed as an essay or long critique of selective studies. • Involves making a critical informed review on the academic credibility of current research	*"The literature review provides a critical discussion on the topic of interest while pointing out similarities and inconsistencies in existing relevant literature."*	Coughlan and Cronin (2017, p. 2)
• Review of paper and electronic sources relevant to your subject area. • Using appropriate search terms to identify relevant sources and devising a way to record and store them.	*"A literature search is a systematic search of the accredited sources and resources."*	Hart (2018, p. 3)
• Purpose is to examine explicit knowledge written about a subject area. • Traditional reviews do not adhere to a prescribed methodology unlike systematic reviews.	*"A literature review is a written appraisal of what is already known – existing knowledge on a topic – with no prescribed methodology."*	Jesson, Matheson and Lacey (2011, p. 10)

(Continued)

Table 8.1 (Continued)

Key points	Definition	Author
• Reviews the academic strengths and potential weaknesses of literature surrounding a certain topic. • Illustrates knowledge and current state of the art of a subject area.	*"Detailed and justified analysis and commentary of the merits and faults of the literature within a chosen area, which demonstrates familiarity with what is already known about your research topic."*	Saunders, Lewis, and Thornhill, (2019) p. 800

Starting your literature review

The literature review is an activity that should begin at an early stage of your project. This point is reiterated by Saunders, Lewis, and Thornhill (2019, p. 74), who state that *"For most research projects, the process of reviewing the literature and starting to draft your review will be an early activity. Despite this early start, it is usually necessary to continue refining your review throughout your project's life."* The literature review should be viewed as an evolving, cyclical, and ongoing process that can continue right up until the end of the dissertation. **UT:** A literature review should be started as early as possible to form a clear research direction.

What is the literature?

Simply stated, the literature can be defined as *" … all sources of published data on a particular topic"* (Collis and Hussey, 2014, p. 76). It is important that you are aware of where and how to locate the relevant sources to conduct your literature review. It would be reasonable to assume that for many games development and computer science students, most literature review sources are to be found online. However, not all useful academic sources will be online. Remember that you can use copies of e-books or their hard-copy equivalent.

As mentioned in Chapter 2, a good place to start is your university library's online catalogue and academic journal databases; you may also seek the help of your subject librarian. Remember that there is no right or wrong literature source for your dissertation. The main point is that you should choose your literature sources carefully to substantiate the primary points you want to make while trying not to overuse them. Table 8.2 gives an overview of sources.

Table 8.2 Overview of literature sources (adapted from Ridley, 2012, pp. 43–46)

Literature source	Why it is useful
Textbooks	Contain relevant facts and explanations regarding issues surrounding specific subject areas.
Edited Books	Include a series of chapters about a specific topic edited by one or more guest editors.
Conference Proceedings	Can be located online via using an online search engine or via your library's online academic database. Conference proceedings are useful for identifying discussions around areas associated with your research.
Academic Journal Papers	Academic journals are dedicated to specific subject areas, are peer reviewed, and should be accessible via your university library's academic database subscription.
Grey Literature	Grey literature can be typically found using an online search. It often includes material such as reports, white papers, theses, blogs, or work not yet in print.
Websites or Online Blogs	Websites or blogs are useful to use when referring to specific organisational bodies associated with a subject (e.g., World Wide Web Consortium, W3C). These often include reports and press releases where the URLs can be included in the dissertation to direct the reader to the website.

Different styles of literature review

There are different types of literature review where the style and approach you adopt are primarily dependent upon the research topic and questions to address.

You might encounter certain categories of literature review during your studies, and it is important to be aware of them. Table 8.3 provides an overview of some additional classifications of literature reviews, though the list is not extensive.

Table 8.3 Overview of classifications of literature reviews (adapted from Jesson, Matheson and Lacey, 2011; Booth, Papaioannou and Sutton, 2012; Hart, 2018)

Literature review type	Purpose
Scoping review	• Used to assess the extent of existing literature in a research area. • Identifies the general academic arguments and debates associated within a certain research area. • Useful for formulating research questions.

(Continued)

Table 8.3 (Continued)

Literature review type	Purpose
State-of-the-art review	• Examines current research including empirical, conceptual, or theoretical work. • Identifies gaps in knowledge associated in a subject area. • Provides potential directions for further research.
Meta-analysis	• Statistical technique used to identify and merge the quantitative results of individual research studies. • Systematic review adopted for quantitative research. • Focuses on numerical data from studies addressing similar research areas.
Qualitative review	• Evaluates empirical results from qualitative research studies. • Presents research themes within individual studies.
Systematic literature review	• Undertakes a structured approach towards evaluating research studies associated with a certain research question.

Traditional literature reviews

Traditional reviews, sometimes referred to as narrative reviews (Booth, Papaioannou and Sutton, 2012), are when a researcher critiques certain studies, focusing upon the research approach used, the theories or hypotheses applied, and the methods and results of the study with a focus on the background and context (Jesson, Matheson and Lacey, 2011). **UT:** Traditional literature reviews are useful for ascertaining background information and can help decide whether your research topic is worth pursuing.

Prior to commencing your dissertation, you need to quickly acknowledge the relevant literature in your chosen field. This will help you complete your project specification form. Traditional literature reviews can also help to formulate your primary research question and research area, as well as your title. In the context of an honour's dissertation, it is usually appropriate to have one research question. A traditional literature review serves the purpose for contextualising your research and informing the reader about the wider academic area of the research (Ridley, 2012).

Though traditional literature reviews are beneficial for gaining a relatively quick and broad overview of the literature surrounding a particular topic, they are viewed as being the least rigorous type of review

(Coughlan and Cronin, 2017). This is primarily because they are often devoid of any predefined methodology for accessing and retrieving the literature. This type of literature review may tend to result in selection bias (Coughlan and Cronin, 2017) or even a biased argument (Jesson, Matheson and Lacey, 2011).

Traditional literature reviews can be useful to perform when researching your dissertation topic and are probably the most common in our experience. The features of traditional literature reviews:

- Are sometimes known as narrative reviews.
- Focus on the research approach adopted and applied in relation to the study's findings.
- Are useful for obtaining background information on a research topic.
- Provide reflection on whether a research topic is worth doing.
- Help to formulate your research question and title.

Systematic literature reviews

A systematic literature review is a more rigorous, methodological, and structured approach. In comparison to a traditional literature review, the systematic literature review is a research process that is usually performed by a team of researchers (Coughlan and Cronin, 2017, Ridley, 2012). The primary purpose of this type of literature review is to answer a specific research question and to identify research in the area that relates to the subject matter under investigation. Similar to traditional literature reviews, systematic literature reviews can locate gaps in knowledge, classify areas of new knowledge, and help to define contributions to knowledge within a certain academic field.

Systematic literature reviews adopt a more coordinated approach when tackling the literature. They require a great deal more effort, but we have seen them performed in honours dissertations when manageable. The features of systematic literature reviews:

- Are more structured in approach in comparison to traditional literature reviews.
- Often involve a team of researchers who are part of a research group ,but can be performed individually.

- Designed to address a specific research question(s).
- Can focus on empirical, theoretical, or conceptual studies.
- Assists toward identifying new research areas.

Literature review and evidence

Useful resources are: academic journal papers, grey literature, conference proceedings, textbooks, edited books, and websites. The key thing is to check source credibility when including them, especially when you are substantiating various arguments or statements provided. Validating the points that you address in your dissertation through evidence is essential. This point is well made by Hart, (2018, p. 157), who states that: *"Evidence is a core requirement for argument, interpretation and recommendations. Evidence is what your discipline and common sense say it is – subject to the rules of proof, authentication and production."* The primary aspect to reiterate here is that the evidence that you provide in your dissertation must be accurate and not consist of false statements. This also relates to the point about academic rigour – that what you are saying is academically credible.

Systematic literature searches

Though many honours dissertations settle with undertaking traditional literature reviews, you may find that a systematic literature review is necessary. We outlined the systematic literature review earlier, but let us reiterate the key features when executing one. Most likely, you will be searching for key words that are pertinent to your research area or for addressing your primary research question. This type of literature search might also be used to answer your secondary research questions that branch off from the primary one. We have summarised the key stages of a systematic literature review in the following guidelines:

1 Identify academic databases to search

It is important to be aware of the academic databases that are relevant to your discipline area. Knowing them in advance will allow you to select the databases that are most likely to contain papers that will contain evidence pertinent to addressing your research question(s). It is important to make it clear why you have chosen these databases, why they will prove beneficial, and why they are relevant to the research.

2 Construct your list of search terms

Devise a list of search terms that are most likely to return academic papers deemed relevant. It is useful to discuss what your search criteria will be with your dissertation supervisor. It is important to ensure that your search terms coincide with the key subject areas of your research. State where your search terms have come from and why you are using them. We provide an example:

Source: *Dissertation E*

The search terms were constructed and conjoined to return the most relevant results when conducting the search. These terms were required to have the focus on narrative and computer games and one of the approaches to capture the player's attention. The following terms were used:

> **("immersion" OR "motivation" OR "engagement") and ("story telling" OR "narrative") and ("computer games" OR "video games")**

Some of the databases searched did not allow the full conjoined search terms to be used; in these cases, the term was broken down to allow gathering of the evidence for all areas, e.g.,

> **"immersion" and "narrative" and "computer games"**

To ensure that the search returned relevant studies appropriate to this project, further criteria were produced as requirements for inclusion. The inclusion criteria were the following:

1   The paper must include empirical evidence on how games affect the player's immersion, motivation, or engagement using narrative.
2   The publication was to be dated between January 2007 and the present.
3   The paper must include a form of study that included participants. No restrictions have been included on the participants that were included in the study or the type of study carried out.

How to review the literature

A number of questions exist on how to review the literature effectively:

- What literature sources should I be looking for?
- What are the salient points I should be extracting from sources?
- How will I know it is relevant to your topic?

When identifying material you deem to be relevant, a core skill to focus on is being critical in your reading. Look for the key arguments made by authors in your research area, whether theoretical, conceptual, or empirical. Try to be concise yet informative when synthesising your literature review.

Empirical research papers present original research and findings that could be related to qualitative or quantitative studies. Theoretical and conceptual papers review theoretical constructs and research positions from prior work to provide new academic perspectives for advancing a particular research area.

You also want to identify any practical applications, i.e., games or software produced. For example, if you were researching whether serious games have potential to teach computer programming concepts, you could review prior work in this area in educational academic databases. In addition to analysing who is saying what, reading the sources you have identified, both critically and analytically, will allow you to acknowledge who the key authors are in your field.

Literature reviews in dissertations vary in length depending upon their scope and focus. Dissertations that are more practical based will inevitably have shorter literature reviews than ones that are more theoretical or conceptual in nature. We have some of the following recommendations:

- Consider how much time have you spent on your literature review. You may not have found everything, but it may be time to draw it to a close as a main activity. You can still look out for new material while you complete other aspects of the project.
- You will not be able to read every source you uncover during your literature review process, and you have to be strategic. Refer to Table 1.2 in Chapter 1.
- A set of criteria can assist you in remaining focused.

We have compiled a list of tips for reviewing the literature in Table 8.4.

Table 8.4 Tips for reviewing the literature

Literature review phases	Tips
Identify relevant sources of information	• Be selective in the material you are going to use to inform your literature review. • Be conscious that you do not have the time to review and use every academic source you find. • Adhering to credible information, whether from books or academic journals, will help strengthen your academic points.
Examine salient points	• Carefully review your sources once you have gathered them as this will help you to evaluate what sources are key to your points. • Quickly scan the titles of your sources, and review the abstracts to assess whether they will be of use to your research question(s).
Cross-examine multiple sources	• Critically review and examine multiple sources against one another to weigh the different stances in your field. Doing so will provide you with an opportunity to reflect upon and become familiar with who is saying what in your chosen area. Academics disagree all the time, and you will often find conflicting opinions.
Organise your sources	• Create a spreadsheet of relevant papers, and categorise them by subject area, research methods used, and whether they are empirical, theoretical, or conceptual. • Organising your academic sources in a centralised location provides accessibility during the writing process. • Use reference-management software tools to collate and organise your references and sources used. • Source material can also be organised in terms of relevancy by year of publication so you have a record of current sources.
Create a spreadsheet of terms and definitions	• Devising a spreadsheet of key research terms and definitions is useful to compare differing viewpoints, and it is easily searchable. • Doing this creates a centralised repository of definitions that you can pick and choose from for defining core concepts in your literature review and aids future work beyond this dissertation.
Annotate and make notes whilst you read	• Make notes while you read, and annotate PDF articles when you discover interesting facts. • Note page numbers so that you remember where you have located important information. • Noting page numbers is useful for when you want to cite an author or a particular source within the main text. • It is useful to complete your references as you write your literature review.

(Continued)

Table 8.4 (Continued)

Literature review phases	Tips
Ensure you reference as you write	• You can make use of software reference-management tools to help formulate your references. • This is a useful activity to undertake because it safeguards against including your references at the last minute and forgetting where your sources have come from.

Summary

Literature reviews are an important part of the research process in a dissertation. There are various types and styles of literature reviews. The kind of literature review and approach adopted for performing it depends on the subject area and discipline of study. Literature reviews are highly beneficial for identifying your research questions and evaluating current research in your discipline area, whether it is conceptual, theoretical, or empirical. One of the most challenging aspects is getting started.

- Certain academic sources will be of more relevance to you than others, so it is important for you to choose them carefully; finding viable evidence is essential. It should be remembered that undertaking a literature review takes time.
- Forward planning, being strategic and systematic in your approach, as well as critically reading your sources will help you present your review in a logical and sequential manner. Though the literature review is hard work, it is – believe it or not – sometimes viewed as an enjoyable activity.

References

Booth, A., Papaioannou, D. and Sutton, A. (2012) *Systematic Approaches to a Successful Literature Review*. London: SAGE Publications Ltd.

Collis, J. and Hussey, R. (2014) *Business Research: A Practical Guide for Undergraduate and Postgraduate Students*. 4th edn. Basingstoke: Palgrave Macmillan.

Coughlan, M. and Cronin, P. (2017) *Doing a Literature Review in Nursing, Health and Social Care*. 2nd edn. London: SAGE Publications Ltd.

Hart, C. (2018) *Doing a Literature Review: Releasing the Research Imagination*. London: SAGE Publications Ltd.

Jesson, J.K., Matheson, L., and Lacey, F.M. (2011) *Doing Your Literature Review: Traditional and Systematic Techniques*. London: SAGE Publications Ltd.

Ridley, D.R. (2012) *The Literature Review: A Step-by-Step Guide for Students*. 2nd edn. London: Sage Publications Ltd.

Saunders, M.N.K., Lewis, P. and Thornhill, A. (2019) *Research Methods for Business Students*. 8th edn. Harlow, United Kingdom; New York: Pearson.

9 Selecting a Software or Games Development Life Cycle Methodology

In this chapter, you will learn about:

- The importance of choosing a development life cycle methodology.
- A methodology and methods.
- Traditional software development life cycle (SDLC) methodologies.
- Games development life cycle (GDLC)methodologies.

Importance of choosing a development life cycle methodology

Games development and computer science dissertations usually entail some form of analysis, design, development, and implementation. This can be in several contexts: a test bed piece of software for testing/evaluation, a new prototype piece of functional software, or a game for educational or entertainment purposes. Creating this implementation objectively and meticulously helps secure marks by showing your thought processes and demonstrating professional development and consideration of an existing model to plan a strategy. This helps contextualise the research, documentation, design, and implementation, assisting to demonstrate competence in all areas. The temptation in a dissertation is to primarily focus on implementation, meaning that academic writing becomes secondary; therefore, it is important to allocate a proportional amount of time to the implementation in relation to allocated marks. A project life cycle methodology helps achieve this goal and demonstrates familiarity with development methodologies, which aids employability.

Methodology and methods

According to the Oxford Learner's Dictionary a '*methodology*' is "*a set of methods and principles used to perform a particular activity*" (Oxford Learner's

DOI: 10.4324/9781003054887-9

Dictionary, 2020). A '*methodology*' is really "*a recommended way of doing something*" (Everett and McLeod, 2007) that has already been tried and tested and can be reproduced. It is the overall strategy outlining the way the activity is undertaken. Nance and Arthur (1988) believe that a methodology should have the following features:

1   Be able to organise and structure the tasks that comprise the effort to achieve the global objectives.
2   Include the techniques and methods for accomplishing the individual tasks within the framework of the global objective.
3   Prescribe an order for making certain classes of decisions and identifying how those decisions are made, leading to the desired objective.

In this context, the methodology is really your overall development methodology, and the methods are a set of complimentary tools to use within the methodology to perform the individual tasks and achieve the overall task. For example, you may use the waterfall model (methodology), but in the implementation phase, use *Unity* or C++ as the method of implementation or tool. Similarly in terms of design, you may select the unified modelling language (UML) class diagram as a method or tool for designing your system. The software/game development methodology is the overall strategy that includes analysis, design, implementation, testing, and maintenance. The methods/tools are constituents used within this strategy to achieve the overall objective.

For your project, you will be constructing functional software or a game. Games, though technically software, have a completely different purpose, different roles in a development team, and slightly different phases. It is possible to use a SDLC for a game, and many games companies prefer using an adaptation of the Agile development methodology.

Several available SDLCs and GDLCs are worthy of consideration, including the traditional models and agile approaches (Vijayasarathy and Butler, 2016); each one has advantages, limitations, and usages (Kumar, 2018). Various GDLCs are available to potentially choose from the grey literature, companies, and academic papers since a game is software for entertainment.

No single SDLC is a one-size-fits-all solution with "*no silver bullet*" or single solution (Vijayasarathy and Butler, 2016 citing (Brooks, 1986); each requires decisions and judgements from people and organisations who generally develop their own development process (Sommerville, 2011). These may be company secrets. Here, we will provide a brief overview of some SDLCs and GDLCs in the literature to potentially select for your dissertation.

Traditional SDLCs

Traditional SDLCs can be categorised into these models:

- **Heavyweight models** – highly structured, disciplined, planned, documentational, and predictable with known user/system requirements. They can be considered to be overly regulated and bureaucratic, sometimes consisting of large quantities of micro-management.
- **Lightweight models** – more unpredictable, gauged toward smaller projects, adaptive and more communicative, permitting changing requirements.

The waterfall model

The waterfall model is the *"traditional"* model of software development (Royce, 1970). It provides a structured, sequential, organised model to address the problematic issues associated with software development; it typically consists of 5 – 7 main stages. These are variable and dependent on the source, and the terms adaptable in terms of detail. Hughes and Cotterell (2009) describe six sequential stages:

- Analysis – analysing the current system, if there is one.
- Specification – producing a requirements specification.
- Design – designing the new required system.
- Implementation – coding and developing the system.
- Testing – executing the program to find errors.
- Maintenance – maintaining the system once it is operational.

The model has been adapted and used by many organisations, including NASA and the air force, where the general idea is that the requirements are finalised before design and implementation begins. It has been adapted to have increased documentation, stringent checking, and integrated risk analysis to overcome some of the shortcomings of the pure model.

The advantages include a great deal of documentation, and transition from one stage to the next only happens through a stringent review process. The major disadvantage is that it is designed for very simple software systems with very little scope for backtracking.

Incremental model/iterative model

The overall system is partitioned into very small components, and each is developed using a waterfall model approach. Several small waterfall models take place delivering each component until all components are converged delivering the entire system. The model can be used in a more focused fashion where a small component of the system or increment is developed in iterative cycles to allow software developers to learn more intently during the development. It has the advantage of being able to produce a prototype quickly allowing increased focus on requirements where issues can be more closely monitored and detected. The main disadvantages are that it is documentation heavy and requires careful planning to partition the system and converge it effectively.

The spiral model

This spiral model is a variation of the basic waterfall model with greater attention to detail at each stage (Boehm, 1986). It is an iterative model demanding critical appraisal of previous passes to be successful and is represented in a spiral where each pass or iteration is investigated. Every time the spiral begins again, there is an intense focus about what could be improved in the iteration. An advantage is that it is an iterative model with a strong emphasis on risk management, which allows constant refinement until the intended results are reached. The main disadvantage is that the project may require a number of passes to produce a software application of acceptable quality, and it is difficult to predict development time. The model is used when great importance is placed on cost and risk evaluation.

Agile model

In the 1990s, several lightweight software development methods were produced to address the issues of heavyweight methodologies considered to be overly bureaucratic. They include: rapid application development (RAD), the dynamic systems development method (DSDM), the unified process (UP), scrum, crystal clear, and extreme programming (XP). After the publication of the Agile manifesto in 2001, all these aforementioned models became integrated under the Agile model umbrella. This integration encompassed all methodologies based on iterative development to address rapidly changing objects, requirements, and market demands that traditional SDLCs were less equipped to do, according to the critics. The Agile model has an enhanced focus on collaboration and teamwork, planning of smaller phases occurs in an iterative fashion with increased emphasis on the quality of the end product. It focuses on speed of production with increased adaptability in relation to changes in requirements. The manifesto was developed by 17 software developers in 2001 with four key values and 12 principles flowing from those values. The values are:

- **Individuals and interactions** over processes and tools
- **Working software** over comprehensive documentation
- **Customer collaboration** over contract negotiation
- **Responding to change** over following a plan

The manifesto has had universal applicability and has since been adapted to disparate areas such as marketing, hospitality, leisure, and recreation. Table 9.1 shows the 12 principles of the Agile manifesto adapted from the Manifesto for Agile Software Development website (available at: https:// agilemanifesto.org/, Accessed: 26 February 2022).

Since the original manifesto, there have been a number of addendums, including addition of project management principles in the Declaration of Interdependence in 2005 (Harris, 2007) and software development principles in the Software Craftsmanship Manifesto (Software Craftsmanship Manifesto Website, 2009). Agile delivery is the contemporary approach to software development incorporating many lightweight models that focus on iterative, incremental development that can be characterised in short sprints of software delivery. Several detailed comparisons of Agile (light) and waterfall (heavy) methodologies are available, and a useful comparison is presented in Table 9.2.

GDLC methodologies

Games (although technically software) have the completely different purpose of providing entertainment; therefore, using a traditional SDLC may not be suitable. Bates (2004) notes that traditional SDLCs are not suitable for developing a game, and, in some instances, merely adopting a SDLC is insufficient (Ramadan and Widyani, 2013). Cardoso, Sousa, and Barata (2017) point out that games are a combination of interleaving

Table 9.1 Agile principles

Principle	Description
1	The **highest priority is to satisfy the customer** through **early** and **continuous delivery** of **valuable software**.
2	**Welcome changing requirements**, even late in development. Agile processes harness change for the customer's competitive advantage.
3	**Deliver working software frequently**, from a couple of weeks to a couple of months, with a preference to the shorter timescale.
4	Businesses and developers must **work together** daily throughout the project.
5	Build projects around **motivated individuals**. Give them the environment and support they need and trust them to get the job done.
6	The most efficient and effective method of conveying information to and within a development team is **face-to-face conversation**.
7	**Working software** is the primary measure of progress.
8	Agile processes promote **sustainable development**. The sponsors, developers, and users should be able to maintain a constant pace indefinitely.
9	**Continuous attention** to technical excellence and good design enhances agility.
10	**Simplicity** – the art of maximizing the amount of work not done – **is essential**.
11	The best architectures, requirements, and designs emerge from **self-organizing teams** that are **proactive**.
12	At regular intervals, **the team reflects on how to become more effective** and then tunes and adjusts its behaviour accordingly.

Table 9.2 Agile and waterfall model differences (adapted from Javanmard and Alian, 2015)

AGILE	*Traditional waterfall*
• Adaptive approach	• Predictive approach
• Success measured in business value	• Success measured in plan conformity
• Suited for small projects	• Suited for large projects
• Decentralised management	• Autocratic management
• Adaptability to change	• Sustainability to change
• Leadership collaboration culture	• Command-control culture
• Low levels of documentation	• High levels of documentation
• Emphasis on being people oriented	• Emphasis on being process oriented
• Has many cycles	• Has limited cycles
• Unpredictable initial planning	• Predictable stages
• Minimal initial planning	• Highly detailed initial planning
• Early return on investment	• End return on investment
• Small/creative team	• Large team

disciplines requiring integration of music, art, implementation, and acting. As a result, SDLCs provide guidelines, methodology, and methods, but they lack game specific criteria and detail. Thompson, Berbank-Green, and Cusworth (2007) alluded to the complexity of game design by presenting the following process: new game proposal, multiple-idea generation, concept selection, game development, game testing, and game launch in relation to the interaction of these different roles: designer, programmer, artist, animator, sound engineer, tester, and manager. The size and constituents of the team depend on the complexity of the game, but as the structure suggests, they depend on the ideas generated. Crawford (1984) also alluded to the complexity of creating games, referring to it as an art that includes the following sequential design stages: choosing a goal/topic, researching and preparation, the design phase (consisting of input/output, game and program structure, design evaluation), pre-programming phase, programming phase, play testing, and a post-mortem.

GDLC components

GDLCs can have components of SDLCs and vice versa. In some cases, SDLCs have been minorly and majorly adapted to create games, and then in other scenarios, simply adopting a SDLC to act as a GDLC is not suitable. Cardoso, Sousa, and Barata (2017) also point out that game development requires "*a distinct development process.*" A comprehensive overview of empirical research performed on GDLC constituents is beyond the scope of this book. However, Aleem, Capretz, and Ahmed (2016) provide one. There are some similarities and major differences in developing a piece of software and developing a game. They are:

- **Overall purpose and creativity** – Games are an entirely different kind of software product since they provide entertainment (Unity 3D Tech Guru, 2018) and a good time with the intention to engage; they sometimes educate and can be used for research purposes centred around the player experience. Software is for some functional purpose where a solution is required for a particular problem. Kasurinen (2016) points out that the purpose of a game is to maximise user involvement where software is attempting to perform a function efficiently, almost minimising involvement. Games require greater creativity to produce the idea and contemplate the innovation, art and writing skills, technical expertise, animation, characters, physics, sounds and collisions (Jain, 2017). Unity 3D Tech Guru (2018) also stated that an SDLC is insufficient for making a game due to various challenges, including: graphics, animations, physics, AI, user input, collisions and gestures.

- **Requirements** – Software requirements are fully or partially known, and while they may change the requirements, they exist initially to develop a solution. With games, the requirements are not apparent, partly because of the overall purpose, and it may not be clear what kind of game is going to be created.
- **Team constituents** – The selection of a team in a SDLC and a GDLC have distinctly different roles, e.g., games can include artists and animators.
- **Deliverables** – An important deliverable in a SDLC is a requirements specification. In a GDLC, deliverables include: a story board, game concept, games design, and technical design document; the process is more creative by nature.
- **Game engines** – SDLCs tend to use recognised high-level languages (HLLs) for implementation such as C++, C#, Java, or Python. GDLCs use these implementation languages depending on the particular game type; however, game engines may be used as well, including *Unity* and *Unreal*. Developing games requires a more bespoke and adaptive approach and extra consideration in terms of which particular "engine" may be the best suited.
- **Testing** – Software testing and game testing can differ since games require play testing, combinatorial testing, and alpha and beta testing, in addition to the functional and structural testing in normal software.

GDLC Example 1

Juego Studios (2017) provide a GDLC consisting of eight stages:

- **Initiation** – Deciding the game type, audience, protagonist/antagonist, theme etc.
- **Team building** – Selecting the game category and hiring the best team consisting of: hiring, developing structure, and defining the work.
- **Feasible study** – Analysing feasibility of requirements, profitability, and technical issues.
- **Pre-production** – Programmers, designers, and artists produce a prototype of the game consisting of: developing the story, game play (mechanics, characters, level designs), script, selection of the correct game development engine, developing the prototype and art documentation, and determining the next technical steps.

- **Production** – Programmers, designers, and artists use the prototype made in the previous process to make the game(s). The programmers begin the coding, and artists produce the models, textures, and animations of the environment and characters. This process includes: coding, layout design, modelling, texturing, animation, and evaluation.
- **Alpha version** – An incomplete playable version of the game is produced with the intention of fixing all gameplay errors.
- **Beta version** – The game is complete with beta testing, balancing, and bug fixing being performed.
- **Release version** – The game is ready to be released to the market.

GDLC Example 2

Summit Games Entertainment (Jain, 2017) produced a GDLC with the following stages, which resulted in the following deliverables:

1 **Idea and Story** resulting in a **Game Concept Document.**
2 **Conceptualisation and Design** resulting in the **Game Design Document.**
3 **Technical Analysis** producing the **Technical Specification Document**.
4 **Development** producing the **Product.**
5 **Testing** producing the **Test Cases and Test Plans.**
6 **Deployment** on the platform producing the **Release Notes and Support Documents.**

Subhash Babu and Maruthi (2013) describe a generic games development framework that describes each stage of the life cycle, taking into account the software and hardware requirements, the availability of software to create the game (including engines), and the duration of its availability. It is generally evident that sticking to a particular framework is a challenge due to the evolutionary nature of creativity and idea generation.

GDLCs for Agile

The Agile methodology has been used and adapted to games development to embrace changing requirements and goals. Summit Games Entertainment (Jain, 2017) points out that game development requires iteration and experimentation, while describing a general Agile GDLC to produce any game genre on any platform. Agile methods are particularly well suited to complex projects where the solution in terms of requirements and goals is fluid and not particularly well specified from the outset. Examples of Agile methods used for games development are XP and SCRUM (Osborne-O'Hagan, Coleman, and O'Connor, 2014; Godoy and Barbosa, 2010). While it may seem easier simply to use a SDLC in an individual project (i.e., a dissertation), many of the principles large teams utilising Agile adopt are still relevant (Clinton, 2020).

Ramadan and Widyani (2013) reviewed four dedicated GDLCs (described in Table 9.3) to identify components of them for their own

Table 9.3 GDLCs reviewed (Ramadan and Widyani, 2013)

Lifecycle name	Type	Stages	Description
Blitz Game Studios	Linear	**Pitching**	Create game concept/initial design
		Pre-production	Game design, concept art, and GDD
		Main production	Realisation of the concept
		Alpha	Internal team members testing
		Beta	Third-party testing
		Master	Game launch
Arnold Hendrick's	Linear	**Prototype**	Initial design, concept art, n prototypes
		Pre-production	Production of GDD
		Production	Construction/integration of assets/source code
		Beta	Testing for user feedback
		Live	Playable game ready
Doppler Interactive	Iterative	**Design**	Initial design and GDD
		Develop/Redevelop	Develop a game engine for current game
		Evaluate	Test the game out and if satisfactory move to test phase or to redevelop phase
		Test	Testing with internal team and third party
		Review release	Repeating iterative process from stage one
		Release	The game is released
Heather Chandler's	Iterative	**Pre-production**	Game design and project planning
		Production	Creation of technical and artistic aspects
		Testing	Testing and fixing bugs
		Post-production	Deliver documentation/Post-mortem activity

GDLC. The compiled GDLC (Ramadan and Widyani, 2013) consists of six development stages and applies an iterative approach with a high emphasis on evaluating the quality of each prototype.

Summary

Requirements analysis, design, implementation, testing, maintenance, and all associated activities must be brought into the proper context. In this case, it is not working in a company but rather on an individual academic project basis to produce the best quality, design, implementation, and associated documentation possible. You can use it as an opportunity to demonstrate to future employers that you have expert knowledge about the methodologies, tools, and options in your field and can weigh up pros and cons of the life cycles, make an appropriate selection, and apply that methodology. The main factors to consider in your dissertation are:

- For the purposes of academic completeness, look at all the alternatives available, weighing the advantages and disadvantages to make an informed choice. This demonstrates that you are able to research both SDLCs and GDLCs and produce a comprehensive overview, which will form part of your literature review (demonstrating a high standard of academic writing). It also demonstrates knowledge in this area, which is exceptionally useful for postgraduate study and interview preparation.
- Working individually to rapidly develop a prototype drastically narrows your choices, and the majority of dissertation students select some aspect of the Agile methodology or rapid application development, in our experience.
- GDLCs are a bit newer, and again, we have given an overview of some options in the grey literature and an overview of the main SDLCs for computer science students. You can select any one of these as long as you can objectively justify the selection for your purposes.
- Ask if there is a necessity for accompanying documentation, which really depends on how you wish to guide your thought processes. As outlined in the chapter, some SDLCs are very heavily documentation based, and this may be a suitable alternative if you feel that you need a disciplined approach. Alternatively, there are also Agile options and GDLC options, and some of these are based on SDLCs and adapted from Agile methods.
- The main conclusion – and coincidentally our tip for the chapter – is: **UT:** Select a SDLC or GDLC methodology for your project to plan and contextualise development.

References

Aleem, S., Capretz, L.F. and Ahmed, F. (2016) 'Game development software engineering process life cycle: A systematic review', *Journal of Software Engineering Research and Development*, 4(6). doi: 10.1186/s40411-016-0032-7

Bates, B. (2004) *Game Design: Second Edition*. Thomson Course Technology. ISBN 1-59200-493-8.

Boehm, B. (1986) 'A spiral model of software development and enhancement', *ACM SIGSOFT Software Engineering Notes, ACM*, 11(4), pp. 14–24. doi: 10.1145/12944.12948

Brooks, F. (1986) 'No silver bullet: Essence and accidents of software engineering', *IEEE Computer*, 20(4), pp. 10–19. doi: 10.1109/MC.1987.1663532

Cardoso, T., Sousa, J.P. and Barata, J. (2017) 'Digital games' development model', *EAI Endorsed Transactions on Serious Games*, 4(12), doi: 10.4108/eai.8-12-2017.153399

Clinton, K. (2020) *Agile Game Development Build, Play, Repeat*. 2nd edn. Pearson Addison-Wesley.

Crawford, C. (1984) *The Art of Computer Game Design*. United States: McGraw-Hill/Osborne Media.

Everett, G.D. and McLeod Jr, R. (2007) *Software Testing: Testing Across the Entire Software Development Life Cycle*. John Wiley & Sons, Inc. IEEE Press.

Godoy, A. and Barbosa, E.F. (2010) 'Game-Scrum: An Approach to Agile Game Development', In Proceedings of *SBC 2010, 9th Symposium on Computer Games and Digital Entertainment*, 8–10 November, Florianópolis, Santa Catarina.

Harris, M. (2007) 'Agile and the declaration of interdependence: A new approach to process improvement', *David Consulting Group*, Available at: https://premiosgroup.com/agile-declaration-interdependence/ (Accessed: 18 November 2020).

Hughes, B. and Cotterell, M. (2009) *Software Project Management*. 5th edn. McGraw-Hill Higher Education.

Jain, S. (2017) *Game Development Lifecycle*. Available at: https://www.linkedin.com/pulse/game-development-life-cycle-sumit-jain/ (Accessed: November 2021).

Javanmard, M. and Alian, M. (2015) 'Comparison between Agile and Traditional Software Development Methodologies', In Proceedings of *Science Journal (CSJ)*, 36(3), Special Issue (2015) ISSN: 1300-1949.

Juego Studios (2017) *What is the Game Development Life Cycle?* Gamedeveloper: Available at: https://www.gamedeveloper.com/business/what-is-the-game-development-life-cycle- (Accessed: 20 November 2021).

Kasurinen, J. (2016) *Games as Software: Similarities and Differences between the Implementation Projects, CompSysTech '16*, Available at: https://www2.it.lut.fi/GRIP/publications/compsystech_Kasurinen.pdf (Accessed: 25 November 2020).

Kumar, M. (2018) 'A comparative study of universally accepted SDLC models for software development', *International Journal of Scientific Research in Science and Technology (IJSRST)*, 4(5), pp. 1084–1092. ISSN: 2395-6011.

Manifesto for Agile Software Development Website (2020) Manifesto for Agile Software Development. Available at: http://agilemanifesto.org/ (Accessed: 28 September 2020).

Nance, R.E. and Arthur, J.D. (1988) 'The Methodology Roles in the Realisation of a Model Development Environment', In Proceedings of the *20th Conference on Winter Simulation*, pp. 220–225, San Diego, California, United States.

Osborne-O'Hagan, A., Coleman, G., and O'Connor, R.V. (2014) 'Software development processes for games: A systematic literature review', *21st European Conference on Systems, Software and Services Process Improvement (EuroSPI 2014)*, CCIS Vol. 425, Springer-Verlag, June 2014, pp. 182–193. doi: 10.1007/978-3-662-43896-1_16

Oxford Learner's Dictionary (2020) Oxford *Advanced Learner's Dictionary Online.* Available at:: https://www.oxfordlearnersdictionaries.com/definition/english/methodology?q=methodology (Accessed: 25 August 2020).

Ramadan, R. and Widyani, Y. (2013) 'Game Development Life Cycle Guidelines', In Proceedings of the *2013 International Conference on Advanced Computer Science and Information Systems (ICACSIS)*, Bali, 2013, pp. 95–100. doi: 10.1109/ICACSIS.2013.6761558. IEEE.

Royce, W. (1970) 'Managing the Development of Large Software Systems', In Proceedings of the *IEEE WESCON 26*, pp.1–9, 1970.

Sommerville, I. (2011) *Software Engineering.* 9th edn. Addison Wesley.

Software Craftsmanship Manifesto (2009) Available at: http://manifesto.software-craftsmanship.org/ (Accessed: 30 September 2020).

Subhash Babu, K. and Maruthi, R. (2013) 'Lifecycle for game development to ensure enhanced productivity', *International Journal of Innovative Research in Computer and Communication Engineering*, 1(8), pp. 1490–1503.

Thompson, J., Berbank-Green, B. and Cusworth, N. (2007) *The Computer Game Design Course: Principles, Practices and Techniques for the Aspiring Game Designer.* London: Thames and Hudson Ltd.

Unity 3d Tech Guru (2018) *Game Development Life Cycle.* Available at: http://www.unity3dtechguru.com/2018/01/gdlc-game-development-life-cycle.html (Accessed: November 2020).

Vijayasarathy, L.R. and Butler, C.W. (2016) 'Choice of software development methodologies: Do organizational, project and team characteristics matter?', *IEEE Software*, 33(5), pp. 86–94. Sept-Oct. 2016. doi: 10.1109/MS.2015.26

10 Selecting a Software Design Modelling Language (SDML)

In this chapter, you will learn about:

- What a model is.
- What a SDML is.
- Why a SML useful for a dissertation.
- Typical SDMLs that are used in games and computer science dissertations.
- Guidelines to assist your selection.

What is a model?

The term *"model"* in the traditional sense is to construct a representation, mock-up or convenient way of representing something else in real life on a different scale – usually smaller, but not always. Models have been used throughout human history, from ancient civilizations to now, for generating and conveying ideas, planning, and providing verification and validation of design in all areas: architectural design, designing machines and inventions, mapping out the proposed view of the solar system (geocentric and heliocentric modelling), recreating historical landscapes using VR and game engines (Kontogianni, and Georgopoulos, 2015), special effects in movies and games, and even modelling human motivation and behaviour. With computers, we can of course be considering simulations or projections of mathematical concepts, simulations of characters, or historical landscapes in museums or computer games. Simulations represent an aspect of reality or even fantasy in another way to provide clarification for other humans. It is in the spirit of the age-old idiom that a *"A picture is worth a thousand words (Henrik Ibsen)."* The Tech Model Railroad Club from MIT used electronic components to build model railways in the 1960s before greatly contributing to the development of the first computer game for entertainment: *Spacewar!*

DOI: 10.4324/9781003054887-10

(Glancey, 1996). West and Stowell (2000) investigate the term "*model*" in depth and cite Ackoff and Sasieni (1968), who use four main categorisations:

- **Iconic** – generally representing the real thing where scale is altered, such as maps, drawings, photographs, or actual physical models, which cannot be manipulated for experimental purposes.
- **Analog** – the use of one set of properties to represent another, such as a graph or electrical circuitry/mechanical, thermometer or speedometer.
- **Symbolic** – using symbols for variable representation and manipulation, such as equations or formalisms.
- **Conceptual** – preliminary representations of either the current system or the required system, which is iteratively revisited to derive the solution.

Pidd (1996, p. 15) defines a model as: "*an external and explicit representation of part of reality as seen by the people who wish to use that model to understand, to change, to manage and to control that part of reality.*" Figure 10.1 shows that the term "model" can in fact appear in many guises and different representations of reality.

Wilson (1999, p. 251) states that a model "*may be prescriptive or illustrative, but above all, it must be useful.*" We suggest that diagrams and models are a highly effective tool for describing the software, game algorithms, levels, and characters in a dissertation.

SDML

A dissertation in games or computing science generally requires some software implementation. The IEEE (1990, p. 24) defines software as "*computer programs, procedures and possibly associated documentation and data pertaining to the operation of a computer system.*" In Scotland, it is a requirement of level 10 SCQF that an honours degree must have some form of software product produced, thus reducing purely investigative projects. Projects can have varied goals depending on particular degree specialism and title, where subdisciplines have a particular focus. Perhaps you are developing a newer, better algorithm, a web-based application, an app in iOS or Android, a database application, or a computer game. All of these software-based systems can be modelled in various ways to convey concepts; in a dissertation, you are producing an outline or design of the preliminary work that will serve as a plan for the final software. The main goal of selecting a SDML is to produce a concise overview of the system you are going to create,

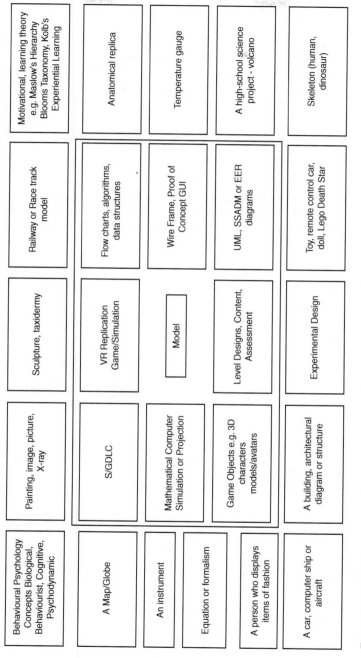

Figure 10.1 A model.

allowing the reader to easily interpret the goals, objectives, data, and structure of what you are designing and implementing. A plan has to manifest itself somewhere, and this may be just a question of capturing it quickly, and, most importantly, showing your thought processes in an ad hoc, even informal, manner. A full overview of modelling languages, notations and techniques, and useful methodologies is beyond the scope of this book. Many books have been written on these topics, but we encourage you to consider the conceptual models available. Johnson and Henderson (2002, p. 2) define a conceptual model as: "*a high-level description of how a system is organised and operates.*" They specify:

- Metaphors and analogies used (if any).
- Concepts the system exposes to the user, including operations and attributes of manipulatable data objects users have created for tasks.
- The relationships between these objects and concepts and mappings between the concepts and the task domain.

Johnson and Henderson (2002) also point out that the use of conceptual models for the design of interactive systems (software products/systems) provide the required functionality where 'less is more'.

Typical SDMLs used

In our experience, the most useful conceptual design models used from methodologies, languages, or notations are attempting to represent the real-world entities, classes, stakeholders, or actors in the software application eventually implemented, or they are well-known diagrams for representing algorithms including:

- Structured Systems Analysis and Design Methodology (SSADM)
- Unified Modelling Language (UML)
- Extended Entity Relationship Model (EER)
- Flowcharts
- Rich Picture Diagrams
- User Interface Design Modelling

SSADM

SSADM is a particular implementation of the waterfall model. This methodology uses several notational diagrams. Systems analysis and design is considered to be a very challenging and satisfying field. Its long history of development approaches ranges from the 1970s with SSADM being popular in the 1980s, formulating a structured approach to systems design (Cosmas et al., 2018). The word '*methodology*' is referring to a formalised approach to utilising and implementing the SDLC (in this case, the waterfall model). SSADM was widely used in the UK, where it was often specified as a requirement for governmental information systems projects; it has been adopted by the public sector in Europe. The method is very comprehensive, enabling the investigation of the current system, the defining requirements, logical design, and physical design with an assortment of sequential techniques to record textually and diagrammatically. Projects can use only the relevant parts of the method, allowing flexibility (Ramakrishnan, 2012).

SSADM has the following main diagrams (Meldrum, Lejk and Guy, 1998)):

- **Logical data structure** – diagram displaying the entities of the system, attributes, and relationships between entities.
- **Data flow diagram** – diagram displaying the flow of data or information, which can either be physical (representing physical transactions and files) or logical (representing the flow of electronic information).
- **Entity-life histories** – diagram can be constructed from an entity event matrix, which allows the specification of the type of operation (sequential, iterative, etc.) and represents the life of the entity as it is created, modified, and removed from the system.

Unified modelling language (UML)

The UML has an extensive history and evolution (Platt and Thompson, 2015). It has been under developmental revision since the 1990s and is inextricably interconnected to object-oriented programming (OOP) due to its origins. The UML is the unification and extension of the methods of Booch, Rumbaugh, and Jacobson, which began in 1994 when the primary concern was to unify the Booch and OMT methods (Booch et al., 1998). After many drafts, UML version 1.0 was offered for standardization to the Object Management Group. In 2005, it was published by the International Organisation for Standardisation (ISO) as a recognised and approved standard. It is currently working toward improvement of the published version of UML 2.5 with the Object Constraint Language version 2.4. Bennett, McRobb, and Farmer (1999) stated that the UML was becoming important in the 90s and has since become the '*de facto*' industry standard (Connolly and Begg, 2014) for object-oriented software engineering products. They also state that

UML is becoming increasingly popular in academia for teaching object-oriented analysis and design/implementation and can be used to model database systems.

The UML is designed to perform four main functions (Booch et al., 1998):

- **Visualising** – Using models, the UML is designed to enhance the understanding of the end user and provide communication in software development teams.
- **Specifying** – Models specifying the analysis, design, and implementation decisions made during development are provided.
- **Constructing** – Use of the UML enables mapping models constructed (particularly class diagrams) to an object-oriented implementation language such as C++, Java, Visual Basic, etc. Mapping to a relational database is also possible to enable fast implementation.
- **Documenting** – This includes facilities for the documenting of every system detail.

UML 2.0 (https://www.uml.org/) has a total of 13 diagrams to represent static, dynamic, and behavioural parts of a system that are split into three distinct categories:

- **Structure diagrams** for viewing the static parts of the system – consisting of class, objects, component, composite structure, and package and deployment diagrams.
- **Interaction diagrams** for viewing dynamic parts of the system, i.e., interactions – consisting of behaviour, sequence, communication, timing, and interaction overview diagrams.
- **Behaviour diagram** for general types of behaviours – consisting of use case, activity diagrams, and state machine diagrams.

UML is versatile, well-known, and adaptive to use in a dissertation, regardless of subdiscipline. Booch, Rumbaugh, and Jacobson state "*you can model 80 % of most problems by using 20 % of UML*" (1998). UML is a highly logical and popular choice when considering analysis, design, and implementation models in computer science-related dissertations as it is closely and conveniently linked to object-oriented programming. We have asked a number of experienced dissertation supervisors who say that UML use case diagrams are popular for requirements capture, and class diagrams are popular for identifying entities, their relationships, and their functions for various systems. In computer games, the trend seems to be that academic institutions teach UML, but smaller games companies tend to use rough notation, as required for:

- class diagrams to identify entities, functionality, and relationships.
- state machine diagrams detailing what the entity is doing and detailing transitions.
- rough flowcharts/activity diagrams due to blueprints/templates, meaning that generally programmers are familiar with this notation, particularly for things like audio logic.
- sequence diagrams for use when considering networking and concurrency.
- use case diagrams for an overview of a game; these generally consist of a list of actions and stick figures next to each.

This is typically done in a company setting using a rough notation to appropriately convey the idea and consolidate it for the developer/development team. Considering a small game such as *Hungry Shark Evolution*, we can draft a very quick class diagram, as displayed in Figure 10.2.

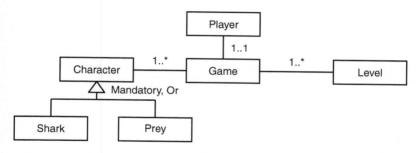

Figure 10.2 Rough class diagram of *Hungry Shark Evolution*.

Classes can have differing levels of detail, including scope, data types, data members, and member functions, depending on requirements. A typical exam question in object-oriented design provides a description and asks the students to draft a diagram. Here is an example description:

A game can have a number of characters/players who have certain demographics, such as name, sex, age and height. In the game, the character may carry one or more inventory items, which are classified into weapons, health and magical items. The game has a number of enemies in it, which are of particular types and can be either a vampire, gargoyle, or werewolf each with different food sources.

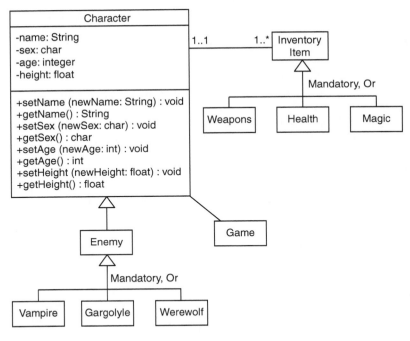

Figure 10.3 Class diagram constructed from textual description.

Figure 10.3 shows a draft class diagram.

The UML has been used to model educational and entertainment games as well. De Lope and Medina-Medina (2016) propose using UML for educational games and suggest the best diagrams for modelling video game aspects. Table 10.1 shows the correspondence between game element and appropriate UML diagrams for educational game development.

Table 10.1 Video game element and diagram (De Lope and Medina-Medina, 2016)

Video game elements	UML diagram
General structure	Class diagram
Game acts, scenes and scenarios	Package and state diagrams
Actions within a scene	Activity diagram
Educational challenges	Sequence diagram
Within the action	Sequence diagram

Bethke (2003) discusses UML in game development and production to a very detailed degree. In relation to requirements capture use, case diagrams can be used to document the core interaction of the player and the game and to formulate test scenarios. A use case diagram of *Pac-Man* split into the display system, player input, game object interaction, and miscellaneous is provided as an example. We are also strong supporters of using the UML in general in software development and computer games development, as demonstrated in Figures 10.2 and 10.3, similar to the diagram in the Pac-Man example. Bethke (2003) also describes the use of other diagrams in the technical design document, including: structural modelling diagrams such as the package model and object model, dynamic modelling diagrams such as activity diagrams, and architectural diagrams such as sequence and deployment. A UML "survival guide" detailing the notation and forward and reverse engineering from class diagrams is in Chapter 17 of his book.

The extended entity relationship model (EER)

The entity relationship model (ER model) was first proposed in 1976 as a model to incorporate some of the important semantic information about the real world. It was a new diagrammatic technique in the field of database design (Chen, 1976). According to Connolly and Begg (2014), the model was more than adequate for capturing the semantic meaning for simple transaction-based database applications at the time. What prompted the introduction of the extended entity relationship model (EER model) was the increase in the development of database applications such as computer-animated software engineering (CASE) tools and multimedia systems since the 1980s. These types of applications have more demanding database requirements, leading to the need for additional semantic modelling concepts. Some of these were incorporated into the EER model (Teorey, Yang and Fry, 1986).

Flowcharts and structure charts

Flowcharts, structure charts, pseudocode, and plain language statements are popularly utilised by programmers to find a solution to a problem, plan the structure of a modular algorithm or a menu structure in games or user-interface design. Reddy and Ziegler (2010) define a flowchart as something that "*uses standard symbols to show different operations and the order of execution steps in an algorithm.*" We will discuss pseudocode in Chapter 11 because the overall objective is to make the code understandable for readers. When thinking of an algorithm, which is really just a logical sequence of steps to solve a problem, a flowchart can assist in organising these steps. If you consider the following example of a simple conversion of Fahrenheit to Celsius, you have the following steps:

1	Take number of degrees in F scale
2	Subtract 32
3	Divide by 9
4	Multiply by 5 – result is in Celsius scale

None of these steps require any specialist skill or ability and can be represented in the following flowchart (Figure 10.4) for the purposes of clarification:

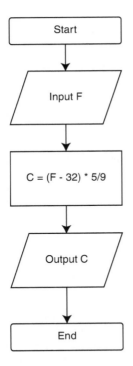

Figure 10.4 Flowchart algorithm example.

Flowcharts for algorithms can become far more complex than this to demonstrate thoroughly planning an algorithm in a dissertation. Hollands (2020) illustrates the process of writing an algorithm for a game, designing the algorithm using a flowchart and implementing that algorithm using Scratch to support children to learn key concepts in relation to programming and computational thinking. The algorithm is the following:

When the broadcast play is received.
Set the size of the dragon to 30%.
Make the dragon move to the location x: -170 y: 0.
Show the dragon so the player can now see him on screen.
If the player tilts the micro:bit to the right, change the dragon's x position by 3.
If the player tilts the micro:bit to the left, change the dragon's x position by -3.
If the player tilts the micro:bit to up, change the dragon's y position by 3.
If the player tilts the micro:bit to up, change the dragon's y position by -3.
Repeat the process.

Figure 10.5 shows the flowchart.

Structure charts are used to represent algorithms as well to identify the individual consecutive steps in terms of modularity. They can also be used in relation to graphical user interface (GUI) design to indicate a menu structure in a computer game or software application (Dennis, Wixom and Roth, 2009).

Rich picture diagrams

If you veer more toward the soft systems approach for research and are more of a qualitative researcher, you may consider the previous models to be too prescriptive and restrictive. Rich picture diagrams (RPDs) were originally gradually formulated from recommendations by Peter Checkland in his development of soft systems methodology (SSM) (Checkland, 1972; Checkland and Scholes, 1990). The idea is that as rich a picture as possible should be constructed in the time available. RPDs have been used in many areas to better understand ill-defined problems, and this applies to modelling information systems (Bronte-Stewart, 1999). They have a very interesting history and generate academic debate around their use independently from the SSM and their interpretation due to lack of standardisation. Some may argue that this is

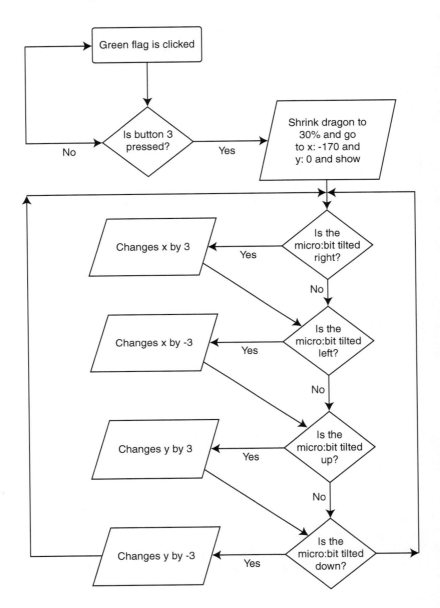

Figure 10.5 Flowchart (Hollands, 2020).

the RPD's greatest advantage – that it can really be used to model anything and to increase understanding of a particular problem. Berg (2013) discusses RPDs in detail with the aim of improving their interpretation; Berg has also recently co-authored a book utilising RPDs: *Encouraging Resilient Communities* (Bell, Berg and Morse, 2016).

User interface design modelling

It may be appropriate to model and design the user interface (UI) and consider it in the first instance as it is the communication mechanism between the user and the underlying software. Ramdoyal, Cleve, and Hainaut (2010) illustrate the reverse engineering of a database system UI to form a conceptual model for analysis; it can be a suitable strategy for the development of software. Game engines and IDEs are capable of reverse engineering a number of diagrams with relative ease. Various models exist to convey the conceptual, physical, and functional design of different user views of systems (Benyon, Green and Bental, 2012). Essentially everything has an interface, including operating systems, IDEs, game engines, software applications, cars, aeroplanes, Smart TVs, and VR headsets. Some designers believe that the best interface is to have no boundary between the user and software. Bad interface design begins to irritate the users by not functioning correctly in terms of fulfilling their requirements and what users expect. Successful UIs are intuitive enough for the user to operate without mental effort and interference. Usability Geek (2016) has compiled a list of GUI principles from highly reputable companies, including Amazon, Apple, Google, IBM, and Microsoft. Figure 10.6 shows a class diagram being forward engineered into a UI and vice versa:

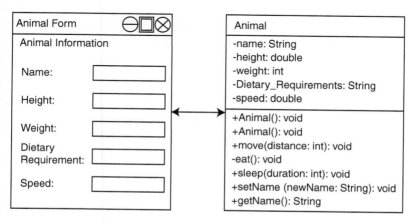

Figure 10.6 Class diagram and UI.

Summary

This chapter has given an overview of some of the methodologies, notations, and languages available. You do not necessarily need to stick to one since there are examples of studies that look at the transfer between modelling techniques as early as the 90s (Oei et al., 1992). We advise that the best modelling language, methodology, or notation for you is based on:

- What your subject discipline is and what design modelling notations, languages, methodologies, and techniques are standard in your area. You will have encountered these in your degree, and where possible, you should use familiar tools you are comfortable with. In summary: **UT:** Use familiar design models to conceptually model software and games efficiently and effectively to add technical precision to your dissertation.
- The nature of the software product you are developing. If attempting to develop a software program for C++, then object-oriented modelling languages and notations may be useful. If you are developing a database, then use ER modelling.
- If there is a current system that you are attempting to model or improve, then you might use a modelling language that has an appreciation of this, such as SSADM.
- Your supervisors' background and the subjects they teach, since they will no doubt have a design preference based on their background.

To conclude, a SDML is a recognised, concise, design notation, methodology or language in your discipline to potentially relay your ideas and illustrate your thought processes. **UT:** Good analysis and design will lead to a better implementation and an overall cohesion in the dissertation, and we encourage you to apply meticulous thought to this as it will pay dividends.

References

Ackoff, R.L. and Sasieni, M. W. (1968) *Fundamentals of Operations Research.* New York: John Wiley And Sons Ltd. ISBN 10: 0471003344 / ISBN 13: 9780471003342.

Bennett, S., McRobb, S. and Farmer, R. (1999) *Object-oriented Systems Analysis and Design Using UML.* McGraw-Hill.

Bethke, E. (2003) *Game Development and Production.* Texas, USA: Wordware Publishing Inc. Plano.

Bell, S., Berg, T. and Morse, S. (2016) *Rich Pictures: Encouraging Resilient Communities Earthscan.* London: Taylor and Francis.

Benyon, D., Green, T. and Bental, D. (2012) *Conceptual Modeling for User Interface Development.* London: Springer, ISBN: 9781447107972, 1447107977.

Berg, T. (2013) Understanding iconography: A method to allow rich picture interpretation to improve. Phd Thesis. Heriot-Watt. doi: 10.13140/RG.2.2.20445.61923

Booch, G., Rumbaugh, J. and Jacobson, I. (1998) *The Unified Modelling Language User Guide.* 1st edn. Addison Wesley.

Bronte-Stewart, M. (1999) 'Regarding rich pictures as tools for communication in information systems development', *Computing and Information Systems,* 6, pp. 83–103.

Checkland, P.B. (1972) 'Towards a systems-based methodology for real-world problem solving', *Journal of Systems Engineering,* 3(2).

Checkland, P.B. and Scholes, J. (1990) *Soft Systems Methodology in Action.* Wiley.

Chen, P.P.S. (1976) 'The entity relationship model – Toward a unified view of data', *ACM Transactions on Database Systems,* 1(1), 1, pp. 9–36.

Connolly, T.M. and Begg, C.E. (2014) *Database Systems: A Practical Approach to Design, Implementation and Management.* 6th edn. Global Edition, Pearson.

Cosmas, N.I., Christiana, A.F., Jeremiah, O.O. and Ikechukwu, A.C. (2018) 'Transitions in system analysis and design methodology', *American Journal of Information Science and Technology,* 2(2), 2018, pp. 50–56. doi: 10.11648/j.ajist.20180202.14

De Lope, R.P. and Medina-Medina, N. (2016) 'Using UML to Model Educational Games', In Proceedings of the *8th International Conference on Games and Virtual Worlds for Serious Applications (VS-GAMES),* Barcelona, 2016, pp. 1–4. doi: 10.1109/VS-GAMES.2016.7590373

Dennis, A., Wixom, B.A. and Roth, R.M. (2009) *Systems Analysis & Design.* 4th edn. John Wiley & Son, Inc.

Glancey, P. (1996) 'The complete history of computer and video games', *Computer and Video Games,* Available at: book_complete_history_of_video_games.pdf (digitpress.com) (Accessed: 5 December 2020).

Hollands, R. (2020) *Expressing Algorithms as Flowcharts: Supporting Children in Writing Algorithms, Sequencing, Selection and Repetition.* Available at: https://blogs.brighton.ac.uk/reh42/expressing-algorithms-as-flowcharts/ (Accessed: December 2021).

'*IEEE Standard Glossary of Software Engineering Terminology,*' in IEEE Std 610.12-1990, vol., no., pp.1–84, 31 Dec. 1990, doi: 10.1109/IEEESTD.1990.101064

Johnson, J., and Henderson, A. (2002) 'Conceptual models: Begin by designing what to design', *Interactions,* 9(1), pp. 25–32. doi:10.1145/503355.503366

Kontogianni, G. and Georgopoulos, A. (2015) 'A realistic gamification attempt for the ancient Agora of Athens', *Digital Heritage, Granada,* pp. 377–380, doi: 10.1109/DigitalHeritage.2015.7413907

Meldrum, M., Lejk, M. and Guy, P. (1998) *SSADM Techniques an Introduction to Version 4.* Studentlitteratur. ISBN 91-44-38061-5.

Oei, J.L.H., van Hemmen, L.J.G.T., Falkenberg, E.D. and Brinkkemper, S. (1992) 'The metamodel hierarchy: A framework for information systems concepts and techniques', *Technical Report, Department of Informatics, Katholieke Universiteit,* 92(17), pp. 1–30.

Pidd, M. (1996) *Tools for Thinking; Modelling in Management Sciences*. John Wiley and Sons Ltd.

Platt, R. and Thompson, N. (2015) 'The Evolution of UML', In: *Encyclopaedia of Information Science and Technology*, 3rd edn. (pp. 1931–1936). IGI Global.

Ramakrishnan, S (2012) 'System analysis and design', *Journal of Information Technology & Software Engineering*, S8, p. e001, doi:10.4172/2165-7866.S8-e0017

Ramdoyal, R., Cleve, A. and Hainaut, J.L. (2010) 'Reverse Engineering User Interfaces for Interactive Database Conceptual Analysis', In: *Advanced Information Systems Engineering*. (ed. Pernici, B.). CAiSE 2010. Lecture Notes in Computer Science, vol 6051. Berlin, Heidelberg: Springer. doi: 10.1007/978-3-642-13094-6_27

Reddy, R.N. and Ziegler, C.A. (2010) *C Programming for Scientists and Engineers with Applications*. Boston, Toronto, London, Singapore: Jones and Bartlett Publishers.

ShellPuppy (2020) *Large Scale Rubik's Cube Simulation - Solving 65536 Layers, 11.54 mins* Available at: https://www.youtube.com/watch?v=y7J3sNR8aC4 (Accessed: December 2021).

Teorey, T., Yang, D., and Fry, J.P. (1986) 'A logical design methodology for relational databases using the extended entity-relationship model', *ACM Computing Surveys*, 18(2), pp. 197–222.

Usability Geek (2016) *Official Usability, User Experience And User Interface Guidelines From Companies*, Available at: https://usabilitygeek.com/usability-user-experience-user-interface-guidelines-companies-2016/ (Accessed: December 2021).

West, D. and Stowell, F.A. (2000) 'Models, Diagrams, and Their Importance to Information Systems Analysis and Design', In: *Systems Modelling for Business Process Improvement*. (eds. Bustard, D. Kwawalek, P., and Norris, M.). Boston: Artech House, pp. 295–311.

Wilson, T. (1999) 'Models in information behaviour research', *Journal of Documentation*, 55(3), pp. 249–270.

11 Design

In this chapter, you will learn about:

- High-level objectives.
- A requirements specification.
- Pseudocode.
- Games design documents (GDDs).

There is no real standard format for a design section, and it is really up to you and your supervisor to decide. The purpose of this chapter is to provide ideas to construct a concise design chapter and show you some useful approaches, including producing high-level objectives and writing a requirements specification, pseudocode, and GDD. Conceptual modes can be used from Chapter 10. It may be a combination of these approaches for clarification, and extra details can go into an appendix or be provided online. A concise design should allow the dissertation to stand on its own without readers having to play the game or run the software, or without breaking the overall flow. We have had students produce 30 pages of character descriptions, narrative, and story, going into infinitesimally small details in the middle of the dissertation, blatantly trying to use up the word count; we secretly dub them *"documentationalists."* Allocate a proportional amount of effort to design, and if is worth 20% of a 10,000-word dissertation and you have 5000 words, then you need to be selective. We will now discuss some approaches, some of which are more suitable to games development or computer science, but they are not entirely mutually exclusive and can be used in combination; for example, a requirements specification is typically used for computer science, where a games design document is used for computer games.

DOI: 10.4324/9781003054887-11

High-level objectives (HLOs)

In many cases, the software developed is experimental and can be implemented in various ways, providing HLOs are met. A brief may be provided to create the software using your own creativity. Formulating HLOs for a dissertation in our experience happens in one of three ways, or a combination of these ways:

- Deriving them from a brief from a supervisor or company. If it is to improve current software, it may require analysis of what current software lacks.
- Performing a literature review to identify what has been done and what best practice principles can be implemented, e.g., identifying what level design principles should be integrated into a realistic survival horror game.
- Using a survey, focus group, or interviews to gather preferred requirements for the target group.

HLOs from a description (Case study)

Source: *Dissertation B*

Description: Current CASE tools are incredibly complicated to use and are not dedicated only to one diagram. The ER model has become similar to the UML class diagram to make the EER model. A database designer uses a conceptual schema in conjunction with the diagram to produce a relational schema, which is the basis for the relations in a DBMS. Diagrams can easily become cluttered with additional details.

Identified HLOs:

Build a dedicated software tool to:

- Display entities and relationships in UML notation.
- Load, save, and print the ER diagram.
- Produce a relational schema from the diagram.

HLOs from a literature review

Source: *Dissertation E*
Description: Gather empirical evidence and identify best practice principles.
Search terms: *("immersion" OR "motivation" OR "engagement") and ("story telling" OR "narrative") and ("computer games" OR "video games")*
Results: 2,051 papers identified 17 relevant
HLOs

1 Capture the player's interest from the start.
2 Allow the player freedom to create their authorship on the story.
3 Challenge the player within their ability.
4 Provide the player with clear goals to accomplish.
5 Support the player, do not control them.

HLOs using a survey

Source: *Dissertation F*
Description: A survey asked about the effectiveness of a computer game to teach programming concepts. Data structures identified were arrays, multidimensional arrays, vectors, and stack/queues.
Implemented game demo: CODE: S.P.A.C.E (Lana, 2020: Available at: http://maurolana.co.uk/work.html#space Accessed: 26 February 2022).

Requirements specification

Producing a requirements specification is extraordinarily complex and has never been perfected, despite being part of the most important initial stages of the SDLC. The IEEE standard glossary for software engineering terminology (1990) defines a requirement as "*a condition or capability needed by a user to solve a problem or achieve an objective*" or "*a condition or capability that must be possessed by a system to satisfy a contract standard, specification or other formally imposed document."* The IEEE provides recognised, highly detailed templates of requirements specifications. Many dissertations we have supervised are primarily concerned with functional requirements expressed first as user requirements and then as more detailed system requirements for a component breakdown. Berezin (1999) proposes an overview stating the commonly accepted objectives and then functional requirements to state precisely what the application will do.

Example requirements specification

Source: *Dissertation B*
Requirements specification (Overview of objectives)
The entity relationship editor will provide the user with the following base functionality:

1   Produce entities in the UML notation.
2   Produce relationships in the UML notation.
3   Provide the ability to load, save, and print the ER diagram.
4   Produce a relational schema from the diagram.

1. Produce entities (Statements of functionality)

1.1 The ability to draw, delete, and edit entities.
1.2 The ability to select a drawn entity.
1.3 The ability to drag an entity to any position on the screen.
1.4 The ability to add the following to entities.

 • Attributes.
 • Attribute types – simple, multi-valued, derived or composite.
 • Primary key.
 • Alternate keys.

1.5 The ability to delete and edit attributes, attribute types, PK and alternate keys.
1.6 The ability to resize entities.

Pseudocode

Pseudocode can be very useful for computer scientists due to its versatility – there are no real standards unless you work for a company that has a preferred format. It can deviate from appearing as natural language to being close to a programming language – so close it may be that language. It is nonlanguage specific, can be used at a high level, low level, in object-oriented and agent-based applications, and can detail the entire program logic or portions of it. Pseudocode allows production of unambiguous, precise algorithmic descriptions and allows professional programmers to implement the algorithm in any programming language. Bennett (2019) provides a list of pseudocode guidelines. Bennett also emphasises that some leading computer scientists do not recommend using it, instead prefering syntax in common programming languages. We recommend that if it helps you organise your code, then use it to demonstrate your work. It can be useful for demonstrating complex algorithms.

Example pseudocode

Source: *Dissertation B*
1:1 Relationships mapping algorithm

```
For each relationship
    If relationship is 1:1 then
            If partial: total participation then
                    Identify the sides
                    Map partial total one to one
            End if
            If total: total participation, then
                    If both entities are present in the schema, then
                            Combine the two relational schema objects
                    End if
                    If one entity is present in the schema, then
                            Add the new entity to the relational
                            schema object
                    End if
                    If none of the entities are present in the schema
                            Create a new relational schema object
                            Combine the entities into the relational
                            schema object
                    End if
            End if
    End if
End for
```

Game design document (GDD)

GDDs should contain as much relevant detail as possible, split into various sections for reading ease where the amount of effort put into these sections is dependent on dissertation focus. In some cases, the GDD and the technical design document (TDD) are separate but can be combined as well. We discuss TDDs in Chapter 12.

Kramarzewski and De Nucci (2018) describe the GDD as providing the team with a detailed description of what needs to be done (communication), acting as an encyclopedia of the game to keep track of what has been done, how it has been done, and what has changed (memory). Good GDDs are modular, multimedial, available in different formats and sizes, and a result of a discussion leaving space for creativity and debate. Interestingly, it is more open-ended than a requirements specification but has similarities, i.e., goals, requirements, is clear, brief, and concise. It can be (in a team) a living, constantly changing document; however, in a dissertation, it is of course individual, and we recommend emphasising relevant parts that are your focus. Pedersen (2009) defines a GDD as *"the designer's entire vision spelled out in detail, which includes all of the storyline, character dialogue, world maps, city views, and detailed room specifications such as sample wallpaper, artwork and rug designs. It also includes audio content for background or ambient sounds, sound effects, character dialogue (with accents and speech patterns), programming and AI considerations."* O'Luanaigh (2006) provides a detailed template for a GDD displayed in Table 11.1.

Table 11.1 GDD sections (O'Luanaigh, 2006)

Section	Possible sub-sections
Overview	Design Summary, USPs, Game Objective, Visual Style, Target Audience/Platforms, Expected Age Rating
Gameplay	Typical Game Example, Game Modes, Key Gameplay Mechanics, AI Description, Difficulty Systems, Controls, Camera Descriptions, Interface/GUI, Audio/Music, Multiplayer/Online, Front End, Saving and Loading System
Game Detail	Back Story, Storyline, Mission List/Game Geography, Key Character Descriptions, Key Vehicles/Objects
Project Issues/Risks	FMV/Cut Scene Technology, Licenses/Product Placement, Languages/Localisation, Schedule Overview, Team, Middleware, New Technology, Key Project Risks, Key Design Risks
Summary	Summarisation of the GDD

Table 11.2 Proposed GDD Structure

Section	Possible sub-sections
Game Overview	Idea, Influences, Competition, Target Audience.
The Game World	Setting, Levels, Level Design, Topologies.
Story	Back Story, Game Narrative.
Game Objects	Characters, Hero/Protagonist, Allies/NPCs/AI, Enemies, Objects – Power Ups, Obstacles, Conceptual Diagram e.g., UML Class Diagram.
Music and Sound Effects	Background music and sound effects.
User Interface	Graphical User Interface, Control Schematic, e.g., Mobile Phone Application Interface, Use Case Diagram.

We recommend a GDD template in Table 11.2.

We provide descriptions of some of the common sections in GDDs from dissertations with some examples:

Game concept and theme

With a brief game description, its size is dependent on its nature and the scope of the project. Games produced in tandem with dissertations for research tools may demonstrate the application of some design or implementation aspect to improve the game, such as enhance realism, immersion, or enjoyability. An overview of the game can range from a short paragraph to a full page where the first line should be exciting and concise to pique interest. Summing up your game in one sentence or paragraph is popular. Here is an example:

Source: *Dissertation G*

"The game is a 3D platformer called Foxy's Adventure, which has a whimsical, bright, and colourful cartoon style. The main character is a cute bushy-tailed fox called Foxy, who is tasked with saving animals trapped by an evil mastermind. Foxy will need to travel to various worlds, depicted by different themed levels, and collect berries and gems, and rescue the trapped animals from a devastating fate."

Look and feel

This section extends the previous one or can be combined with more detail about the game look. Try to help the reader visualise the game by providing examples of similar existing games to enhance their understanding. Provide enough detail to allow the reader to visualise the game/software. Here is an example:

Source: *Dissertation G*

"The game takes inspiration from various games of the same style, such as Crash Bandicoot, Spyro the Dragon, Yooka-Laylee, Ratchet & Clank, and Conker's Bad Fur Day. The game aims to portray the same style as these types of games but with a modernised aesthetic so that it can be enjoyed by people who did not play the games originally, as well as those who did, so it is similar and gives them a nostalgic feeling, although it is still modern with a fresh look."

Genre, format, target audience, and competitor analysis

Many game genres exist (Arsenault, 2009), and this is where to specify the genre(s) and type of game you are developing. You can also specify the format(s) you intend the game to be played on, such as PC, console, or mobile device.

Target audience can also be specified; so, for example, is the game for children? Is it for computing students at university? It is useful to use age certification, such as Pan European Game Information (PEGI) (https://pegi.info/). It should be noted that different countries use different rating systems.

When creating a game, find out if similar games exist; these could be potential competition as well as help you generate ideas. For a serious game, looking at existing games helps identify previous research and empirical evidence. It is always good practice to find out what has been done already, either in a business or research context, to verify originality and avoid duplication by:

- Performing a simple *Google* search. Adding 'pdf' at the end of the search terms will bring up papers associated with similar games.
- Searching your institutional electronic journals.

- Looking on *Steam* (https://store.steampowered.com/) and searching for relevant tags. This shows ratings, games reviews, and player likes and dislikes to generate ideas of what to add to your game.

Characters (Main character/NPCs/enemies)

This can include descriptions and images of characters, such as protagonists, antagonists, NPCs, teachers, or guides. We recommend showing blueprints and early drawings in an evolutionary way, leading up to the finished design if you create your own assets; if you're using existing assets, add them and acknowledge the source. You may add in character alterations and new characters at a later stage, and we recommend showing character evolutions that illustrate your progress. Regardless of whether the game is 2D or 3D, an assortment of images can be added and range from 2D sprites in graphical software, screenshots, to a 3D render of a constructed model. If you are not able to create your own characters, then it is fairly common to get them from a source, e.g., *TurboSquid* (https://www.turbosquid.com/Search/3D-Models/uk).

Empathising with characters may be important in a game, so back story, behaviour, mannerisms, appearance, and a defined role may be required. **UT:** Always ask if it is crucial that the reader knows this to produce a concise design document and place supplementary information in an appendix.

Level design

Level design is part of game design but distinct and defined as "*the process of constructing the experience that will be offered directly to the player using components provided by the game designer*" (Adams, 2014, p. 439). It is genre dependent and varies in size depending on the game scope and focus. In a dissertation, every level relevant can be listed with screenshots and the game objects placed in the levels. This can show some form of evolution from a hand-drawn 'blueprint' to an intermediary mock-up, and finally, the finished level through the project course. Level design typology layout is commonly specified in terms of selected type(s), such as linear, semi-linear, parallel, ring layouts, network layouts, hub, and spoke layouts.

Pacing

Pacing is popularly mentioned in GDDs because it keeps the player in the flow and immersed. Davies (2009) describes various potential aspects:

- **Movement impetus** – the player will to move through the level.
- **Threat** – the notion of danger.
- **Tension** – level atmosphere, mood or perceived danger reflected in the player.
- **Tempo** – action level currently being experienced by the player.

Flow is well known to game designers, players, and researchers. As well as the eight isolated factors identified by Czikzentmihalyi (1998), it entails offering interesting choices for optimum challenge, allowing control over their actions and leading to a pleasurable state. Isbister (2017) touches on flow in games in terms of making interesting and meaningful choices in her book '*How Games Move Us*'. Affecting pacing can be done, altering the skill required (pacing the difficulty or frequency of the enemies) or the setting (having different types of levels/settings).

Player experience

Computer games are not just described in simple user-interface design terms but also in terms of user-experience design. The goal is not to simply present screens and menus but to adopt a player-centric approach where every design decision is questioned in relation to how it makes the player feel and whether it entertains them. The concept of the player experience is broad and '*creating the user experience*' is covered extensively in the book '*Fundamentals of Game Design*' by Ernest Adams (2014).

Adams (2014) states that *"the software, art, and audio assets that present the game to the player and interpret his inputs are collectively called the user interface (UI). Designing the players experience via the UI is one of the game designer's most important jobs. It has an enormous effect on whether the player perceives the game as satisfying or disappointing, elegant or graceless, fun or interesting."*

Hence, it is common to discuss:

- **Interaction models** (avatar-based, omnipresent, party-based, contestant, and desktop).
- **Camera models** (how the player views the game world, what the camera focuses on, what the perspective is (first-person, third-person, top down, isometric)).
- **Input devices** (keyboard/mouse, controller, Oculus Touch controller).

Gameplay and mechanics (Game features)

It is common to describe gameplay features and game mechanics, which can encompass challenges within the levels, actions, and character/avatar interactions. We recommend focussing on the most important features and game mechanics in the main body since you can provide a complete list in an appendix of everything, including character(s), vehicle(s), weapon(s), and object(s). Games are a unique form of medium as events are not directly authored as in movies and books. The player interacts with rules/mechanics to alter the game state and produce gameplay. Mechanics can be unlocked as rewards for increasing skill or facing harder difficulties. We present several categorisations of game mechanics that can be used to organise this:

- Core, primary, and secondary mechanics (Sicart, 2008)
- Core and satellite mechanics (enhancement, alternative, and opposition mechanics) (Maranhao et al., 2016)
- Physics, economy, progression, tactical manoeuvring, and social-interaction mechanics (Adams and Dorman, 2012)

Mechanics are genre specific. Here are some well-known examples:

Super Mario jumping
Sonic the Hedgehog spinning
Rotation, randomisation of blocks, scoring and incremental speed of blocks falling in *Tetris*.
Movement of chess pieces, e.g., a pawn can only capture diagonally.
Blocking, punching, kicking, jumping in *Street Fighter* or *Mortal Kombat*. Fatalities are game specific.

User interface design (UID) – Menus, HUD, screen flow diagram

The user interface (UI) is different from the player experience and is concerned with menu screens, button functionality, responses, and where they navigate the user in terms of different levels and scenes. It is really the functionality and navigation around the game, very much like navigating through *Netflix* using the GUI. You can include images of menu screens and button descriptions, and if the game has a HUD (heads-up display) (a common UI for digital games), you can display

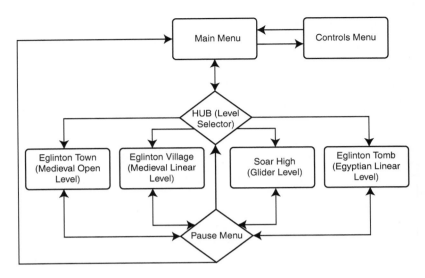

Figure 11.1 Navigation flowchart example.

Source: Dissertation G.

information to the player without distraction, such as ammunition, health, and map. Then this is a good place to describe screen shots and functionality. UID elements can be: non-diegetic, meta, spatial, and diegetic (Norrman, 2020). An example of a navigation flowchart is in Figure 11.1.

Photo reference, research, and inspiration

Previously, you may have mentioned inspirations when comparing your game to other similar games, and here, you can expand on this idea using:

- Screenshots from other games.
- Images from movies, books, comics, models, posters, or even real-world objects.

This can contribute to a sort of digital mood board allowing the developer to convey what they want the game to look like and can include:

- Game post-mortems, design fan sites, review sites, and professional sites.
- Gathering first-hand digital images (abandoned warehouses, racecourses, castles, forests, volcanos, structures, mountains, your environment) to represent styles, mood, aspirations, and ideas.
- Identifying real-life game inspirations.
- Specifying environmental concepts, such as atmospheric effects (fog, storms, game mechanics), lighting, setting, to what extent they represent the real world, time setting (past, present future), and what mood is to be created.

Audio design

Sound effects and music are important parts of any game and fundamental to mood creation. For an entertainment game, e.g., *Super Mario* you may wish to have cartoon-like jumping sounds. For a game like *Resident Evil,* you may wish to have sombre music playing during a narrative sequence, music such as Beethoven's *Moonlight Sonata.* We recommend describing all sound effects and musical pieces used by providing links to sources, e.g., *YouTube.* We have had dissertations where studying audio is the main focus, such as how it affects the player experience. In this case, audio design would be more important, and larger. game audio is an intricate topic and can have different categorisations:

- **Diegetic sounds** – occurs within the game, e.g., character footsteps.
- **Non-diegetic** – occurs out with the game and heard by the player but not the characterm e.g., background music.
- **Interactive audio** – audio in response to player reaction.
- **Adaptive audio** – the game alters the audio playback.
- **Dynamic audio** – combination of interactive and adaptive audio.
- **Kinetic gestural audio** – gestural movement for game control.

Students often create audio by composing their own music and making their own sound effects, employing an independent audio designer, or using internet resources. Popular resources to royalty-free sound effects/music include:

(All websites were accessible via these URLs dating from 26 February 2022).

- Audacity (https://www.audacityteam.org/)
- digccMixter (http://dig.ccmixter.org/)
- Freesound.org (https://freesound.org/)
- PlayOnLoop (https://www.playonloop.com/)
- Bensound (https://www.bensound.com/)
- FreeSFX (https://www.freesfx.co.uk/)
- Twin Musicom (http://www.twinmusicom.org/)
- ZapSplat (https://www.zapsplat.com/)
- Incompetech (https://incompetech.com/)
- MusOpen (https://musopen.org/)
- Boom Library (https://www.boomlibrary.com/)

Audacity® is a very popular open-source, multi-track editor for Windows, Mac, and Linux; it is used quite often by games students. Sometimes, for each level to have a unique feel, it has to have unique audio to fit the theme, ensuring coherence and style. Here is an example:

Source: *Dissertation G*
Music
"Crash Bandicoot and Spyro the Dragon both have amazing and memorable soundtracks, and the hope is that Foxy's Adventure can follow in their footsteps. The music in Soar High, Eglinton Village, and Egyptian Tomb were created by a Sound Engineer based near Barcelona – the music was made specifically for this game only. The music in Eglinton Town and the menu were part of the Ultimate Game Music Collection asset pack on the Unity Asset Store by John Leonard French.

A video compilation of the music is on YouTube: https://youtu.be/ Kwg6IUc9zDg."

Sound effects

"Various sound effects were used throughout the game including: Foxy's footsteps, the sound of the berry box smashing when the player rolls into it, the sound of the TNT box exploding when the player touches it, the sound of the catapult bomb exploding, the sound of the bugs being squashed when the player jumps on them or rolls into them, the sound of the waterfall, the sound of the rotating platforms rotating, and menu button presses."

3D modelling

A 3D modelling section can be added, particularly when assets are created from scratch to ensure appropriate recognition. A dissertation involves phenomenal hours of effort, which can be in various directions, whatever they may be – so highlight the work performed. Past dissertations have used images providing evidence of: rendering of areas/levels, textured boxes modelled in *Autodesk Maya*, and textures created in *Adobe Photoshop* with occlusion and normal maps.

Animation

If you perform work on animations, demonstrate it by providing evidence and explain what you have done. If the animations are acquired, then it may just be an acknowledgement of the source, even if that means acknowledging a fellow animation student. If they are specially constructed, then provide evidence. This may entail: describing the animations in the game and displaying screen shots of the animation implementation, e.g., using the animator in *Unity*. Some pieces of evidence included in previous dissertations have been:

- Character animation transitions.
- Screenshots of the conditions required for transitions set up in the games engine.
- Images of keyframes of particular animations when keys are pressed.

If a number of animations have been created, we recommend that you only detail the most important ones to prevent the GDD within the dissertation becoming cluttered. Detailed descriptions of a few important animations will be sufficient and list the rest or allocate put them in an appendix.

Concept art

Concept art is generally utilised from the beginning of a larger games project and is littered throughout the GDD. Optimistically, it allows an accurate visualisation of the final product, and pessimistically, it allows pinpointing of where things have gone awry.

Example games design documents

Nuclino (2021) provides excellent tips on what a GDD is, what it should include, and how to use a template, providing that you sign in and are part of a team. An extremely useful part of this process is access to real-life GDDs for:

(URLs accessible dating from 26 February 2022).

- Grand Theft Auto (https://www.gamedevs.org/uploads/grand-theft-auto.pdf)
- Silent Hill 2 (https://drive.google.com/file/d/1nxvdXasP-HsRCt62cHK3wF_pIrJpYx5T/view)

Summary

This chapter has provided a number of examples and mechanisms of how to present your design section of a dissertation. This chapter has encompassed HLOs, requirements specifications, pseudocode, and GDD elements specifically for games. While there really is no format, we recommend that you seek guidance from your supervisor. UT: Make the design section concise and attempt to make it proportional to the marks available.

References

Adams, E. and Dorman, J. (2012) *Game Mechanics: Advanced Game Design*. New Riders Games.

Adams, E. (2014) *Fundamentals of Game Design*. 3rd edn. New Riders.

Adobe Inc. (no date) *Adobe Photoshop* (version 23.2) [Computer Programme] Available at: https://helpx.adobe.com/uk/photoshop/using/whats-new.html (Accessed: 27 February 2022).

Arsenault, D. (2009) 'Video game genre, evolution and innovation' *Eludamos, Journal of Computer Game Culture*, 3(2), pp. 149–176. Available at: https://septentrio.uit. no/index.php/eludamos/article/view/vol3no2-3

Audacity® software is copyright © 1999-2021 Audacity Team. The name Audacity® is a registered trademark.

Autodesk Inc. (no date) *Autodesk Maya* (version 2022.1) [Computer Programme] Available at: https://www.autodesk.co.uk/products/maya/free-trial (Accessed: 27 February 2022).

Bennett, N. (2019) *Introduction to Algorithms and Pseudocode*. Available at: https://ddc-java. github.io/assets/pdf/Introduction%20to%20Algorithms%20and%20Pseudocode.pdf (Accessed: March 2021).

Berezin, T. (1999) *Writing a Software Requirements Document*. Available at: https:// home.adelphi.edu/~siegfried/cs480/ReqsDoc.pdf (Accessed: 17 March 2021).

Czikzentmihalyi, M. (1998) *Finding Flow: The Psychology of Engagement with Everyday Life*. Basic Books.

Davies, M. (2009) *Examining Game Pace: How Single Player Levels Tick*, 12 May. Available at: Feature: 'Examining Game Pace – How Single-Player Levels Tick' (gamedeveloper.com) (Accessed: December 2021).

Foxy's Adventure Music (2020, April 9). Available at: https://www.youtube.com/ watch?v=Kwg6IUc9zDg (Accessed: 27 February 2022).

'IEEE Standard Glossary of Software Engineering Terminology,' in IEEE Std 610.12-1990, vol., no., pp.1-84, 31 Dec. 1990, doi: 10.1109/IEEESTD.1990.101064.

Kramarzewski, A. and De Nucci, E. (2018) *Practical Game Design: Learn the Art of Game Design through Applicable Skills and Cutting Edge Insights*. Packt Publishing.

Maranhao, D.M., Menddonca, G.M., da Rocha Franco, A. and de O. Maia, J.G.R. (2016) 'Towards a Comprehensive Model for Analysis and Definition of Game Mechanics', In Proceedings of the *SBGames*, São Paulo.

Norrman, A. (2020) 'User Interface's Impact on Player's Immersion', *Masters Thesis*. Available at: http://urn.kb.se/resolve?urn=urn:nbn:se:umu:diva-170644 (Accessed: February 2021).

Nuclino (2021) *Games Design Document Template and Examples*. Available at: https://www. nuclino.com/articles/game-design-document-template (Accessed: December 2021).

O'Luanaigh, P. (2006) *Games Design Complete*. Paraglyph Press.

PEGI *Pan European Game Information* (2017) Available at: https://pegi.info/ (Accessed: 27 February 2022).

Pedersen, R.E. (2009) *Game Design Foundations*. Wordware Publishing Inc.

Sicart, M. (2008) 'Defining Game Mechanics', *Game Studies*, 8(2), Available at: Game Studies – Defining Game Mechanics

Shutterstock (2022) *TurboSquid: World's Best 3D Model Collection* Available at: https:// www.turbosquid.com/Search/3D-Models/uk (Accessed: 26 February 2022).

Steam (no date) Available at: https://store.steampowered.com/ (Accessed: 26 February 2022).

Unity Technologies (2022) *Unity* (version 2020 LTS + 2021.2 Tech Stream) [Computer Programme] Available at: https://unity.com/releases/release-overview (Accessed: 27 February 2022).

12 Implementation

In this chapter, you will learn about:

- Technical design documents (TDDs).
- Presenting basic functionality.
- Presenting advanced/interesting functionality.
- The benefits of version control.
- Producing a show reel.
- Demonstrations.

This chapter will describe various optional constituents of an implementation section for games development and computer science including: the TDD, basic implementation/functionality, advanced and interesting functionality, version control, presenting a show reel and screen shots, and preparing a demonstration. In a dissertation, this involves conveying what you have developed so that anyone can read and understand. It is not enough to develop a game or software application; you must also document it sufficiently for the reader to comprehend simply by reading the dissertation. This chapter will provide an easy structure for generating ideas that we have developed for dissertation students over many years.

Technical design document (TDD)

The process of technical requirements analysis involves detailed planning of the development, such as development platform, game-engine selection, framework, and implementation details, which produce a TDD. This is primarily for computer games and is described as follows:

DOI: 10.4324/9781003054887-12

- It is separate from the GDD and written in conjunction with it; it is a working blueprint written by the technical lead for the game and focussing on mechanics (Ryan, 1999).
- It is part of the GDD; there can be GDDs of various types, including a concept, proposal, level design, and technical design. Study tonight (2021) presents the TDD as part of a production plan and where the TDD is a subset of the overall GDD (production plan), including: the concept/vision document, project schedule, software testing plan, risk–mitigation plan, artistic design document, and, of course, the TDD.

The overall idea of the TDD is to provide a software blueprint that developers can produce the game from. It is similar in that respect to the software requirements specification (SRS) in computer science. Table 12.1 shows possible features of a TDD.

Table 12.1 Features in a TDD (adapted from Ryan, 1999)

Features	Description
Platform and OS	Hardware platform, operating system, and versions supported.
External Code	Source and purpose of code used (include OS code, drivers, code libraries).
Code Objects	Purpose of code objects coded, complied, and built into EXE.
Control Loop	Document functions in the core loop (e.g., collision, movement, rendering routines).
Game Object Data	Data structures and identifiers (i.e., to support attributes, functions, behaviours), OOP show class inheritance tree, class–interface properties and functions.
Data Flow	Storage of data, how it is loaded, transferred, processed, saved, and restored.
Game Physics and Statistics	Movement, collision, combat. Defining and describe the purpose and function of each procedure, the stats that control their behaviour (e.g., constants, variables).
Artificial Intelligence	Methods of manipulating the AI; path finding, target selection, events and decisions made by characters.
Multiplayer	Connection methods and protocols supported, client–server or peer-to-peer, packet sizes and how often sent.

(Continued)

Table 12.1 (Continued)

Features	Description
User Interface	GUI programming, game purpose to be separate from GUI function, document how GUI objects will work.
Game Shell	Screens that make up game shell, screens, and windows, excluding main play screens.
Main Play Screen(s)	Screens where core of game is played; low-level mechanics perspective.
Art and Video	Specify details relevant to the artists such as: resolutions, palettes, file formats, compression, and any other data the artists need.
Graphics Engine	Describe functions of sprites, voxels, 3D-polygon rendering.
Artist Instructions	Document how the art and video will be stored, loaded, processed, and displayed in the game.
Sound and Music	Loading and playing of sound; address requirements in functional specification.
Level Specific Code	Details of code implementation specific to levels (based on functional specification).

Study tonight (2021) presents possible constituents of a TDD and a link to a good example TDD by college students: (https://computergamesmmu.files.wordpress.com/2012/10/technical-design-document-final.pdf). It includes sections displayed in Table 12.2.

Table 12.2 Sections in a TDD

Section	Description
List of Features	Summarising the main GDD points, allowing a synthesis between documents, e.g., first person, game-world objects, character, AI, multiplayer, HUD, menus, format. If the TDD is going to be used in the future as a standalone document, this can be useful.
Game Engine Selection	*Unity, Unreal Engine, Game Maker Studio2* features, pros and cons.
Schedule	A Gantt chart outlining detailed development or a basic document. *Trello* is a popular tool for games.
High-level Diagrams/ Software Design	Layout of levels, technology diagram contributing to the game, design diagrams in terms of roles assumed, implementation diagram as another mechanism of illustrating the schedule and gameplay diagrams to illustrate how to play the game.
Art tools	Listing software version, description, and what it is being used for. Popular software may include: *Paint, Adobe Photoshop, Autodesk 3ds Max, Blender and Audacity®*. It

(Continued)

Table 12.2 (Continued)

Section	Description
	may also be beneficial to have links to where you got assets, e.g., The *Unity* Store (https://assetstore.unity.com/).
3D Objects, Terrain, and Scenes Management	This can list all objects utilised, organised in a table giving an image of the object, description, and the source. These can include doors, control panels, weapons, computers, tables, and interactive objects. Terrain from an indoor and outdoor perspective can be described, even if that is a virtual real-life reconstruction such as The Museum of Natural History. Terrain can be described, e.g., desert, snow, rocky, plain, procedural terrain generation. Scene management refers to efficiently loading and rendering scenes effectively utilising system resources including: culling and occlusion, utilising lower levels of detail in objects that are further in the distance, and clipping objects not in the players field of view.
Collision Detection, Physics, and Interaction	Outlining the mechanisms specifying what happens when two game objects intersect. This also applies to software, e.g., drawing tools. How are the physics of the game implemented, e.g., objects falling, characters jumping and encountering obstacles? Is a physics engine going to be utilised, and if so, which one? It may be useful to specify what happens when the player interacts with objects, doors, or NPCs.
Game Logic and AI	This can entail visual scripting (a programming language, development environment that allows the manipulation of programming objects via graphical images) or perhaps *Blueprints* in *Unreal Engine* or *Bolt* in *Unity*. AI can vary in complexity and can be a very small description of what governs enemy NPC behaviour or can take up far more space if the AI is the focus such as in **Dissertation C**.
Networking	Is networking facilitated in terms of multiplayer, and if so, what particular dynamics are catered for: cooperative or competitive?
Audio and Visual Effects	These can be effects free from the internet or purchased effects, as long as it is acknowledged, e.g., the *Unreal Engine Asset Store* (https://www.unrealengine.com). This can also include recorded effects using *Audacity*® or free effects from, for example, Epidemic Sound (https://www.epidemicsound.com/).
Delivery Platform & Hardware and Software Requirements	Format the game is delivered on, e.g., PC, console, or mobile device. The minimum hardware specification for the game to run smoothly and what software is required to run is such as *Windows 10* and versions of *Direct X*.

In addition to these categories, we have had seen TDDs in game dissertations with some of the following:

- Hardware and software.
- High level diagrams and design patterns illustrating software design.
- Artificial Intelligence (AI).
- Optimisation.
- Code and Pseudocode.

Hardware and software

This can include a detailed hardware specification outlining the minimum requirements of a machine to run your software. This can encompass RAM, storage requirements, graphics cards, whether the PC is VR active, and what peripherals are best suited to the player experience/user experience (UX). The software is also specified, such as the choice of games engine, e.g., *Unity or Unreal Engine,* as well as plugins and any frameworks used. Any software utilised in the development of the application can be specified, such as: Adobe *Photoshop*, *Substance Painter*, *Autodesk Maya*, *Blender* or *Audacity®*. A computer science dissertation can include description of the technical specifications required to run the software and the programming language or IDE. To summarise, we recommend at least mentioning a delivery platform and hardware and software requirements for running your implementation. **UT:** Provide a rationale for the selection of development software such as it was selected to develop your skills. You may also state that you used it because you were familiar with it, or you may specify a particular technical reason for the selection such as: C++ was utilised because the project involved the use of pointers. This can also be illustrated in a diagrammatic form showing how all of the technologies have contributed, e.g., Figure 12.1.

High-level diagrams and design patterns illustrating software design

Design notations were described in chapter 10 and can be used to demonstrate knowledge of the structure of the application and programming. In a TDD, UML diagrams such as use case, sequence, class or state transition diagrams are popular choices. It can be advantageous to explain design patterns using state patterns or factory-pattern diagrams, showing code examples or screenshots of the code with some explanation of how it is utilised. This can also encompass highly detailed level-design diagrams in relation to layout, e.g., the layout of particular

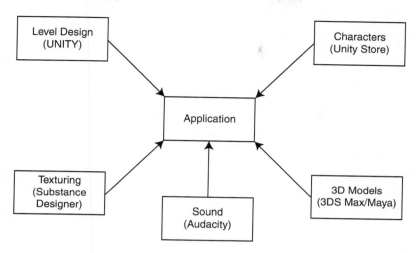

Figure 12.1 Technology contribution diagram.

areas such as buildings. This may also include wireframes for websites or mobile apps to be delivered either on the web or via mobile device.

Artificial intelligence (AI)

We have seen a number of games where AI is addressing autonomous reactions of NPCs, whether they are animals, zombies, attacking ships, racing cars, enemies that are targeting, patrolling, fighting, etc. Here is an example:

Source: *Dissertation G*

AI description

The bug enemy in the Medieval open level and the scorpion, spider, and beetle enemies in the Egyptian linear level behave differently; these enemies follow the player when the player is within a certain distance, which can cause problems such as enemies walking through objects or even getting stuck behind walls. To ensure these enemies behave more intelligently, they use the NavMesh system in Unity. The NavMesh can be used to set pathfinding and tweak global behaviour of pathfinding and obstacle avoidance.

The first step is to create a Navigation Mesh, which approximates the walkable surfaces of the level that appears as a blue overlay on the ground, while the Navigation Window is open in the editor. Things that can cause an obstacle to the enemies need to be marked as a NavMesh Obstacle by adding the NavMesh Obstacle component on each of the objects. In the image below, for example, the walls, doors and the boxes are all marked as obstacles; this then leaves a gap so that the enemy does not touch them and get struck or walk through objects. The obstacles need to be carved into the baked NavMesh. Once the NavMesh walkable surface is set up, each enemy needs to have a NavMesh Agent component attached to them to ensure they use the NavMesh. Each NavMesh Agent's settings, such as radius, height, offset, speed, and acceleration need to be set up since all enemies will be different. There is also an option to add Auto Repath, which means the enemy will pick the closest route to the target, similar to how a Satnav works.

Optimisation

Optimisation is more common in games dissertations and can be covered if any steps have been taken to optimise your game. These steps can include: setting up occlusion culling and occlusion areas within *Unity*, for example, to improve optimisation. An example of a descriptive video is provided by Black (2020). Here is an example of an optimisation section:

Source: *Dissertation H*

Optimisation description

"The performance of the prototype was a very important part of the development since participants who are testing the game might have a less powerful system than the one the game was intended to be played on.

During the development period, the frame rate of the game was constantly dropping below 30 frames per second (FPS), and the reason behind that was the large amount of assets and lights sources. To fix this, an optimisation process was made to the game by switching all the lights in the game from moveable to static, and by doing this, the shadows are being built into the memory before the game starts. In addition, instead of placing hundreds of trees and grass assets, all the forest assets were placed into the foliage tool system, which was used to paint them around the level. This helps by combining all the forest assets into one asset. Lastly, the foliage culling was used to disable assets at a distance when the player is far away from them."

One example of optimisation in software engineering involved the dragging and dropping of software controls. It was in this case more efficient to allow dragging of an outline rather than the actual control itself.

Code and pseudocode

Screenshots of the code (for the main parts of the game), along with a brief explanation of what the code does or pseudocode, is common in a TDD and very useful. **UT:** It is important to draw a fine line between being thorough and drowning the reader in technical diagrams, blueprints, and jargon. Try to keep in mind that some readers may be coding and technical laymen or not interested in your code at all – so only include what is necessary.

Implementation functionality

TDDs are game specific but the rest of the sections can be used for games and computer science. We recommend splitting functionality into basic and advanced implementation functionality to provide a distinction between the implementational aspects that were relatively easy to complete and those requiring far more thought, time, and effort. It may be necessary to develop a basic implementation for a pass and more advanced features are integrated into the first-class section of the project specification. The implementation typically becomes more complex as time progresses and depends on how much you can get done. There may be a number of different prototypes or games, and you may be implementing several smaller applications for research purposes.

Basic functionality

This part can contain the description of the fundamentals of your implementation or game along with associated screenshots, code segments, state diagrams, etc. **UT:** It is only necessary to convey the basic functionality of the application without looking as if you are deliberately trying to fill space. For example, if this is a 3D platformer game, you may be describing a game such as *Super Mario*. The basic functionality is jumping, walking, running, climbing, collecting, achieving health, etc. Describe this and show screen shots of it happening, as well as how these things are executed via the controls and perhaps diagrams and blueprints. It is reasonable to show the control mechanism of the game from both and instructional and descriptive point of view, and therefore, it is common to see the W,A,S,D keys, mouse, and keyboard controls in this section.

In the case of functional software, you can focus on the menus, UI, and describe the functionality of the buttons, e.g., a metronome app for a musician, or a calorie tracker for a fitness enthusiast, or even a basic calculator. Here are examples:

Computer science dissertation example

Source: *Dissertation B*

Basic functionality description

It was necessary to be able to draw entities and relationships and also define the entity names, attributes, and relationship cardinality to enable the basic functioning program to exist. This was all contained within a drawing canvas. The user had to be able to select the various entities within a bounding box, and these were stored in an underlying data structure with their positions, sizes, primary keys, attributes, composite keys, and data types etc. Selecting a relationship was far more difficult and required the use of vectors to highlight the lines (relationships) to any degree of specificity. This allowed testing of the more advanced mapping a relational schema functionality based on the diagram.

Computer games dissertation example

Source: *Dissertation C*

Basic functionality description

The basic functionality entails implementing a racing game where a player can select a car, character, racetrack, and race against other players where there is the possibility of finishing in a certain place in a certain time.

Advanced/interesting functionality

This is functionality that you want to stand out and is original or the focus of your dissertation such as: procedural-level generation, advanced AI, mapping algorithms, more advanced algorithm, an enhanced morality-based selection system, the scaffolding/tutoring system, enhanced mechanics, or highly tricky implementation issues.

This allows elaboration on the interesting focus of your implementation and augments the basic implementation to enable the complex functionality. Ironically, despite the fact that it has been far more work from an implementational perspective, it will most likely be far smaller in documentation.

Computer science dissertation example

Source: *Dissertation B*

Advanced functionality description

The mapping of the relational schema was highly complex and required mapping 1:1, 1.M, M..M, aggregation and composition. Extra layers of complexity included specialisation/generalisation types with membership constraints, completeness constraints, and disjoint constraints, e.g., (Mandatory, Or)

Computer games dissertation example

Source: *Dissertation C*

Advanced functionality description

The AI of the NPCs (other cars) is customisable to either be quite friendly or highly aggressive.

The previous examples can of course be expanded to illustrate exactly how this functionality has been accomplished through code, screenshots, and blueprints etc. Sometimes an extensive list of basic and advanced functionality is all that is provided. **UT:** When you have done the work and put in a significant amount of effort – writing about your own creation can become effortless. The challenge is then refinement.

Version control/source control

Version control and source control are interchangeable terms. A number of challenges exist in software development, such as collaboration (a number of individuals sharing and changing the software at geographically disparate locations) and storing versions since the project is not complete in a single version. It may be necessary to restore previously working versions of software to track down a problem. *Git* is a version-control system that maintains a progressive database of all the changes that are made in your files or folders, enabling you to view all changes, view progress at particular stages, and allow restoration of previous versions. Version control is good to mention and use in a dissertation. You may wish to discuss it and demonstrate it by providing links to show the process and demonstrating meticulous thoroughness. Software developers, engineers, and games programmers/developers all use version control, so use this as an opportunity to increase your employability prospects, despite the fact that this is an individual effort. Version control can be:

> - **Centralised,** where the main files are stored on a server. The main disadvantages are that if the server copy goes awry, it is catastrophic, and all programmers have to be online.
> - **Distributed,** where there are still files on the main server repository, but every individual can also pull their own local repository. If anything goes wrong in the server repository, it can be restored from any local repository; sustained online access is not required since you only require connection when you wish to pull the repository or push the changes.

(All websites were accessible via these URLs dating from 26 February 2022).

Version control tools include:

- Unity Teams (https://unity.com/products/unity-teams)
- Git Hub (https://github.com/)
- Git (https://git-scm.com/)
- GitLab (https://gitlab.com/)
- Beanstalk(https://beanstalkapp.com/)
- PerForce (https://www.perforce.com/)
- Apache Subversion (https://subversion.apache.org/)
- AWS CodeCommit (https://aws.amazon.com/codecommit/)
- Mercurial (https://www.mercurial-scm.org/)
- Bitbucket (https://bitbucket.org)

Version control is a highly beneficial to become familiar demonstrating consideration of collaboration, backup, and project restoration.

Regardless of whether version control is used – UT: always back up your work, whether it is on the cloud, USBs, external hard disks, or even saved by emailing it to yourself. We have had disasters during the years where students have stored all of their project work on one laptop, and the unthinkable has happened.

Apple Play Store and Google Play

Publishing your App (game or functional software) on the *Apple* or *Google Play Store* is an excellent demonstration and easy download for assessors and readers. A number of our students have published their applications on *Google Play,* e.g., (MafMih, 2021). If you plan to do this, then look into what it is required to understand the intricacies and time.

Producing a video/show reel

In our institution, particularly in games, it is standard practice to have a mark associated with an online portfolio, and as a result, a short show reel or video of a game or software is necessary. Stevenson (2020) provides an excellent example of a game online portfolio. This can be used to demonstrate any computer science dissertation. This can be a critical reflection, a description of your game, or simply an entertaining video to be part of a greater portfolio.

To effectively produce this, you will need appropriate software. Whether you are a Windows, Mac, or even Linux user, there will be a stable and reliable video-editing software available for you to use. We recommend the following to consider:

(All websites were accessible via these URLs dating from 26 February 2022).

1 Adobe Premiere Pro (https://www.adobe.com/uk/products/premiere.html)
2 Sony VEGAS Pro (https://www.vegascreativesoftware.com/)
3 Wondershare Filmora (https://filmora.wondershare.net/)
4 Lightworks (https://lwks.com/)
5 Shotcut (https://www.shotcut.org/)

There are pros and cons to the different recommendations. There are purely free versions available that offer a great piece of video-editing software, but there may be limitations such as video watermarking on the final product. Remember to share your final show reel and upload to either *Vimeo* or *YouTube* and share it on *LinkedIn*. (*Producing a video/ showreel material kindly produced by Alan Williams Associate Lecturer UWS*).

Demonstrations

Sometimes, you have to perform a live demonstration of the game or software, and the only advice that we can give follows:

> - Take your own laptop or computer, if possible.
> - Perform deployment tests on other computers to make sure that the software runs successfully.
> - Produce a readme.txt file outlining system requirements and how to open the application if you are not present.
> - We recommend recording a successful demonstration as a backup to the live one.
> - Try not to worry – your supervisor and assessor are familiar with the pitfalls of trying to perform live software demonstrations. Everything is working until the live event and then catastrophe – it is expected, considered to be funny, and a rite of passage, so best of luck!

Summary

In this chapter, we have provided a basic structure and examples of content that can be put into every section, and we have included some practical examples. For games students, we have presented what we would expect in a TDD, and for computer science students, we have recommended a basic-to-advanced functionality structure. The two are not mutually exclusive, and the structure is designed to help with idea generation. We have also covered show reel and version-control software.

References

Adobe Inc. (no date) *Adobe Photoshop* (version 23.2) [Computer Programme] Available at: https://helpx.adobe.com/uk/photoshop/using/whats-new.html (Accessed: 27 February 2022).

Autodesk Inc. (no date) *Autodesk Maya* (version 2022.1) [Computer Programme] Available at: https://www.autodesk.co.uk/products/maya/free-trial (Accessed: 27 February 2022).

Autodesk Inc. (no date) *Autodesk 3ds Max* (version Autodesk 3ds Max 2022) [Computer Programme] Available at: https://www.autodesk.co.uk/products/ 3ds-max/features (Accessed: 27 February 2022).

Adobe Inc. (no date) *Adobe Substance 3D* (version 2021.1 (7.1.0) [Computer Programme] Available at: https://www.substance3d.com/ (Accessed: 27 February 2022).

Black, J. (2020) *Occlusion Culling – Optimising Unity Scene*. Available at: https://youtu.be/ 1brpOOECoa8 (Accessed: December 2021).

Blender Foundation (no date) *Blender 3.0* (version 3.0) [Computer Programme] Available at: https://www.blender.org/ (Accessed: 27 February 2022).

Epic Games (2004–2022) *Unreal Engine* (version 5 UE5) [Computer Programme] Available at: https://www.unrealengine.com/en-US/unreal-engine-5 (Accessed: 27 February 2022).

Git (2005, April 7) *Git* (version 2.35.1) [Computer Programme] Available at: https://git-scm.com/ (Accessed: 27 February 2022).

MafMih. (2021) *High Rise – Offline Hack Slash* [Video game]. Available at: https:// play.google.com/store/apps/details?id=com.ChessersStudios.HighRise&gl=GB (Accessed: December 2021).

Ryan, T. (1999) *The Anatomy of a Design Document, Part 2: Documentation Guidelines for the Functional and Technical Specifications*. Available at: https://www.gamedeveloper.com/ design/the-anatomy-of-a-design-document-part-2-documentation-guidelines-for- the-functional-and-technical-specifications. (Accessed: 4 December 2021).

Stevenson, K. (2020) *Down Below – Demo*. Available at: https://kristoferstevenson. itch.io/down-below (Accessed: December 2021).

Study tonight (2021) *Technical Design Document and Game Design Document*. Available at: https://www.studytonight.com/3d-game-engineering-with-unity/tdd-and- gdd (Accessed: December 2021).

The Audacity Team (2022) *Audacity* (version 3.1.3) [Computer Programme] Available at: https://www.audacityteam.org/ (Accessed: 27 February 2022).

Unity Technologies (2022) *Unity* (version 2020 LTS + 2021.2 Tech Stream) [Computer Programme] Available at: https://unity.com/releases/release-overview (Accessed: 27 February 2022).

YoYo Games Ltd (2013–2022) *GameMaker Studio 2* (version Studio 2) Available at: https://www.yoyogames.com/en/gamemaker (Accessed: 27 February 2022).

13 Testing

In this chapter, you will learn about:

- Software testing.
- Games testing.
- Software testing techniques.
- Games testing techniques.
- Test plans and test logs.

Testing is important in any computer science or games development project requiring some skill to integrate into a dissertation. It can be confused with evaluation, in our opinion, due to the introduction of UX (user experience) testing that covers the overall player experience. This chapter defines software and games testing, techniques available, and how it can be documented in a dissertation involving reviewing available techniques and making an objective selection.

Testing a game has extra complexity and can involve play testing, alpha testing, beta testing, combinatorial testing, test flow diagrams, ad hoc testing, and positive and negative testing. We will show examples of test plans/logs that can be included in an appendix section.

Software testing

Software testing is a highly creative and intellectually stimulating process requiring a little bit of a mindset shift if you intend to do it professionally. In 1979, Glenford Myers published his classic book: "*The Art of Software Testing*" defining testing as "*the process of executing a program with the intent of finding errors.*" One primary purpose being to improve the quality of the software rather than to simply prove that the software functions as expected with safe inputs for anticipated outputs. Software is written by humans who, of course, make mistakes, ergo software has

DOI: 10.4324/9781003054887-13

many mistakes! You may be thinking: *"it's only software – what's the worst that can happen?"* Do an internet search of *"top software disasters"* and the answer is: loss of life, disaster, and billions of pounds of damage. It would in fact take an infinite number of tests to prove that software is bug free. One of us once, many years ago, implemented a ferry booking system in C for an assessment, and the lecturer came in and immediately bashed the keyboard randomly to try and break the program. The error checking thankfully held up to scrutiny, but coming up with a test plan/ log in advance would have been impossible. A *"successful"* inventive test case is one that has a high probability of detecting as-yet undiscovered errors. Software testing is a large area, and there are excellent resources presented by the International Software Testing Qualification Board (ISTQB, 2021) with the possibility of applying for recognised certification who identify seven principles:

1	Testing shows presence of defects but never really proves if a product is defect free.
2	Exhaustive testing is impossible since all possible conceivable combinations, preconditions, or scenarios cannot be tested.
3	Early testing should occur to identify bugs early in the lifecycle because the earlier they are revealed – the more cost effective.
4	Testing is context dependent, and different domains have a number of applications with different user requirements, functions, and purpose.
5	Defect clustering means the majority of the errors are generally in a small number of modules, and this should concentrate testing effort.
6	Pesticide paradox means the same sets of tests are repeated in a system, and if they are unable to uncover any bugs, then the tests need to be reviewed.
7	Absence of errors does not mean that software is defect free.

Games testing

Games testing or Gameplay testing is different form testing normal productivity software since games have a different purpose entirely. This is where we may look at the overall experience of a game. You may choose to perform play testing for others to identify bugs for you to fix and analyse and report them. Politowski, Petrillo, and Gueheneuc (2021) have recently performed a survey of video game testing, pointing out that games have particularities in relation to normal software, such as: user experience, fun, balance, difficulties with automated testing, AI testing, and multiplayer and network testing. They present seven main findings:

- Particularities of games with regard to traditional software require convergence of well-known testing strategies to form new strategies.
- Games players are not software testers, requiring them to work with software testers as a team to enhance testing knowledge and strategy.
- Game development and testing is reliant on human testing and, as a result, automation is overlooked.
- Games testers search for the fun factor and balancing of the game, which is difficult to automate.
- Games are diverse and can differ greatly, meaning no one size fits all.
- Acknowledged importance of testing by game studios should open the door for open-source initiatives.
- Lack of planning and coverage call for early testing.

Software testing techniques

Software testing should be considered in context as it is involved at every SDLC stage:

- **Unit testing** – testing the smallest components, units, modules of the software.
- **Integration testing** – testing the interfaces between the units and how they interact.
- **System testing** – looking at the quality of the system in entirety including: the functional requirements from the requirements specification and non-functional requirements such as security.
- **Acceptance testing** – delivery of the completed system to the users to gain confidence.

For software engineering/computer science dissertations, unit and integration testing to demonstrate that you can test your software appropriately are popular enhancements to your skills and demonstrate your skill set in a holistic way. In a dissertation context, it is probably rare that you will be at an advanced enough stage or be happy enough to move to acceptance testing. The software may be specialised, and as a result, we have not seen a lot of system testing. If you test your software with participants, it is good but always have ethical approval. We recommend reviewing some techniques in Table 13.1 as a starting point.

We advise describing each technique, listing the advantages and disadvantages, and then objectively selecting the correct one(s). Sawant, Bari and Chawan (2012) provide a quick comprehensive reference guide for a number of techniques discussing advantages and disadvantages, including:

- **Performance testing** – consisting of **load testing** where an application is tested to the work level approaching the limits of the specification and **stress testing** beyond those limits to determine failure level.
- **Reliability testing** – reliability relates to many aspects of the software. Software may fail and still be strictly speaking correct and therefore the nature of how the software fails is important. Software that fails and recovers gracefully is robust.
- **Security testing** – ensuring only authorised personal can access the functions provided by the software at their security level and there is no information leakage or software compromise.
- **Grey-box testing** – a combination of black and white-box testing that has 10 steps to test software against its specification and using internal knowledge.
- **User acceptance testing**
  - **Alpha and Beta testing** – In alpha testing, the user tests the software at the developer's site where developers observe and document outcomes. In beta testing (also known as field testing), the users test the software at their own site to improve the software before official release.
  - **Operational acceptance testing (operational readiness/ preparedness testing)** – This process ensures that all required components and processes are present for the user to appropriately utilise the system.
  - **Contact and regulation acceptance testing** – This is where the system is tested to ensure that it meets all contractual obligations, adhering to regulations, standards, governmental, local authority, and legal requirements.

Table 13.1 General techniques to review

Testing technique	Description
Review Techniques (Manual Testing)	Based on small peer groups reviewing the program analysis, design, and code documentation. Two popular methods are Formal Technical Reviews and Structured Walkthroughs (Collofello 1987; Yourdon, 1989). The approaches involve inspection steps requiring members of the inspection team to be assigned certain roles. An advantage is applicability during any lifecycle stage.
Functional Testing (Correctness Testing, black box)	Uses the requirement specification and documents produced during development to derive test cases. Popular methods of functional testing are Equivalence Partitioning and Boundary Value Analysis (Patton, 2001). The advantages of these techniques are that the focus is on specification-based tests and the techniques are well suited to applications, which have a very large input and output domain. The disadvantage is there is no real standard for selecting the test cases and is left to the creativity of the tester and has no reference whatsoever to the logic of the code.
Structural Testing (Correctness Testing, glass box)	Focuses on the program logic to derive the test cases. These include Logic Coverage, Basis Path Testing, and Linear Code Sequence and Jump. Logic coverage is the simplest form of structural testing and can involve the construction of a flow graph to aid different levels of structural coverage such as 'statement' where every source statement in the code has to be executed and 'branch' where all possible decision outcomes have to be executed (Cline, 1995).
Error Oriented (Fault-Based Techniques)	Focus on assessing the presence of specific errors in the program. Two popular error-oriented testing techniques are error based and fault-based testing (Chu, 1997). Error-based testing identifies errors and then asks the question of how these errors manifest themselves as faults in the implementation. Methods of fault-based testing include weak and strong mutation testing. Mutant testing is when a mutant program is produced differing from the original in one small detail and the program is assessed to see if it can tell the difference.

- **System testing** is really a series of different tests falling into the category of functional testing to evaluate the completed, integrated systems compliance with the requirements specification; it includes recovery, security, GUI, and compatibility testing.

Game testing techniques

In games, software bugs are commonly referred to as glitches. Any of us who have played games to any great degree know there have been many glitches. Testing games can be more complicated and time consuming due to the fundamental nature and idea of the software, i.e., get the player to engage with it for as long as possible. Even considering input variables such as button presses, audio, and motion in comparison to a normal piece of functional software, it becomes more complex before we even consider multiplayer environment interaction.

Frequently, we see functionality testing and internal and external play testing in dissertations to fix bugs either by doing it personally or utilising the target audience with play testing. This is usually performed with the players in their own environment, using a basic online questionnaire to gather some empirical evidence. Play testing and game user experience testing muddies the waters between testing and evaluation. For this book, testing is looking at the functionality of the game or the software product, even if that means looking at the full player experience, immersion, presence, fun, enjoyability, controls, interface, and playability. Evaluation is really taking the full completed game and ascertaining if it is doing what it is supposed to do or answering your overall research question, which may be "does this NPC character scaffolding method lead to greater enjoyability?" This makes it easier to formulate a convincing, stringent, valid evaluation experiment to ascertain if your game fulfils its purpose, such as increasing knowledge or providing greater player satisfaction by introducing a new mechanic. We will discuss evaluation in the next chapter (Chapter 14). In terms of games testing, there are no standard methodologies but well-known techniques and a number of choices.

Game user research/user experience (GUR/UX)

GUR and UX academic disciplines themselves integrating and encompassing several fields, including psychology, interaction design, human factors, ergonomics, software development, and computer science. Usability is defined in the ISO 9241-11 (1998) as "*the extent to which a product can be used by specified users to achieve specified goals with effectiveness, efficiency and satisfaction in a specified context of use.*" It encompasses learnability, regular use, error protection, accessibility, and maintainability. GUR/UX testing, like user-centred design, is of course verifying that the product or game is providing a great experience to the player. Essentially, you are giving a version of the game to players to try out and provide detailed feedback in a number of ways: either a constructed survey or a standardised test, with metrics and measurements or through observational analysis. Using this method, the developers observe the players playing the game to look for anything that could improve the experience, ensuring it compares against the designers' intended responses. GUR and UX testing covers the holistic user experience – playability, immersion, fun, enjoyment, interaction, realism, and cost effectiveness – to look for bugs and make the game experience better. This area is vast and can fill entire books or courses, but in a dissertation, you may choose one of several methods. Drachen, Mirza-Babaei and Nake, (2018) discuss a number of methods at different stages of the GDLC and look at attitudes and behaviours. These include:

Envisioning – interviews, focus groups, ethnographic field study
Design/build – usability test, RITE test, narrative usability, review, heuristic evaluation, initial and extended play testing
Release – benchmark play test, usability play test
Post-release – alpha/beta testing

Play testing

In our dissertation experience, students commonly perform internal play testing and external play testing. Internal is allowing the game testers within the company to test the game, and external play testing is the target audience. In the context of a dissertation, this means individual testing or student peer testing until a polished product is produced and then making it available to a target audience. We have seen internal testing consisting of white- and black-box testing by the student and then external play testing involved games students/players used from their course; these students were considered subject experts, providing that ethics had been approved. Kramarzewski and De Nucci (2018) in their book *Practical Game Design* define play testing as *"the process in which you expose your game to the members of your target audience in order to uncover issues and design flaws and gather actionable feedback that can help improve the game."* They provide a detailed guide with many different aspects to consider including:

- **What to playtest?** – controls, mechanics, whether people are motivated or care about the characters?
- **What playtest format?** –individual, group, public, or remote play testing solutions (which became more frequent during COVID-19) or supervised individual sessions.
- **How to run sessions?** – introducing yourself, making the player feel at ease, encouraging interaction, post-session interviews, and play testing questionnaires guidance.

In game dissertations, bug reports can be compiled in a spreadsheet, and in some instances, these are automatically generated using tools such as *Firebase Crashlytics* (https://firebase.google.com/products/crashlytics/).

Mirza-Babaei, Moosajee, and Drenikow (2016) note the challenge associated with play testing is effectively gathering, analysing, interpreting, and visualising qualitative and quantitative data, which is more of a challenge for Indie Game companies (closer to a dissertation scenario). They outline the most common GUR methods:

- **Behavioural observations** – Players are asked to perform a task while being recorded or observed, which can be time consuming but also cost effective.
- **Think-aloud protocols** – Players are asked to talk through their actions to gain insight into the players' thought processes.
- **Heuristic evaluation** – This formal accessibility and usability evaluation method, with several heuristics added, is available in different versions that are applicable to games. The primary difficulty is that is suffers from subjective interpretation.
- **Questionnaires** – This paper-based or online approach can efficiently be sent to many participants to ascertain what they do.
- **Interviews** – These are utilised to gain more detailed and thorough information, but as a result, are time consuming.
- **First Time User Experiences (FTUE)** – For a game, the first few minutes of play are especially critical where the rate of attrition is at its highest. Generally, if a game passes the test at this point, then players will engage in prolonged participation.
- **RITE (Rapid Iterative Testing and Evaluation)** – This employs both observations and think-aloud techniques to iteratively, rapidly alter design after usability testing.

Alpha and beta testing

Alpha testing is really a form of internal user acceptance testing generally done onsite by potential users of the system or game before the release or the beta test. Beta testing is external-user acceptance testing where the game is released to a controlled population, or even the entire population, to receive feedback. It is similar to internal and external testing – so we would recommend that **UT:** If play testing in a dissertation context, then internal testing is either yourself as the developer or student peers, and external testing is making the game available to the intended audience.

Simulation demonstration

It may be that your project is so technical in nature that the only way to test it is to implement a series of demos/simulations, run them, and record the result. For example, procedural terrain generation, running algorithms for efficiency, 3D lighting demonstrations, 3D object rendering, rotation demonstrations, and platform compatibility testing.

Combinatorial testing

Kuhn et al., (2015) state that combinatorial testing has gained popularity in the past decade due to *"improved algorithms and practical successes."* It is a method of generating test cases for commercial software testing, which can, of course, be applied to video games (Sagi and Silvestrini, 2017). It probably is not really suitable for a dissertation; however, you should not discount the possibility and at least review the options if only to say this is for automatic test generation of a large-scale system and not suitable. Several tools to automatically generate test cases are identified by Sagi (2016) for further reference if you wish to research further. Combinatorial testing allows a systematic, formulaic scrutiny of all possible combinations of inputs and outputs for a game and is considered effective due to the combination of parameters. A mock example is show in Table 13.2 to give you a quick idea.

Test flow diagrams

Test flow diagrams (TFDs) are useful graphical representations of the behaviour of a game from the player perspective; they allow a tester to construct appropriate tests in a logical, systematic way by traversing the

Table 13.2 Mock combinatorial testing example

TEST	Character moving speed	Armed with weapon	Fire button pressed	Target hit	Result
1	Slow	YES	YES	NO	PASS
2	Medium	NO	NO	NO	FAIL
3	Fast	YES	NO	YES	FAIL
4	Slow	NO	YES	YES	PASS
5	Medium	YES	YES	YES	PASS
6	Fast	NO	YES	NO	PASS

diagram and executing the game in expected and unexpected ways. They have a variety of components, and the entire notation is outlined in Chapter 9 of *Game Testing All in One* by Charles P. Schultz and Robert Denton Bryant (2016).

Test plans and test logs

Testing a game or piece of functional software requires planning and thought. Generally, we find test plans and test logs in computer science dissertations as well as game dissertations. Additionally, games dissertations have play testing and user experience testing.

The **Test Plan** is a record of the entire test-planning process and is described by the ISTQB as *"the scope, approach, resources and schedule of intended test activities."* It identifies test items, features to be tested, testing tasks, assignment of tasks, degree of tester independence, environment, design techniques, entry and exit criteria to be used, rationale for the selection, and any risks requiring contingency planning.

The **Test Log** contains information about test cases and whether the test has passed or failed. The log is microscopic in detail, breaking tests into processable components.

Here are two examples from computer science and from games.

Example 1: Computer science

Console-based application menu structure
The menu has the following basic structure:

1   Create a character.
2   Create an item for the character.

3 Display all character and item details.
4 Save the game.
5 Load the game.
6 Exit the game.

A test plan for this is displayed in Table 13.3:
Table 13.4 shows possible individual tests for *test 2*.

Table 13.3 Test plan example

Test no.	Test purpose	Program modules
1	Testing the menu display	MenuDisplay()
2	Testing the menu for input	MenuSelection()
3	Testing the character creation	CreateNewCharacter()
4	Testing the item creation	CreateNewItem()
5	Testing whether all details are displayed	PrintCharacterDetails() PrintItemDetails()
6	To test if the character(s) saves	SaveCharacter()
7	To test if the characters(s) loads	LoadCharacter()
8	To test if the program saves the Item data structure	SaveItems()
9	To test if the program loads the Item data structure	LoadItems()

Table 13.4 Individual tests example

Test no.	Inputs	Anticipated outputs	Actual outputs	Results
2 a)	"1" in the MenuSelection()	CreateNewCharacter() functionality reached		Pass
2 b)	"2" in the MenuSelection()	CreateNewItem() functionality reached		Pass
2 c)	"3" in the MenuSelection()	PrintAllDetails() functionality reached		Pass
2 d)	"4" in the MenuSelection()	SaveGame() functionality is called		Pass
2 e)	"5" in the MenuSelection()	LoadGame() is called		Pass
2 f)	"6" in the MenuSelection()	ExitGame() is called		Pass
2 g)	"a" in the MenuSelection()	MenuDisplay()	Program Crash	Fail

Table 13.5 Test plan excerpt

Test no.	Test purpose	Program modules
1	Drawing an entity.	EntityDraw MouseDown, MouseMove, MouseUp
	Mapping Algorithm Testing	
31	Mapping of Diagram with Specialization/Generalization.	CmdGenerate_Click

Table 13.6 Test log excerpt

Test no.	Inputs	Anticipated outputs	Actual outputs	Results
1A	Select entity check box and click on the screen	An entity of a default size will be drawn on the screen, and the user will be asked to specify an entity name		P

Example 2: Computer science

Source: *Dissertation B*
Test plan segment
Table 13.5 displays a test plan excerpt including Test 1 and 31 in this project for drawing an entity and mapping a complex relationship illustrating that test inputs can be complex.

Table 13.6 shows the test log for test 1A.

Here is an example test log entry for the complex test:

Test log 31 A

Inputs
Multiplicity, participation, and disjoint constraints of the specialisation/generalisation are being tested with Figure 13.1.
Anticipated outputs
The participation of 1:1 relationships are Total: Total so all of entities will combine to create one large relational schema object with all attributes.
Result – Pass

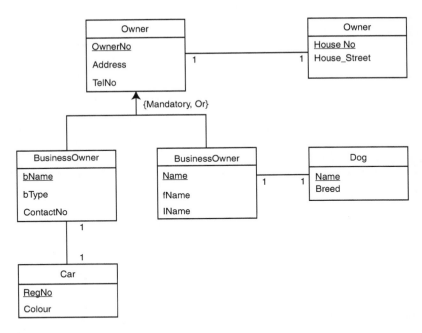

Figure 13.1 Test input diagram.

Example 1: Games development

In games dissertations, we have seen examples of initial play testing to gather preliminary data to determine how to move forward with the implementation using questionnaires.

Source: *Dissertation A*

1   The game controls were easy to use.
2   The objective of the game was clear.
3   The game play was immersive.
4   The game was too easy.
5   Did you make it to the second level?

    a   Why did you not make it to the second level?
    b   What it was like to reach level 2 e.g., easy, difficult, challenging?

6 Did you encounter any bugs, glitches, or errors?
7 How in your opinion, would you improve the game?

The results were analysed and described in pie charts and bar graphs, with the qualitative data processed. Figure 13.2 shows the analysis of question 1.

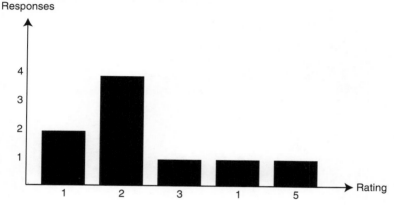

The game controls were easy to use

Figure 13.2 Example analysis.

Example 2: Games development

This example is two rounds of play testing of various incremental game implementations investigating typology preferences:

Source: *Dissertation G*
What is your favourite level design type?

- Open World
- Linear
- Semi-Linear
- Hub and spoke
- Network
- Parallel

- Ring
- Other

Please elaborate on why this particularly level typology is your favourite.

Figure 13.3 shows an analysis of the results:

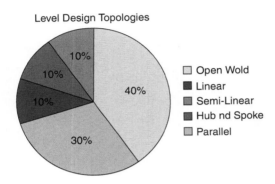

Level Design Topologies

- ☐ Open Wold
- ■ Linear
- ▨ Semi-Linear
- ▨ Hub nd Spoke
- ☐ Parallel

Figure 13.3 Example analysis.

Summary

In this chapter, we have reviewed the concepts of software testing and games testing, as well as listing a number of well-known techniques to get you started and to consider. We have also provided detailed examples from computer science and games development as a point of reference. We recommend that when beginning the testing part of your dissertation, you ask some of the following questions:

1   What exactly are you testing? The functionality or nonfunctional attributes, such as playability, interface, balance, enjoyment, immersion, or engagement?
2   Are you going to use internal or external testing or both?
3   Are their automated tools to generate reports or test cases?

In the dissertation, we recommend to UT: Perform a review of software testing techniques for computer science and additional games testing techniques/approaches for games, as well as traditional software testing and objectively select the appropriate one(s) with justification.

References

Chu, D-H (1997) 'An Evaluation of Software Testing Techniques', In: *Reliability, Quality and Safety of Software-Intensive Systems.* (ed. D. Gritzalis). Springer Science +Business Media Dordrecht, pp. 259–262.

Collofello J.S. (1987) 'Teaching Technical Reviews in a One-Semester Software Engineering Course', In Proceedings of the *Eighteenth SIGCSE Technical Symposium on Computer Science Education*, 19(1), pp. 222–227.

Cline, M. S. (1995). An Empirical Study of the Branch Coverage of Different Fault Classes in Computer and Information Science. PhD thesis. University of Santa Cruz.

Drachen, A., Mirza-Babaei, P. and Nake, L.E. (2018) *Games User Research*. Oxford.

Firebase (no date) *Firebase Crashlytics* [Computer Programme] Available at: https://firebase.google.com/products/crashlytics/ (Accessed: 27 February 2022).

ISO 9241-11 *Ergonomic requirements for office work with visual display terminals* (VDTs) – Part 11 Guidance on usability (1998).

ISO CD 9241-11: *Ergonomics of human-system interaction – Part 11: Usability: definitions and concepts* (2015).

ISTQB (2021) *References*. Available at: https://www.istqb.org/references.html (Accessed: December 2021).

Kramarzewski, A. and De Nucci, E. (2018) *Practical Game Design: Learn the Art of Game Design through Applicable Skills and Cutting-Edge Insights*. Packt Publishing.

Kuhn, D.R., Bryce, R., Duan, F., Ghandehari, L.S., Lei, Y. and Kacker, R.N. (2015) 'Combinatorial Testing: Theory and Practice', *Advances in Computers*, 99, pp. 1–66. doi: 10.1016/bs.adcom.2015.05.003

Mirza-Babaei, P., Moosajee, N., and Drenikow, B. (2016) 'Playtesting for Indie Studios', Proceedings of the *20th International Academic Mindtrek Conference*, pp. 366–374 doi: 10.1145/2994310.2994364

Myers, G. (1979). *The Art of Software Testing*. John Wiley & Sons.

Patton, R. (2001) *Software Testing*. SAMS.

Politowski, C., Petrillo, F. and Gueheneuc, Y-G. (2021) *A Survey of Video Game Testing*. Available at: https://arxiv.org/abs/2103.06431v1 (Accessed: 31 July 2021).

Rajkuma (2021) Software Testing Material: Game Testing 101 – The Ultimate Beginner's Guide. Available at: https://www.softwaretestingmaterial.com/game-testing/ (Accessed: December 2021).

Sawant, A.A., Bari, P.H. and Chawan, P.M. (2012) 'Software testing techniques and strategies', *International Journal of Engineering Research and Applications (IJERA)*, 2, Issue, May – Jun 2012, pp. 980–986. ISSN: 2248-9622.

Sagi, B.R. (2016) Experimental Design in Game Testing. PhD thesis. Rochester Institute of Technology. Available at: https://scholarworks.rit.edu/cgi/viewcontent.cgi?article=10170&context=theses (Accessed: December 2021).

Sagi, B.R. and Silvestrini, R. (2017) 'Application of combinatorial tests in video game testing', *Quality Engineering*, 29(4), pp. 745–759, doi: 10.1080/08982112.2017.1300919

Schultz, C.P. and Bryant, R.D. (2016) *Game Testing All in One*. 3rd edn. Dulles, Virginia, Boston, Massachusetts, New Delhi: Mercury Learning and Information.

Yourdon, E. (1989) *Structural Walkthroughs*. 4th edn. Yourdon Press.

14 Evaluation

In this chapter, you will learn about:

- Evaluation.
- Formative evaluation.
- Summative evaluation.
- Questions for performing an evaluation.
- Presenting an evaluation in a dissertation.

Evaluation and testing can often become blurred and grouped together in computer science and games dissertations. We encourage you to look at testing techniques and individual tests as components or constituents of evaluation. Just as methods can be used as tools in a methodology, tests can be used as tools in an evaluation. Where evaluation is forming an overall conclusion about a game or software artifact, this may entail many tests or techniques, which may be quantitative and qualitative in nature. Testing can be several small steps to verify acceptable, correct behaviour of functionality at the micro level just as assessment can be a small measurement of student learning at the micro level. Evaluation looks at the macro, holistic level and can take many things into account: cost effectiveness, design, satisfaction, interface, intellectual stimulation, usability, immersion, efficiency, and many more. We tend to view evaluation as a far more thorough and deep analysis. In this chapter, we will discuss evaluation, types of evaluation, and where evaluation research can fit into a dissertation in terms of answering your research question or verifying that your game or software is effectively addressing an issue. We will highlight what to specify in relation to participants, instruments, design, and results.

Evaluation

Evaluation is not easy to define, but we (as educators and students) are subconsciously familiar with it on a modular, programme, and

DOI: 10.4324/9781003054887-14

institutional level. We are familiar with some of the processes and instruments, such as course evaluation questionnaires or the NSS (National Student Survey) to ascertain if a programme is performing properly, worth keeping, in need of improvement, and if it should be removed. Crompton (1996) citing Thorpe (1993) in "Implementing Learning Technology" by The Learning Technology Dissemination Initiative (http://www.icbl.hw.ac.uk/ltdi/index.html) states that *"evaluation is the collection, analysis and interpretation of evidence about the effects and outcomes of a particular activity or system of provision. It includes both intended and unintended outcomes and should support the making of judgements about the value of what is being evaluated, and how it might be improved."* Gavin (2008) defines evaluation as *"research involving systematic appraisal of organisations, processes or programmes leading to feedback on improvement or performance."* Essentially evaluation can occur for programmes of study or interventions, and therefore, software and games can be evaluated as well, and various types can be performed. Frey (2018) defines an evaluation as *"a systematic and purposeful collection and analysis of data used to document the effectiveness of programs or interventions. Rigorous evaluation can determine if programs or interventions should be maintained, improved, or eliminated."* There are many purposes of evaluation, and historically, this debate started in the 1960s. Phillips (2018) presents a comprehensive overview of the development of evaluation terminology from Cronbach's (aiding decision-making approach) to Scriven's (making value-judgements) leading to the distinction of formative and summative evaluation. Philips also presents Stake's example elaborating the distinction: *"when the cook tastes the soup, this is a formative evaluation; when the customer tastes the soup, this is summative evaluation."*

Formative evaluation

Formative evaluation is performed throughout a course, software, or game development. This is where data is collected before and/or during instruction or development to improve the course or application. During a 12-week implementation/development process, you may have three formative evaluations in 4-week intervals to improve your software/game. This allows for the improvement of your implementation and the evaluation process, including the evaluation instruments, e.g., the questionnaire. Sometimes it is wise to perform a pilot study, as well to verify the details. Variations of formative evaluation exist:

- **Expert reviews** conducted very early, where the primary goal is to offer correctional advice. For example, using experienced game players to provide feedback on your game.
- **One-to-one** utilising potential users of the software/game to gauge their reactions.
- **Small group evaluations** where a developer/instructor interacts with a small group of potential users in the targeted context to refine content and rectify errors involving the collection of descriptive and quantitative feedback.
- **Field trials** are larger scale trials to ascertain if the changes made from small group evaluation were effective and to gauge suitability for the intended context. The evaluator observes intervention interaction in a larger group (e.g., 20–40).

Summative evaluation

Summative evaluation is performed at the end of the development period, course, software trial, or game play test to assess the product, usually using external evaluators. Considering that assessment is a small micro constituent of evaluation, summative assessment and evaluation usually mean a large exam to test individual/collective knowledge of a large body of students. Bhat and Bhat (2019)) state that "*summative assessments evaluate student learning, knowledge, proficiency, or success at the conclusion of an instructional period.*" According to Frey (2018), summative evaluation is more outcome focused rather than process focused and is usually undertaken at the end when the program or intervention is in a state of stability. Harpel (1978) describes two main orientations of summative evaluation: **research-oriented** to validate and improve programmes and **management-oriented** to assess cost and whether the programmes did what they were supposed to.

Questions for performing an evaluation

Ainsworth (2003) identifies important questions to ask when performing an evaluation

What is to be done with information collected?

This is determined by the research question(s) and overall purpose of the software or game to allow collection of relevant data. If you have implemented a new game mechanic to increase immersion, you may wish to gather information on the usability of the mechanic and conduct a test to measure immersion before and after playing the game. You may wish to use a similar control condition game without that mechanic to draw comparisons. If you have developed a new algorithm, you may wish to compare your algorithm to other algorithms so that you can make a case for efficiency. It is worthwhile to consider what to collect in relation to what it will allow you to ascertain and discern.

What are the appropriate forms of measurement?

It is possible to measure a great many things as long as you use your own judgement and be able to justify what you are measuring and why. These can include: usability, user satisfaction, motivation, heuristic evaluation of the interface, enjoyment, immersion, balance, fun, whether learning has taken place if it is serious game, learning styles, or personality types when making moral choices in a simulation. The list is endless, and you can measure several aspects to reach an overall conclusion. If we select motivation as an example, ask yourself "*how do you measure motivation levels?*" and there will be tried, tested, and recognised questionnaire examples or inventories in existence already that you can use or draw inspiration from or academic rigour. For behavioural models, we have seen dissertations utilise the Felder-Silverman and Myers-Biggs models of learning and personalities.

What is the most appropriate experimental design?

Evaluation may involve an intervention and participants will try your implementation at some point, and there are several experimental designs to consider:

- Experimental or quasi-experimental?
- Pre-test (possibly to determine if the population sample is adequate)
- Intervention → post-test
- Pre-test → Intervention → post-test
- Pre-test → Intervention → post-test → long term follow-up post-test (Figure 14.1)

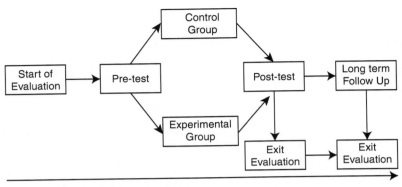

Figure 14.1 Evaluation experimental design.

What is an appropriate form of comparison?

To illustrate, here are some examples:

- Different software usability, efficiency, and user preference.
- VR game vs. normal game, comparing presence, immersion, or engagement.
- Relational database vs. object-oriented database.
- Algorithm efficiency.
- Serious game vs. paper-based vs. role-playing.
- Uses of alternative audio effects.
- Level typologies: linear vs. branching vs. open ended.
- Comparing tutorials and scaffolding, e.g., NPCs and navigational pointers vs. control with no guidance.

See some examples of experimental designs in Figure 14.2 and 14.3.

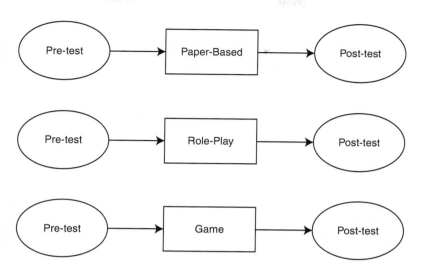

Figure 14.2 Serious game vs. role-play vs. paper-based experimental design.

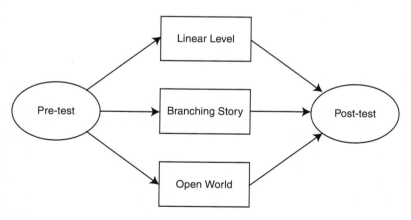

Figure 14.3 Level preference comparison experimental design.

What is an appropriate context?

Where is the evaluation to be performed, such as: a business/company, industrial setting, a classroom, lecture, computer lab, remote/online? During the pandemic, evaluations were done remotely, if practically possible, and interviews could be recorded and transcribed in *MS Teams*.

Suggested presentation of an evaluation in a dissertation

Evaluation type

Specify if the evaluation will be formative, summative, or both. We tend to see a demonstration of both where formative evaluation improves the software/game and summative evaluation ascertains that it has fulfilled its primary function by logically gathering data that the student has selected using their own judgement. In a dissertation, a formative evaluation may be several experts providing improvement advice at various stages, and a summative evaluation your main experiment and review of the final product. The main thing is to show the process.

This can also present a number of quantitative comparisons in relation to algorithmic efficiency performed using software that outputs a detailed graph of the comparison.

Procedure

The procedure section can provide:

- An overview indicating the specific aspects being evaluated such as learning effectiveness, immersion, engagement, fun, usability, preferences, perceptions. You can simply say the evaluation will investigate, for example, *"procedural efficacy in VR"* and collect quantitative data, learning analytics, and some qualitative data.
- When and where the evaluation is going to take place. This can be in a classroom, a business, remotely or on Steam (https://store. steampowered.com/). You can specify a date and estimated time that the evaluation will take place.
- Whether there is an experimental and control group. This occurs when a pre or a post-test is going to be deployed and what techniques are going to be used to analyse the data.
- Information about questionnaires or interviews involved. Here is an example:

The questionnaire was made available through an online survey package for a two-week period during March 2021. Participation was voluntary, and participants were notified of the questionnaire through email and the Institutional VLE. Notices were also posted across the university. Respondents completed the questionnaire online at their convenience during this period. Access to the questionnaire was controlled using the students' VLE usernames and passwords, and the students' unique identification number was used to ensure a student only completed the questionnaire once.

Materials/instruments used in the study

If questionnaires or interviews are involved, then describe their constituent sections with actual instruments added in an appendix. This does not have to be a duplication but rather a description and justification of the section of the instrument such as:

- Demographic questions.
- Reasons for playing computer games using a recognised framework such as: Malone and Lepper's intrinsic motivation framework (Malone and Lepper, 1987) or mechanics, dynamics, and aesthetics (MDA) framework (Hunicke, LeBlanc, and Zubek, n.d.).
- Types of games/software used in terms of recognised genres/types.
- Measuring levels of immersion, engagement, motivation using a recognised inventory.
- Type of learner/teacher based on a specific learning model such as: Kolb's Experiential Learning model (Kolb, 1984).

It is good practice to provide a basic description of all of the sections of a questionnaire or interview and any previous frameworks or references to the academic literature used to enhance academic rigour.

Participants

This should be a detailed account of the participants that have taken part and should (at this stage) be an account of what has taken place including, for example:

- Numbers of participants
- Demographics

  Gender
  Age
  Name of Course
  Level of education
  Occupation
  Status (part-time or full-time)

- Proportion – if you targeted many potential participants, how many participated and how many responded?

This allows grouping the information for analysis (see Chapter 15). It may also be the case that there are no participants to report because the dissertation was heavily development, algorithmic, or simulation based.

Methodology

Specify the overall methodology in this section, i.e., survey/questionnaire, experimental, interview, observational case study, etc. Most evaluations at honours level are either case study, survey/questionnaire, or intervention experiments. You can specify:

- The methodology.
- The experimental/intervention design e.g., pre-test → intervention → post-test.
- How the participants were randomly assigned to each group.

UT: The intervention in this context will be the software/game you have created.

If there is a control group, it is either a piece of software for comparison, a game without the new functionality you have created for comparison, or possibly a traditional form of approach, e.g., role-play or lectures. It may also be a simple comparison of efficiency in relation to an algorithm or a particular software solution such as comparing DBMS.

Results

In our experience, at this level, reporting evaluation results is a breakdown of each individual piece of data gathered for each question of the questionnaire/ interview or some form of efficiency/comparative measurements of algorithms for software products. We encourage you to adopt a structured approach rather than robotic, plain reporting. It is very useful to interpret and contextualise the results by stating what they indicate and what they mean for your research area and findings. An acceptable structure would:

- **Report basic demographic results.** It is acceptable to use sensible charts and graphs. A pie chart showing 100%, or 50% and 50% is perhaps too obvious. Showing percentages, numbers, means and ranking tables is a good way to report findings and data.
- Have a section **answering the research question(s)** in some way typically involving:
    - A comparison of a pre-test and post-test to measure change, such as levels of learning or fun.
    - A comparison of two post-tests of a control or experimental group, e.g., for a usability preference comparison, or a knowledge comparison or enjoyability comparison if comparing two alternatives such as drawing software or level types.
    - Incremental formative evaluations to measure improvement of an application in a development process.
    - A report of a post-test test questionnaire or interview.
    - A description and the quantifiable results (timing, efficiency, optimisation) of several runs of a simulation.

Evaluation is a process demonstration at this level and probably not a full randomised controlled trial (RCT) with 30 participants per group. Dissertations in these disciplines are highly implementation based, and it is rare to have rigorous statistical analysis, which is more of a requirement for say a psychology dissertation; however, it is still good practice to present and interpret evidence objectively. We tend to see graphical comparisons or basic quantifiable evidence such as percentages and means compared or ranked data. This is generally backed up with qualitative open-ended data that is gathered through field notes, observations, or open-ended questions. Evidence is presented, organised, and highlighted to synthesis the main findings. If, for example, you were running a comparison of a pre-test before intervention and a post-test after intervention, and example is presented in Table 14.1.

Table 14.1 Example data

PRE-TEST SCORES	POST-TEST SCORES
2	5
4	4
5	7
3	8
2	6
5	8
8	7
7	8
3	9
5	6
MEAN = 4.4	MEAN = 6.8
SD = 2.01	SD = 1.55

Despite no inferential statistical analysis performed here, you can still say results indicated that the intervention increased scores between pre and post-tests. Various charts (bar charts, pie charts) can be presented if there is only a post-test or scatter graphs for simulations and algorithms. You may present additional sections in tables to provide supplementary evidence, for example, by asking the following questions: What do you like or dislike about traditional approaches? What do you like about the experimental approach (your implementation)?

Example evaluation: Computer science

Source: *Dissertation J*
This involved the comparison of performance tests of 12 DBMSs, including using PHP to measure the performance on various operations such as:

- INSERT
- SELECT
- UPDATE
- CREATE
- DROP
- DELETE

The execution times were presented in a bar graph for each DBMS and an overall matrix was compiled to evaluate the best DBMS for a particular companies' requirements.

Example evaluation: Games development

Source: *Dissertation G*

A play test intervention with three different level configurations and a post-test with a questionnaire instrument asking specialised questions with results was reported in various ways. A formative approach at three different intervals was used throughout development. Table 14.2 shows the questions, collection, and reporting methods used.

Table 14.2 Question descriptions, collection and reporting methods

Question description	Collection method	Reporting method
Age	Multiple choice – single selection (Under 18, 18–21, 22–25, 26–30, 31–34, 35+)	Pie Chart
Type of games usually played	Multiple choice – multiple selection (FPS, MOBA, Platformers, Platformer, MMO, RPG, Simulation, Puzzle, Horror, Other)	Bar Graph (Vertical)
The players most preferred level	Multiple choice – single selection (Medieval Open, Medieval Linear, Glider)	Pie Chart
Elaboration of the players most preferred level	Qualitative explanation open-ended question	Table displaying qualitative quotes for each respondent if no answer is given then this was reported
The players least preferred level	Multiple choice – single selection (Medieval Open, Medieval Linear, Glider)	Pie Chart
Elaboration of the players least preferred level	Qualitative explanation open-ended question	Table displaying qualitative quotes for each respondent
Additional themes in terms of future level design and development	Multiple choice – multiple selection (Ice/Snow, Jungle, Egyptian, Arabian, Futuristic)	Bar Graph (Vertical)
To what extent the unique music developed for the game suited the levels	An ordinal scale ranging from Strongly Agree to Strongly Disagree from 1–5	Bar Graph (Horizontal)
Suggestions for additional future puzzles in the open-ended level of the game	Qualitative explanation open-ended question	Table of results

(Continued)

Table 14.2 (Continued)

Question description	Collection method	Reporting method
Suggestions for the name of the main character	Qualitative explanation open-ended question	Table of results
Additional question addressing things that may have been missed or not covered	Qualitative explanation open-ended question regarding some of the following: feedback regarding the character, gameplay/mechanics, enemies, level types, music, likes or dislikes or if there is anything that could be added	Table of results
The participants favourite type of level design structure	Multiple choice – single selection (open world, linear, semi-linear, hub and spoke, network, parallel, ring and other)	Pie Chart
Justification of favourite level design	Qualitative explanation open-ended question	Table of results
What part of the Mechanics-Dynamics-Aesthetics framework was most important	Multiple choice – single selection (Mechanics, Aesthetics, Both Equally Important)	Pie Chart
If you with to elaborate on design and aesthetics	Qualitative explanation open-ended question	Table of results
The most important types of sound from various sources	Multiple choice – multiple selection (Interface (from the HUD, menu button clicks), Effect (sound triggered in the game world from the player), Zone (sound relating to the setting in the game world such as weather), Affect (sound to reflect the emotional state of the player)	Pie Graph (Vertical)

After each play test, a synthesis of actions were written up from the results with changes being implemented and further play testing performed.

Summary

This chapter has outlined the different kinds of evaluation, as well as what important questions to ask when performing an evaluation. We have also provided our recommended structure to allow you to focus your evaluation section and detailed examples of how to collect your data and report it within a dissertation.

References

Ainsworth, S. (2003) 'Evaluation Methods for Learning Environments', *A tutorial for the 11th International Conference on Artificial Intelligence Education*, Amsterdam Available at: https://slideplayer.com/slide/777067/ (Accessed: December 2021).

Bhat, B.A., and Bhat, G.J. (2019) 'Formative and summative evaluation techniques for improvement of the learning process', *European Journal of Business & Social Sciences*, 7(5), ISSN: 2235-767X. https://www.researchgate.net/publication/333633265_Formative_and_Summative_Evaluation_Techniques_for_Improvement_of_Learning_Process.

Crompton, P. (1996) 'Evaluation: A Practical guide to methods', *LTDIL Implementing Learning Technology*, Available at: http://www.icbl.hw.ac.uk/ltdi/implementing-it/eval.pdf (Accessed December 2021).

Frey, B. (2018) *The SAGE Encyclopaedia of Educational Research, Measurement, and Evaluation*. (Vols. 1–4). Thousand Oaks, CA: SAGE Publications, Inc. doi: 10.4135/9781506326139

Gavin, H. (2008) *Understanding Research Methods and Statistics in Psychology*. London: SAGE Publications Ltd. ISBN: 9781412934411.

Harpel, R.L. (1978) 'Evaluating from a management perspective', *New Directions for Student Services*, 1, pp. 19–33.

Hunicke, R., LeBlanc, M. and Zubek, R. (n.d.) *MDA: A Formal Approach to Game Design and Game Research*. Available at: https://users.cs.northwestern.edu/~hunicke/MDA.pdf (Accessed December 2021).

Kolb, D. (1984). *Experiential Learning*. New Jersey: Prentice-Hall Inc.

Learning Technology Dissemination Initiative (no date) Available at: http://www.icbl.hw.ac.uk/ltdi/index.html (Accessed: 27 February 2022).

Malone, T.W. and Lepper, M.R. (1987) 'Making Learning Fun: A Taxonomy of Intrinsic Motivations for Learning', In *Aptitude, Learning and Instruction, Volume 3: Conative and Affective Process Analysis*. Hillsdale, NJ: Lawrence Erlbaum, pp. 223–253.

Phillips, D.C. (2018) 'The many functions of evaluation in education', *Education Policy Analysis Archives*, 26, p. 46. doi: 10.14507/epaa.26.3811

Thorpe, M. (1993) *Evaluating Open and Distance Learning*. Harlow: Longman.

15 Statistical Analysis
Techniques

In this chapter, you will learn about:

- Types of data.
- Identifying statistical techniques.
- Descriptive and inferential statistical analysis.
- Dependent and independent variables.
- Parametric and non–parametric criteria.
- Sample design.
- Common techniques.
- Recommended software.
- Qualitative analysis.

A basic understanding of statistical analysis techniques and qualitative analysis is an excellent caveat skill to obtain during your degree and can assist you in the next stage of your academic career. Few dissertations at this level in these disciplines utilise statistical techniques or qualitative analysis, and if they do, it is highly impressive. Whether it is from a questionnaire or the results of performing an intervention experiment, you may find yourself in the fortunate position of having a sizable amount of data to analyse that is worthy of academic publication. This can be a brilliant opportunity to learn some basic statistical analysis or qualitative analysis. It is, of course, very wise to plan what data you wish to collect so that you can have it in the correct format, know what techniques to apply, what software to do this in, and how to report the findings. This becomes second nature when you have experience and have conducted a number of research projects, but probably at the moment, you are a novice. This chapter will get you started with the basics of statistical techniques and how to select and apply them with a small overview of qualitative techniques.

DOI: 10.4324/9781003054887-15

Type of data

There are two pertinent questions to ask about data:

- Where did the data come from? Is it returned as a result of a questionnaire/survey, experiment, or an interview?
- What kind of data will be returned?

When you are more experienced you can ask: What kind of data do you want to get? What are you trying to find out? Where did the data come from? This could be the first time you have analysed data like this, and chances are that in all likelihood, you have some data from a particular source (which is a bit of a fortunate accident). These sources, in our experience, include a survey questionnaire, an experiment, or interviews. For a questionnaire/survey, it is most likely going to be quantitative analysis with descriptive statistics and various charts for the quantifiable questions and identification of themes for the open-ended questions. Inferential statistics can be used to split groups of participants. In an experiment, this is relatively similar, but if there is a pre-test and post-test that have comparable questions, then you can use inferential statistical tests to compare within groups, and if there is more than one group, you can compare between groups. Questionnaires and experiments can also have some qualitative analysis usually consisting of open-ended questions to allow the participants to provide some explanation to the quantifiable, numerical answers they have provided. Generally, interviews require some form of qualitative analysis, such as thematic analysis. Basically, when numbers are involved, quantitative methods are used, and when language analysis happens, such as with interviews, conversation, broadcasts, etc., then qualitative methods are used (Field, Miles, and Field, 2012).

What kind of data will be returned?

The type of data you get back determines how that data is analysed. Five main data types will be returned, split into categorical and continuous data (Field, Miles and Field, 2012). They are:

- **Categorical variables** are composed of unique categories.
    - **Binary** – two distinct types, e.g., single or multi-player.
    - **Nominal** – names or labels for certain characteristics, e.g., igneous, sedimentary, metamorphic.
    - **Ordinal** – describes order, but not relative size or degree of difference between the items measured, for example, in a race.

Use of an ordinal-scale question may be: How strongly do you agree games are educationally beneficial? Strongly agree, Agree, Neutral (Neither Agree nor Disagree), Disagree, and Strongly Disagree.

- **Continuous variables** – There are two different kinds of continuous variable which are **discrete** (can be counted) and **continuous** (cannot be counted). An example of discrete is the number of characters in our *POP!* Figures collection in the office, which is vast at this point – but still countable. It is impossible to represent discrete variables in decimal form (Mishra et al., 2018). An example of a continuous variable is when your personal trainer pretends to speak into a recorder to give you motivation saying: "day: 1 million – his power grows!" This is not countable as you would have to be 2,739 years old.

  - **Interval** – is measured along a scale and is numerical, can be categorised and ranked where each position is equidistant from one another, and as a result, we can say that the difference between 20°C and 30°C is the same as the difference between 40°C and 50°C.
  - **Ratio** – has all the properties of an interval variable but also has a nonarbitrary definition of 0. One of the best examples of the distinction between interval and ratio data is temperature. Celsius, Centigrade, or Fahrenheit are all intervals since they have no point of absolute zero, meaning the point of zero on these scales is actually not as low as it can go. The Kelvin and Rankine temperature sales set their zero points at absolute zero by definition, which is the lowest point of the thermodynamic temperature scale. −273.15°C is 0°K (Kelvin).

Identifying statistical techniques

To identify what statistical techniques to perform, you have to go through a process of asking the following questions:

- Do I use descriptive, or inferential, or both?
- What are the dependent and independent variables?
- Is the DV parametric or non-parametric?
- What is the sample design?
- What are the specific techniques?
- What software should I use?

Descriptive, inferential statistical analysis, or both?

Internet resources can be accessed to quickly decipher the differences between descriptive and inferential statistics. For now, just ask: do you simply want to describe the data that you have collected from the population, or do you want or use it to make inferences on the general population? If you just want to describe the data, then you will be using descriptive statistics, and if you want to draw inferences, then you will probably use a combination of the two.

Descriptive statistics present the numerical data in a manageable form, generally involving a measurement of central tendency (mean, median, mode), standard deviation (SD), and charts (bar, scatter, and line graphs). There is generally some form of distribution, which is a summary of frequencies for the individual values for a variable. You may remember from school that a Normal/Gaussian distribution of frequencies is the shape of a bell curve, which is important if you are using measures of central tendency. Here is a brief description of measures of central tendency:

* Mean
    * Probably the most often used
    * Sum of observations/number of observations
* Median
    * Divides a distribution in half where one half of the scores is <= median and one half of scores is >= median
    * Odd 4, 7, 8, 11, 15, Even 4, 4, 5, 6, 8, 14
    * 1, 3, 3, 4, 5, 5, 5, 5, 7, 8
* Mode
    * The value of the most frequently occurring observation
    * 4, 5, 9, 3, 6, 1, 3, 5, 9, 7, 1, 5, 2, 7, 5, 4, 6, 3, 2, 8
    * 1, 1, 2, 2, 3, 3, 3, 4, 4, 5, 5, 5, 5, 6, 6, 7, 7, 8, 9, 9

The question then becomes what measure of central tendency? If the distribution is completely symmetrical, then mode, median, and mean are equal. If the distribution is skewed, then it is better to use the median than the mean. The mean is really the most preferred, and it is a good indication of the balance point for most normally distributed data; it also has numerical properties that allow it to be manipulated in useful ways. The mode is more suitable for qualitative data.

Laerd statistics (2021) provides a very useful overview of methods of central tendency, as well as providing a summarisation of the best measure of central tendency to use in relation to the type of variable collected, i.e., nominal (mode), ordinal (median), interval/ratio, which is not skewed, (mean) and interval/ratio, which is skewed (median).

What are the dependent and independent variables?

Scientists are in agreement that the most effective and unambiguous method of revealing and establishing a cause-and-effect relationship is utilising the experimental methodology to test some form of prediction involving the manipulation of the independent variable (IV) and observation of the result in the dependent variable (DV). Here are some general examples of independent and dependent variables:

- Plant growth – IV (exposure to sunlight), DV (growth rate).
- Animal size – IV (protein intake), DV (muscle mass).
- Drink driving – IV (alcohol intake), DV (reaction time, blood alcohol level).

Foster et al., (2018) presents a number of examples of the IVs and DVs and describes the difference between quantitative IVs and qualitative IVs. There is also a discussion of levels of independent variables, meaning that if you have a number of experimental groups, e.g., an experiment to find out which piece of gym equipment was best for burning calories out of a cross trainer, treadmill, spin bike, or rowing machine, then you would have four experimental groups and the IV would have four levels.

It is important to give some thought to what the IV and DVs are. In your context, the IVs are the software, software component, or the game you have developed. Here are some examples.

Example 1: A new algorithm is developed to improve efficiency of an existing algorithm. The new algorithm is the IV, efficiency is the DV, and the existing algorithm is the control.

Example 2: A serious game has been created to teach programming at undergraduate level. The game is the IV, the learning effectiveness is the DV, and traditional approaches, such as lecturing and classes, are the control.

Example 3: A new game mechanic has been developed to ascertain if it has a positive effect on the player experience. The game mechanic is the IV, the player experience is the DV, and a control group may have a game without the new game mechanic.

Example 4: A new EER drawing tool has been created to generate a relational schema from the diagram. The drawing tool is the IV, and perception of usefulness may be the DV. Other CASE tools may be used as a method of control.

Example 5: A new app has been developed for empathy training in COVID-19. The IV is the App, and the DV is level of empathy and believability in relation to the stories presented.

The following three factors should be obvious:

- Sometimes there is no evaluation, and the development of the software can be sufficient. Or, it may never reach a stage where it can be evaluated since this is an exploratory journey, and it may be that an evaluation is not going to be performed.
- Sometimes a control group is not feasible, or the idea is too new to have a control group in existence, as in Example 5.
- It should also be relatively clear that the IV is something that can be manipulated in an experiment, and there will be IVs that can be manipulated and changed and others that can merely be measured and perhaps quantified. For example: "Do male or female Fortune 500 CEOs make more money?" In this scenario, it is not possible to manipulate the gender variable – you can only measure it.

Does the DV determine parametric or non-parametric?

The nature of the DV (result) determines whether parametric or non-parametric statistical tests are utilised. The DV has to adhere to the following three pieces of criteria:

- Parametric tests assume a **normal distribution** of values, i.e., the Gaussian distribution or the bell-shaped curve. Several tests for normality are designed to complement the visual inspection of a graphical representation of data (Ghasemi and Zahediasl, 2012).

SPSS provides the Kolmogorov-Smirnov test (for larger samples) and the Shapiro-Wilk's W test (for smaller samples).

- **Homogeneity of variance** (homoskedasticity) is an assumption where the population variances – the distribution of scores around the mean of two or more samples – is considered equal (Salkind, 2010). So, it is considered that populations under observation, such as games students, will be similar. Levene's test of homogeneity of variance can be used to test for this.
- **Interval** level or **ratio** level data.

> **UT:** If the DV adheres to normality, homogeneity, and is interval or ratio, then parametric tests can be used; otherwise, use the non-parametric equivalents.

This is quite difficult to fully process and takes practice and time. There is a plethora of online resources and *YouTube* videos to perform the necessary tests for normality and homogeneity. It is important to go through the process and check for normality and homogeneity, but essentially, if you are returning ordinal and nominal data, then you can probably conclude that you are going to be using non-parametric tests.

What is the sample design?

When selecting statistical analysis techniques, the sample design must be considered (Miller, 1974). The sample designs can be a one-sample design, two-sample design, k sample designs, and correlations. In one-sample design, a single sample is used and then compared with already established data. Two-sample designs can be divided into related and independent samples. With related samples, some effort has been made to make sure that the participants' characteristics are equal. In in-dependent samples, two entirely different groups of individuals are se-lected. In k sample design, there can be multiple groups or different levels of the independent variable. In correlations, the researcher mea-sures the IV rather than manipulating it.

Common techniques

Parametric tests are more stringent, and if you have the opportunity to use them, then you should. Despite the fact that you may think you know what types of tests you are going to use, it is still important to go through the process of checking for normality and homogeneity and then ascertaining the type of data. There are non-parametric equivalents of parametric tests that can be used. Since you are going to have the data lined up in a package to analyse, you may as well just try both parametric and non-parametric equivalents to see if there is any difference in the level of significance. Most people starting to learn elementary statistics do, and there is generally very little difference. Table 15.1 displays selection criteria and several common specific techniques adapted from Chan (2003), Stojanović et al. (2018), and Kataike, Kulaba, and Gellynck (2017).

Table 15.1 Selection criteria and common techniques

Criteria	Parametric	Non-parametric
Distribution	Normal	Any (normal or skewed)
Variance	Homogenous	Any
Type of Data	Interval or Ratio	Ordinal or Nominal
Measure of Central Tendency	Mean	Median/Mode
Advantages	Stringency	Less affected by outliers
Group Dynamic	**TESTS**	**TESTS**
Repeated Measures, 2 groups	Dependent t-test	Wilcoxon matched paired signs rank test
Independent Measures, 2 groups	Independent t-test	Mann–Whitney U test
More than 2 conditions	ANOVA	Kruskal Wallace test

Recommended software

There are a number of open source and proprietary packages available for statistical analysis listed in Wikipedia (https://en.wikipedia.org/wiki/List_of_statistical_software). From a student perspective, the determining factor for deciding is probably whether the software is free or whether your academic institution has a subscription. A number of popular alternatives are displayed in Table 15.2.

Table 15.2 Statistical software

Software	Description
Python®	A good alternative for statistical analysis for computing students as they may have encountered it before in programming classes. It is free to download and install for Windows machines and is pre-installed on most Linux distributions.

(Continued)

Table 15.2 (Continued)

Software	Description
R®	Popular alternative for computing students that can be downloaded from the CRAN (Comprehensive R Archive Network) available at: https://cran.r-project.org/ (Accessed 27 February 2022).
Microsoft Excel®	An excellent choice for data analysis using the Analysis ToolPak add in program. A plethora of instructions exist.
IBM SPSS Statistics®	Now on version 26 and widely used in social science, with many features and resources. If you are familiar with programming languages, then this package is well worth learning. Online survey packages can allow downloading into an SPSS file, and it is worthwhile checking.

We find the most popular packages are *Excel* and *SPSS,* with all the learning resources you require available on *YouTube.*

Qualitative analysis

Qualitative research can produce large amounts of text-based data, such as transcripts and field notes. The systematic arrangement, and thorough analysis of qualitative data, can be time consuming and labour demanding (Zamawe, 2015). However, computer-assisted qualitative data analysis software (CAQDAS) can assist to boost speed and accuracy of the process instead of doing it manually (Bazeley, 2007). NVivo is excellent for researchers working on teams because it facilitates collaboration by merging the work of individuals under a single project. It can capture quantitative and qualitative data and accommodate different types of data, including documents, spreadsheets, images, audio, video, and web pages from any language. In addition, NVivo assists the researcher in recording, storing, preparing, indexing, sorting, coding, and retrieving qualitative data (Bringer, Johnston, and Brackenridge, 2004; Leech and Onwuegbuzie, 2011) using nodes, cases, memo, and framework matrix to find out underlying themes, theories, relationships, and interpretations. NVivo can be synchronized with different reference managers, such as *EndNote, Zotero,* and *RefWorks.*

Unlike statistical software, NVivo is not necessarily dedicated to analysing the data, but rather to fostering the analysis process. CAQDAS are fundamentally treated as data management packages to facilitate the researcher during the data analysis to enhance the quality of the research significantly. (*Qualitative section kindly produced by Sabbir Ahmed Chowdhury, PhD student, UWS*).

Summary

This chapter has provided a brief introduction to statistical analysis in term of providing sufficient information to allow you to select the analysis techniques easily. It is rare for an honour student to use inferential statistics in these disciplines at this level, but we have provided a small starter course in this chapter to get you up to speed and introduce the notion of qualitative analysis.

References

Bazeley, P. (2007) *Qualitative Data Analysis with NVivo*. London: Sage Publications Ltd.

Bringer, J.D., Johnston, L.H., and Brackenridge, C.H. (2004) 'Maximizing transparency in a doctoral thesis1: The complexities of writing about the use of QSR* NVIVO within a grounded theory study', *Qualitative Research*, 4(2), pp. 247–265. doi: 10.1177/1468794104044434

Chan, Y.H. (2003) 'Biostatistics 102: Quantitative data – Parametric & nonparametric tests', *Singapore Med J*, 44(8), pp. 391–396. doi: 10.1016/j.jsurg. 2007.02.001

Clarivate (no date) *EndNote* (version EndNote 20) [Computer Programme] Available at: https://endnote.com/ (Accessed: 27 February 2022).

Corporation for Digital Scholarship (no date) *Zotero* (version Zotero 5.0) [Computer Programme] Available at: https://www.zotero.org/ (Accessed: 27 February 2022).

Durian, D. (2002) 'Corpus-based text analysis from a qualitative perspective: A closer look at NVivo', *Style*, 36(4), pp. 738–742.

Field, A., Miles, J. and Field, Z. (2012) *Discovering Statistics Using R*. SAGE Publication.

Foster, G.C, Lane, D., Scott, D., Hebl, M., Rudy, G., Osherson, D., and Zimmer, H. (2018) An Introduction to Psychological Statistics. Open Resources Collection. Available at: https://irl.umsl.edu/oer (Accessed: 28 July 2022).

Ghasemi, A., and Zahediasl, S. (2012) 'Normality tests for statistical analysis: A guide for non-statisticians', *International journal of endocrinology and metabolism*, 10(2), 486–489. doi: 10.5812/ijem.3505

IBM (no date) *IBM SPSS Software* (version SPSS Statistics 28) [Computer Programme] Available at: https://www.ibm.com/uk-en/analytics/spss-statistics-software (Accessed: 27 February 2022).

Kataike, J., Kulaba, J., and Gellynck, X. (2017) 'What junior researchers must know before and after data collection: Difference between parametric and nonparametric statistics', *International Journal of Science and Research*, 6(6), pp. 653–658. doi: 10.21275/ART20173571

Laerd Statistics (2021) *Measures of Central Tendency*. Available at: https://statistics. laerd.com/statistical-guides/measures-central-tendency-mean-mode-median.php (Accessed: 27 February 2022).

Leech, N.L., and Onwuegbuzie, A.J. (2011) 'Beyond constant comparison qualitative data analysis: Using NVivo', *School Psychology Quarterly*, 26(1), pp. 70–84, doi: 10.1037/a0022711

Microsoft 365 (no date) *Microsoft Excel* (version 2021) [Computer Programme] Available at: https://www.microsoft.com/en-us/microsoft-365/excel (Accessed: 27 February 2022).

Miller, S. (1974) *New Essential Psychology: Experimental Design and Statistics*. Methuen.

Mishra P., Pandey C.M., Singh U. and Gupta A. (2018) 'Scales of measurement and presentation of statistical data', *Annals of Cardiac Anaesthesia*, 21(4), pp. 419–422. doi: 10.4103/aca.ACA_131_18

Proquest LLC (2022) *RefWorks* [Computer Programme] Available at: https://about.proquest.com/en/products-services/refworks/ (Accessed: 27 February 2022).

QSR International (2022) *NVivo* (version 'NVivo') [Computer Programme] Available at: https://www.qsrinternational.com/nvivo-qualitative-data-analysis-software/home (Accessed: 27 February 2022).

Salkind, N.J. (2010) *Encyclopaedia of Research Design* (Vols. 1–0). Thousand Oaks, CA: SAGE Publications, Inc. doi: 10.4135/9781412961288

Stojanović, M., Apostolović, M.A., Milošević, Z.G., and Ignjatovic, A.M. (2018) 'Parametric versus nonparametric tests in biomedical research', *Acta Medica Medianae*, 57, pp. 75–80 doi: 10.5633/amm.2018.0212

Zamawe, F.C. (2015) 'The implication of using NVivo software in qualitative data analysis: Evidence-based reflections', *Malawi Medical Journal*, 27(1), pp. 13–15. doi: 10.4314/mmj.v27i1.4

16 Discussion

In this chapter, you will learn:

- What a discussion chapter is.
- Why a discussion chapter is relevant.
- What should a discussion chapter should include.
- How to structure a discussion chapter.

A discussion chapter is a central part of the dissertation process because it is where you provide an explanation and interpretation of your findings and place them into context. It is an opportunity for you to elaborate upon any interesting findings that you have identified during your study, but it is important that you do not present any new findings that were not in the original results. The discussion section relates more to contextualising the research findings within the scope of your research aims and questions. It provides you with the opportunity to accentuate the main findings of your study.

What a discussion chapter is

Once you have presented the analysis of your data, whether qualitative or quantitative, you will be required to discuss your research findings. It is important to note that the discussion chapter is not the same as the results chapter. Sometimes, students present their findings and do not elaborate upon them further. Simply copying and pasting your results into your dissertation (e.g., from some online questionnaire software) does not provide any real academic rigour toward interpreting and reflecting upon your findings. The aim of a discussion chapter is to provide a greater degree of analysis, depth, and understanding about what your results mean for your research area. It should draw upon the findings that have been presented in the results chapter.

DOI: 10.4324/9781003054887-16

It is also worth remembering that it differs from the conclusions chapter. The aim is to expand upon the findings of your research in the wider context of the study. In contrast, the conclusions section provides a summary of the research and can also include a section relating to future directions. The conclusion section can provide a summary of the starting point of the research to the end point. A summary of how the research has navigated from A to B from the initial conception of the research question, aims, what was uncovered during the research, and an overview of concluding remarks.

Why a discussion chapter is relevant

A discussion chapter allows you to explain your findings so that the results you have presented in the earlier sections can be analysed and interpreted. This is done with your research questions as the primary focus, where you are explaining to the reader not only what the findings are, but also, the extent to which the findings have addressed the research questions. The discussion chapter should connect to the results and literature review chapters, and you can also compare with other pieces of literature and previous research studies.

What should be included

Though every discussion chapter is unique due to the nature of the study and the results, there are still some generic details that can that are summarised in Table 16.1.

How to structure a discussion chapter

Not all discussion chapters are generic since they depend on the overall presentation of the dissertation and its subject area. We provide some suggested guidelines about how to structure this chapter.

Provide a synopsis of your research area

It is useful to provide a recap of your research area and research questions (Crossley, 2021). This is beneficial for the reader to review prior to reading the primary findings of the research. Doing so also means that the reader does not have to keep referring to the introduction chapter.

Table 16.1 Some discussion chapter features (adapted from Statistic Solutions, 2021; Crossley, 2021; Dissertation-Servive.org, 2021; Proof-Inc., 2017)

What to include	Justification
Provide a brief synopsis of your research area and questions.	This reminds the reader about your research area and aims of your study. The relevancy of your study is also stated to the reader.
Include a discussion relating to what extent you consider you have addressed your research aims.	It is useful at this stage of the dissertation to reflect upon whether you have addressed what you have set out to do. Has the data you have obtained helped you in answering your research topic?
Contextualise your findings and relate them to your results and literature review.	Relating your results to your literature review chapter allows you to substantiate or refute any findings identified.
Provide a comparison between the qualitative and quantitative findings from your results chapter (if you have both).	Providing a comparison between qualitative and quantitative findings ensures you adhered to the principles of mixed methods research.
Include novel interpretations of your findings and what they suggest for your research area.	Stating the research implications of your study allows you to place your findings into the domain of your field.

Address your research questions in turn

Relate your research findings to each of your research questions, and evaluate them based on the evidence provided and whether they have been sufficiently addressed. This is when you integrate and analyse your qualitative and quantitative findings based on your mixed-methods research design, if you have adopted one. Even if you have utilised a monomethod study, using either quantitative or qualitative research, you can discuss your findings and contextualise them based on your research area.

Refer to the literature

It is important that you relate the discussion of your findings to the academic literature, by referring to the literature examined in your literature review chapter (Proofed Inc, 2017). This is important because it provides you with an opportunity to identify and state what the potential research implications are for your study. For example, these could be research implications from a technical or practical perspective. What you can also do is draw comparisons with some of the empirical studies you identified in your literature review. How generalisable are your findings? Have any new research themes emerged during the research?

Provide clarity

Try to provide clarity throughout and present your discussion chapter in a way that is logical and comprehensible for the general reader (Proofed Inc, 2017). Do not use language that is ambiguous, but do provide a sense of structure to the chapter by breaking down the various points you are addressing into identifiable headings and subheadings.

Tense is important

It is also important that you utilise your grammatic style of writing consistently throughout your chapter. This is relevant for when you are explaining your findings. For example, when referring to results and explaining what their current practical implications are, you should use the present tense. Here is an example (Baxter and Hainey, 2019):

> *The methodology used in this research was a mixed methods approach that incorporated both qualitative and quantitative elements via the dissemination of a questionnaire that included a set of closed and open questions.*

In contrast, when providing a synopsis of your results or of a research process that has been completed, it is advisable to use the past tense. Here is an example (Baxter and Hainey, 2019):

> *The overall findings of the research were predominately positive with students indicating that there are beneficial pedagogical uses of VR to be had in an educational context.*

Recommendations and future research

Offer recommendations for future research in your field of study (Statistics Solutions, 2022). This can also sometimes appear in the conclusions section. Doing so allows you to elaborate more about the wider context of your research topic and reflect upon how you envisage it progressing.

Discuss limitations

Acknowledge and mention any potential limitations associated with your study, such as your research or implementation approaches. For example, this could involve aspects associated with your chosen research design, how generalisable your findings are, and any unforeseen limitations related to your developed software and game.

Summary

The discussion chapter is a useful optional chapter that can be used to provide context and interpretation for the reader in relation to your research findings. It can give clarity to the reader, not only about your research results but also about what your findings mean in the wider area of your academic field. It provides a platform to allow you to address your research questions and to reflect upon the extent to which you have tackled them. UT: If writing a discussion chapter, we recommend you reflect on your research question(s), refer to your discovered literature, previous studies, and implications, and state to what extent you have answered your question(s).

In some dissertations, it should be noted that the discussion is immediately after the presentation of the results, but it is a section and not a full chapter. We have observed that a discussion chapter is more frequent, with qualitative analysis, since this requires further elaboration. In quantitative dissertations, there are more frequently smaller discussion sections.

References

Baxter, G. and Hainey, T. (2019) 'Student perceptions of virtual reality use in higher education', *Journal of Applied Research in Higher Education*, 12(3), pp. 413–424. doi: 10.1108/JARHE-06-2018-0106

Complete Dissertation by Statistics Solutions (2022) *Dissertation Chapter 5: Discussion*. Available at: https://www.statisticssolutions.com/academic-research-consulting/dissertation-consulting-services/discussion/ (Accessed: 29 December 2021).

Crossley, J. (2021) *How to Write the Discussion Chapter: The What, Why & How Explained Simply (with Examples)*. Grad Coach International. Available at: https://gradcoach.com/discussion-chapter-examples/ (Accessed: 29 December 2021).

Dissertation-Service.org (2021) *Dissertation Discussion Chapter Writing & Dissertation Discussion Help*. Available at: https://www.dissertation-service.org/dissertation-chapters/discussion/ (Accessed: 29 December 2021).

Proofed Inc. (2017) *4 Tips for Writing Your Dissertation's Discussion Chapter.* Available at: https://getproofed.com.au/writing-tips/4-tips-for-writing-your-dissertations-discussion-chapter/ (Accessed: 29 December 2021).

Further reading

Dissertation Genius (2016, November 5) *12 Steps to Write an Effective Discussion Chapter.* Available at: https://dissertationgenius.com/12-steps-write-effective-discussion-chapter/ (Accessed: 14 February 2022).

Lempriere, M. (2019, June 7) *The PhD Proofreaders: The difference between empirical and discussion chapters (and how to write them).* Available at: https://www.thephdproofreaders.com/structuring-a-thesis/the-difference-between-an-empirical-and-discussion-chapter/ (Accessed: 14 February 2022).

Nicolas, A. (2021, November 8) *Research Prospect: How to Write a Discussion Chapter.* Available at: https://www.researchprospect.com/how-to-write-dissertation-discussion-chapter/ (Accessed: 14 February 2022).

OxbridgeEssays (2020, March 2) *Dissertation findings and discussion sections.* Available at: https://www.oxbridgeessays.com/blog/dissertation-findings-discussion-sections/ (Accessed: 14 February 2022).

17 Conclusions

In this chapter, you will learn about:

- The importance of conclusions.
- What a conclusion should include.
- Answering research questions based on findings.
- Acknowledging limitations.
- Proposing future work and future directions.
- Things to avoid in a conclusion.

The importance of conclusions

When writing a conclusion for your dissertation or any piece of academic work, you may be unsure about what this task entails. It is not simply including a short paragraph of a few lines briefly summarising the research study. Sometimes, students adopt this approach because they run out of steam toward the end of their dissertations. They view the conclusion section as being insignificant since their focus has been predominately on their developed software or game output and its evaluation. The conclusion in a dissertation is relevant because:

- It shows the reader you have understood the research area and have been able to sufficiently reflect upon it.
- It allows you to accentuate the main points or findings of your study and to highlight them to the reader, concisely yet informatively.
- It allows you to identify any gaps in knowledge associated with your subject area and to bring them to the reader's attention.

DOI: 10.4324/9781003054887-17

- It presents you with an opportunity to inform your readers about the wider implications and academic significance of your research.
- It can act as a critical appraisal not just of your research but also on how you felt you performed throughout your dissertation.
- It can allow you to propose future or new directions for research.

What should be included in a conclusion

There is no right or wrong approach toward writing a conclusion in terms of structure, and it will be dictated by the subject area. However, there are several things you can include in a conclusion that can be considered fairly generic, and we provide a set of recommendations:

- Address your research questions or topic, and assess whether you have answered them in terms of your research approach.
- Acknowledge the limitations of your study from a design, development, and evaluation perspective.
- Provide reflection and self-criticality about how the dissertation progressed and review what you might have done differently.
- Allow reflection upon whether there are further research implications for your study, and provide suggestions for future research directions.

Answering research questions based on findings

One of the primary things to include is your assessment of how well, and to what extent, the research questions you set out to answer in the beginning have been addressed. This can include all issues or problems faced and how they were overcome. This should be the focus of a conclusions section. It is very useful to reiterate what your research questions were and then to discuss, in your opinion, to what extent you have addressed them. Furthermore, it is important to substantiate your findings from the literature you cited in your earlier chapters and ascertain if your findings validate the points made in the literature or refute them. So, for example, if you were researching the aspect of challenge and difficulty in video games and how they impact upon players' emotions, you could state the following:

The main aim of the dissertation was to investigate the impact that difficulty and challenge has on a player's emotions, as well as to assess how this affects the immersion within the game play.

The three project aims for this project were to find out:

1   *Why do people play games?*
2   *Has game difficulty evolved over time?*
3   *Does challenge enhance game play and immersion?*

This is a useful way to commence the conclusions section as opposed to providing a quick summary of the research. In doing so, you can revisit the literature articulated in your literature review section and substantiate or refute any of the arguments you made. Remember, you can always summarize your results by stating that they were not fully answered or remain inconclusive. The key aspect is to ensure that you substantiate the points you are addressing with evidence from your findings.

If you are summarising the key qualitative and quantitative results based on your questionnaires or interviews, it is important that you do not introduce any new evidence at this stage of the dissertation. Just provide a brief synopsis or overview of the key themes identified, but do not propose any new ones. This should have been addressed within your discussion section. You need to critique your research questions and to assess to what extent they have been addressed.

Key findings – Qualitative and quantitative results

In this section of the dissertation, you should reemphasise the importance of your qualitative findings, as identified in the discussion chapter, but more specifically, the key themes that you discovered throughout the course of your research, bringing the entirety of the study together based on your qualitative findings. You also want to reiterate the relevancy of the findings in the context of your review of the academic literature in terms of whether the qualitative themes substantiate or refute them.

Like the reporting of your qualitative results, you can briefly reiterate the key findings from your quantitative data and discuss them in the context of your study overall. You can reemphasise for the reader why some of the key quantitative findings are important and incorporate this into the context of the academic literature.

Limitations of the research

The conclusions section should also provide you with an opportunity to reflect upon any acknowledged limitations. This allows you to also consider how you might have done things differently if you were to start over. For example, limitations could relate to your research study being too wide ranging or too narrow in scope. This could correlate to the formulation of the research questions being too straightforward to address or too complex to provide a conclusive answer. Limitations could also be associated with the research design chosen in relation to methodology and methods.

Future work or future directions of the research

It is inevitable that during your dissertation, you may not have time to address everything that you set out to do. This might be the case in terms of your development, especially if you would like to add additional features to whatever it is you have implemented. For example, if developing a website or an app, you might want to improve upon their layout from a user interface (UI) or user experience (UX) perspective or to make the website or app a bit more responsive. Some future developments could be based upon user feedback that, due to time constraints, you were not able to address. In the context of designing a game, future work would involve making further additions to the game to make it more engaging and immersive. This future work might be because of participant feedback that was not implemented. Future improvements for a game might include more open levels with quests, new level themes, new character abilities, or the creation of more boss levels.

Within this section of the conclusions, you can also reflect upon future directions of the research. It is also important to consider the wider implications of your research study and whether you can expand upon any aspect of the research, taking it in a new direction. For example, a game or an app that has been developed for entertainment purposes could be developed for educational uses. This is something that you consider toward the end of your study and could also be pursued at master's level.

Things to avoid in a conclusion

There are a few things to avoid including in a conclusion, so ask yourself what makes a bad conclusion?

- If you provide a short concise summary of about eight lines starting with the phrase "In conclusion ... " then this denotes that the conclusions section has been somewhat rushed. It also signifies that there has been no real proper reflection about the research.
- It is important that you do not introduce any new evidence, such as statistical data or open-ended quotes. You can, however, concisely reemphasise some of the key findings for the reader.
- Do not simply reiterate what the study was about and leave things at that.

The key thing with any conclusion is that it should be reflective and concisely informative at the same time. You are drawing your study to a close, so you want to accentuate the main points from it and to bring them to the forefront. You want to state the salient reasons why your study was worth undertaking and the value that it adds to your research area.

Summary

The conclusions section is important because it is where you get your final opportunity to state the importance and relevancy of your work. It is the most reflective part of the dissertation because you are having to summarise the key achievements and findings from your research. Here are some summary points:

- The conclusion should be a concise, yet informative, reflective summary of your research.
- Only key findings should be summarised.
- Do not introduce any new evidence in this section.
- Be reflective while avoiding the first-person pronoun, and write in the active tense.
- Do not be afraid to acknowledge limitations.
- Consider future work and the potential future directions, particularly with regards to development and implementation.

To summarise: UT: A conclusion should be a concise, informative, and reflective summary of the key findings of your research, using only the evidence you have presented previously, acknowledging limitations, and presenting avenues for future work and recommendations.

18 References

In this chapter, you will learn:

- Essential tips to put finishing touches to the references section in relation to:
  - Format.
  - Completeness.
  - Overall presentation.

Once you have completed the writing of your dissertation, you will need to check the overall formatting and presentation of your document. This not only involves the layout of your headings, subheadings, and general text, but also the consistency of your citations and references. A useful piece of advice is to regularly check the style of your citations and references while you are writing your dissertation. For example, if you are using the Harvard referencing style or APA, you need to check that the referencing style you are using is uniformly portrayed throughout your dissertation. You also need to ensure that you have consistently cited and referenced any images you have used.

To assist you with this task, we have provided some brief guidelines for reviewing the reliability of your citations and references.

Check for uniformity

When reviewing your citations and references, it is important to ensure that the way you have standardised them throughout your dissertation remains uniform and consistent with the citation and referencing style that you are using. Prior to commencing the writing of your dissertation, it is useful to identify the referencing style adopted by your university. Your supervisor will be able to inform you of this style, and if in doubt,

DOI: 10.4324/9781003054887-18

you can always consult with your subject librarian or a member of the library to confirm it.

Review the style of your citations

In addition to reviewing the style of your academic references, you also need to ensure that your citations have been addressed correctly. It would be useful to check the spelling of author surnames, years of publication, page numbers, where relevant, and that the ordering of authors is correct for more than one author. Also ensure that you have used the correct naming conventions for citations – et al. for more than three authors, though this use depends on the referencing style.

Use of external material

It is important that you have referenced any external sources you have used, such as images you have embedded into your dissertation. For example, any images that you have used to illustrate or denote something (e.g., a software development methodology) must be cited from the actual source where you obtained them. This also applies in the context of games development if you have used any free game assets to help develop your game. Remember always to go to the source and reference.

Works in order of author surname

When adding your references in the reference section of your dissertation, it is usually standard convention to list them in alphabetical order of author surname. You can also have separate sections that relate to any online sources you have used. External images can be included in your appendices.

Bibliography

If you have included a bibliography in your dissertation, this should also be properly referenced; it traditionally appears after your reference section. Remember that a bibliography is a set of additional reading sources that you would like to direct the reader toward. However, the material has not been mentioned or referred to within the main body of the dissertation.

Appendices

It is also important that you ensure that the way you have listed your appendices matches the way in which they have been referred within the main body of your dissertation. For instance, be careful to double check that your appendices contain examples of what you have specified in your dissertation and that they relate to one another.

Summary

Make sure that your citations and references are consistent throughout your dissertation. This is something that you should be checking regularly as you are writing your chapters. Your project supervisor will also review your references at the proofreading stage of your dissertation. Overall, though, you should try to observe the following when reviewing your citations and references:

- Be sure that your citations and references are consistent in referencing style throughout your dissertation.
- **UT:** Check that citations are present in your reference section and vice versa.
- Review your references and citations. Though it is a time-consuming process, adhering to the correct referencing and citation style as you write will assist you.
- Any material you include in your dissertation from an external source (e.g., an image or diagram) should have an acknowledgement of where it has originated from, as well as the creator of that material.
- Remember to position your bibliography after your reference section to direct the reader to further reading or additional sources, if required.

19 Appendices

In this chapter, you will learn about:

- What appendices are.
- Things to include in an appendix.
- Referencing an appendix in the dissertation.

What appendices are

You may have encountered appendices before when you included one in an essay or a technical report you had to write. An appendix is usually a section of a document that provides more information about a topic discussed in the main body and is included toward the end of a document. It is important not to disrupt the flow of your written work for the reader. Appendices are useful for including supplementary material that a reader can refer to to support the main body of the text of a document. They can also be used to provide additional examples of something already showcased in the main body.

Appendices are supplementary

An important point to note is that appendices are ancillary and supporting material (extra). This means that if they were removed from your document, then this would not affect the document overall in terms of readability. The reader should still be able to understand the main points communicated in the document without any appendices. Furthermore, appendices are useful to include if you are under constraints of a word count. If you feel that you have written too much for a section, then try not to worry about it and include any extra material in an appendix. UT: Appendices can be used as you can put extra, supplementary work in them, meaning no work is a waste of effort.

DOI: 10.4324/9781003054887-19

Things to include in an appendix

There is no real right or wrong answer regarding what to include. The main thing is that the material provides supplementary insight toward what has been written or portrayed within the main body of the document. Table 19.1 provides an overview of possible items that can be included in an appendix.

Referencing an appendix in the dissertation

Referencing ensures that the reader is directed to the appendix from the main text. The following examples denote this (**Source: *Dissertation C and D***):

- *"The following images display a mock-up of how the user interface may look, and further, individual sketches can be found as an appendix in section 11.4."*
- *"Examples of these documents can be found in appendix 11.2 and 11.3. A collection of signed consent forms has been scanned into a digital format and attached in appendix 11.7."*
- *"Once the images have been sourced and loaded into Blender, the modelling can start by using polygon modelling techniques to match up the reference images to the 3D model. More images relating the cars are in Appendix C."*
- *"Some of the answers made by the participants have been omitted from the evaluation because they were nonconstructive; a full answer set is in the appendix A."*

Table 19.1 Appendix examples

Appendix Examples

- **Questionnaire questions** (e.g., from online questionnaire software packages).
- **Qualitative analysis** (e.g., open-ended questionnaire responses or interview transcripts).
- **Quantitative analysis** (e.g., statistical data, graphs, charts).
- **Illustrations or diagrams** (e.g., wireframes, level design layouts, concept art).
- **Ethics forms** (e.g., consent forms and ethical research statements, ethical approval letter).
- **Coding examples** (e.g., C# or C++, code that denotes how something has been developed).
- **Screen captures** (e.g., when visually depicting a game, app's, or website's development).
- **Presentation slides** (e.g., including an overview of a presentation you have done during your dissertation).
- **Gantt chart** (e.g., created for the purposes of project management).
- **Test plan/log** (e.g., functional testing or play testing results).
- **Evaluation analysis** (e.g., additional data that has been analysed that is extraneous).

The appendices should be placed in your dissertation after the reference section, for example:

Summary

Appendices are not mandatory, but if they are included, they must provide additional supplementary information for the reader separate from the main document. Try to have a maximum of 10 and ensure that they are relevant in terms of contributing to the primary points made. We have summarised the following appendix tips:

- They should provide the reader with supplementary information separate from the main document.
- Clear signposting must be used in the main document to guide the reader to the appendix.
- The dissertation should 'stand alone,' even if your appendices are removed.
- They are included after the references.
- They can be illustrations, tables, charts, details of other documents, or further examples of development work, presentations, or test plans and test logs.
- They must provide an informative purpose and not be included simply for the sake of 'beefing up' the document.

20 Writing Up and Proofreading

In this chapter, we have compiled several friendly tips for the process of writing up and proofreading. They are mainly a combination of common sense and observations from our teaching experience.

In this chapter, you will learn about:

- General project management tips.
- The value of version control.
- Writing up tips.
- Proofreading tips.
- A write-up checklist.

General project management tips

A dissertation is a very complex project, and it is important to formulate a workable plan to make sure that you deliver it on time without putting yourself under pressure. Remember that you will be doing this project over the course of an academic year, and you will have other courses and modules running in tandem. One common mistake that we have observed is a tendency for students to put the dissertation project on the back burner in the first term of study and prioritise the completion of other assessments.

The best piece of advice about writing dissertations revolves around forward planning. Doing so allows you to think of any unforeseen eventualities that might impact the progression of the dissertation. **UT:** Some students find it useful to create a risk-analysis document to identify any issues of a technical and research nature.

It is useful to devise a time frame for when you aim to start the final write-up. The writing process should ideally be a continuous one undertaken concurrently with your practical development. However, there

DOI: 10.4324/9781003054887-20

is a time when you will have to solely focus on the final write-up. This stage will typically commence once you have performed your final testing or evaluation of your game, website, app, or the piece of software you have developed.

We now present other factors to consider when managing the write-up process:

Assessment submissions for other courses

Balancing coursework assignments with writing a dissertation can be challenging. Sometimes students are tempted to focus on other courses, with the logic being that they can concentrate on the dissertation at a later stage. Though this might appear to be a sensible tactic, it can backfire, leaving your with too much to do for the dissertation at such an advanced stage. A sensible approach is to create a timetable designed to allow you to allocate sufficient time to work on all your assignments concurrently and proportionately.

Working hours on the dissertation

Each course should be allocated approximately 8–10 hours of independent study per week, and this should equate to 30 hours of effort per week on everything. This is something to bear in mind when planning the writing of your dissertation since it can be difficult to allocate the appropriate hours to your studies. Forward planning is important, in addition to having a contingency plan should you need to devote more time to certain course works over others.

Holidays and social occasions

Maintaining a life balance and taking breaks from study is advisable to increase productivity and emotional well-being in the long term. Factor in holidays and social occasions during your dissertation year and your academic studies in general. Taking regular breaks allows reflection on what you have completed and the work still to be done. Having suitable breaks will give you a fresh perspective and new ideas.

Writing up tips

To aid you in the writing-up process of your dissertation, we have devised some useful tips:

Tip 1 Try to get an early start

You are under a deadline and want to avoid being in a situation where you exacerbate that pressure by not writing up as you go along. Start early, and try not to procrastinate. Time is precious, so it is important to make the most of it.

Tip 2 Commit yourself to paper

Write a little each day, whether that is a paragraph or a page a day, because it soon mounts up. An assessor can only mark what you produce on paper or what you have developed as a software product.

Tip 3 Remain consistent and keep pressure on the wound

Do not become lax and spend weeks thinking about writing rather than actually writing. Articulating something on a page is more difficult than you think, and it is easy to delude yourself into thinking this is an easy task. You can easily eliminate that confusion by writing something, even if just incrementally.

Tip 4 Create an implementation plan for your dissertation

Keep yourself running to schedule, whether you use a Gantt chart or a simple table denoting timelines and deliverables created using word-processing software. It is also important to adhere to the concept of version control to ensure you are writing from the most current version of your document. Keep track of deliverables pertaining to individual sections, even if this is simply writing your introduction in the first two weeks. Make your writing tasks manageable and achievable.

Tip 5 Plan your meetings with your supervisor

Take notes, minutes, and produce an agenda before attending supervisory meetings. This will minimise irrelevant discussion and will focus the meeting. A dissertation supervisor has only a certain amount of time to dedicate, so use the time wisely. If you have in fact done no work whatsoever and try to commit acts of subterfuge by asking your supervisor irrelevant questions to fill up the time, just remember that your supervisor is an academic far more skilled at coming up with irrelevant discussion than you are.

Tip 6 Fully immerse yourself in the writing process

It takes time to immerse yourself in writing, and if you do not take that time, it becomes blatantly apparent that your work is rushed. Also, if you run out of time, the difference in quality throughout your dissertation will be noticeable. Make sure that the quality of writing remains consistent by planning appropriately.

Tip 7 Your supervisor can only mark what has been given

This is an obvious sentiment that may be expressed by your project supervisor. It goes without saying that your supervisor can only provide a grade for what is presented to them. Therefore, focus on addressing all the sections in the project specification or marking scheme. Failure to do so may result in losing marks or suffering wasted effort on your part.

Tip 8 Utilise illustrations to retain the reader's attention

Instead of writing incredibly long descriptions of models, algorithms, game characters, or back stories, it may be more efficient and eye catching to use a diagram to illustrate what you are discussing. Illustrating the points you are making via diagrams, tables, or charts may capture and retain the reader's attention more effectively.

Tip 9 Give yourself plenty of time for transcripts

If you have incorporated qualitative data such as interview transcripts, then allocate yourself plenty of time to transcribe them as this process is quite time consuming. The fact that you must transcribe everything word for word, literally verbatim, takes time, effort, and commitment.

Proofreading

Proofreading is regarded as being an *"attention-demanding task"* (Pilotti, Chodorow and Thornton, 2004, p. 243). It is, however, a necessary evil to undertake if you intend to submit a dissertation of good academic quality. Proofreading is relevant because it allows you to reflect upon what you have written, as well as what you might want to alter. Regularly reviewing what you have written allows you to also check aspects relating to your grammar and punctuation. Proofreading provides you with an opportunity to review the layout and format to ensure that each section flows logically together. Proofreading is an activity that should be performed regularly after each section. The fact is that your supervisor will read your dissertation, and it is probably a good idea that you do as well. We have proposed the following tips:

Tip 1 Check your citations

Make sure that all the citations appear in full in the reference section. The best way to accomplish this task is using *Microsoft Word's* Find functionality. Highlight the first name in the citation and press Ctrl-F. Doing so will allow you to quickly check whether you have referenced the citation in your references section.

Tip 2 Check your formatting and layout

Take time to review the overall formatting and layout. This could relate to matters such as uniformity in the font you are using. You also need to check for consistency in the format of your headings and subheadings. It is most likely that your academic institution will provide you with a set of formatting guidelines that you must adhere to. It is important that you check the consistency of your font and headings. Inserting a table of contents using word-processing software can help you with this task.

Tip 3 Validate your sources

Ensure that you have properly sourced your images or any diagrams that you might have included from other sources. This needs to be done in-text and within your references section. This is important for copyright purposes and acknowledgment of the work of others.

Tip 4 Check for typographical errors

Taking time to ensure that there are no typos, or typographical errors, such as spelling mistakes or words that have been typed incorrectly. Once you have submitted your work, you will not be able to correct these mistakes.

Tip 5 Use of formal language and no colloquialisms

This is a formal piece of academic work that is expressed within the context of an academic writing style. Avoid the use of colloquialisms, meaning you should not write using informal language or slang within your dissertation. Use formal linguistic structure in your writing and avoid contractions – such as 'it's' or 'there's' or 'don't'.

Tip 6 Justify your text

Review the consistency of how text has been formatted and presented. For example, assessing the spacing within paragraphs is important in addition to trying to ensure that the text in your dissertation is justified. The justification of your text can easily be achieved using this feature on word-processing software. Unjustified text looks messy and does not contribute to a good look and feel. **UT:** Presentation is just as important as content.

Tip 7 Make use of the print preview feature

Go to the print preview and scroll down the finished document to check that it looks professional and doesn't have too many quotes. This is also a useful approach to check the formatting, and you should ask yourself if the document looks professional and whether you would pay money to own it.

Tip 8 Proofreading services

If the dissertation is required to be in English. For those who wish further assistance with spelling, grammar and punctuation – a professional proof reader will be provided/is recommended.

Write-up checklist

We now present a checklist in Table 20.1 to aid you in the write-up process. There is a lot to focus on, and this checklist will help with key aspects to ensure that you have addressed them.

Summary

The writing-up process can be a daunting one involving lots of procrastination before making a start. It takes determination and commitment. You will have your own unique approach toward this process. Make as early a start as possible and steadily work away on various sections of your chapters per day. To avoid things not going to plan, the best thing is to provide your dissertation supervisor with dissertation drafts to ensure the write-up goes smoothly.

Table 20.1 Write-up checklist

Planning considerations	Questions
• Commence the writing of chapters as early as possible. • Devise a realistic timetable to assist in the early stages of writing up your chapters. • Decide when you are most productive during the day for writing. • Have version control in place prior to commencing.	• Have I made a good early start to my dissertation chapters? • Is my timetable realistic in terms of my goals and deadlines? • Am I more productive during the morning, afternoon, or evenings? • Am I saving my files to OneDrive? How regularly is this being done?
Writing considerations • Write manageable sections and do not rush. • Reflect on what you have written, and make revisions where necessary. • Balance out the various sections with text and visuals. • Reference your sources where necessary, including in-text citations, images, and sources from websites. • Use formal language and write in an appropriate academic style.	*Questions* • How much time am I able to devote to writing per day or week? • Write, reflect, and revise – am I following this practice when I am writing up? • Can I exemplify some of the points I am making with the use of diagrams? • Have I referenced sources both directly and indirectly? Have I referenced the sources of images, models, charts, and diagrams? • Have I included any colloquialisms? Have I written in an informal and conversational style?
Formatting considerations • Ensure that your formatting is consistent throughout the dissertation. • Assess spacing within paragraphs, and make sure that the text is presentable and justified. • Make sure that you adhere to and have understood your institution's formatting guidelines.	*Questions* • Have I used the same font throughout? Is there consistency with the layout and use of headings? • Does my text look sloppy and disjointed? Is the layout aesthetically pleasing to the eye? • Have I read, and do I understand, what is being asked of me in relation to formatting guidelines?
Proofreading considerations • Review each new section of your dissertation for any typographical errors. • Check overall consistency of layout in terms of format while proofreading.	*Questions* • Have I proofread my dissertation for any spelling mistakes or words that have been typed incorrectly? • Have I used the print preview feature? Is everything presentable, and does everything flow logically?

Here are our summary points:

- Writing up takes time, commitment, and perseverance.
- The key to a successful write-up is planning and setting yourself realistic milestones and deliverables.
- Try to dedicate at least one hour to writing a day.
- Consistency is also very important in terms of format and layout.
- Use formal academic language and avoid slang or colloquialisms.
- Review and revise what you have written regularly.
- Proofread the entire document once complete.
- Once you have completed a particular section, take the time to proofread what you have written.
- Save and back up your work regularly. Adhere dutifully to the concept of version control.
- Send drafts to your dissertation supervisor.
- Ensure that you provide your supervisor with plenty of time to read the final draft of your dissertation.

Do not be disheartened if the writing process is progressing slowly as it is a time-consuming and incremental activity. You will ultimately get there in the end!

References

Microsoft (2022) *Microsoft Word* (version Office 2019) [Computer Programme] Available at: https://www.microsoft.com/en-us/microsoft-365/word (Accessed: 28 February 2022).

Pilotti, M., Chodorow, M. and Thornton, K.C. (2004) 'Error detection in text: Do feedback and familiarity help?', *The Journal of General Psychology*, 131(4), pp. 242–267. doi: 10.3200/GENP.131.3.242-267

21 Data Collection Mechanisms

In this chapter, you will learn about:

- Using online questionnaires.
- Some online questionnaire tools with *SurveyMonkey* and *Google Forms*.
- Gain an understanding of the benefits of adopting a 'mixed methods' approach via online questionnaires.
- The use of online questionnaires to aid you toward investigating your research questions.

Using online questionnaires

Based on our experience, one of the most common research methods utilised by game development or computer science students is questionnaire-based research, primarily due to circumstances and time. Often, and quite correctly, the dissemination of questionnaires is a quick and easy research method to obtain raw research data. We will discuss questionnaires in Chapter 22. The most convenient and popular approach toward questionnaire dissemination among students is using online questionnaires. This process predominately involves creating a questionnaire online using platforms such as *SurveyMonkey* or *Google Forms* and sending out a link (URL) for respondents to complete at their convenience.

The versatility of using online questionnaires sent via a link through the web to any electronic device instantaneously, completed by participants in their own time, is a large bonus regarding the use of web-based questionnaires.

DOI: 10.4324/9781003054887-21

Survey Monkey and Google Forms

We tend to find that students use either *SurveyMonkey* or *Google Forms* for designing online questionnaires and distributing them.

Google Forms is an online survey platform that is part of the *Google Docs Editors* suite from *Google*. If you have a *Google* account, *Google Forms* comes free with it. It is a web-based app that allows you to create questionnaires to send out to participants to complete in their own time. *SurveyMonkey* is also a popular web-based survey tool that allows you to create questionnaires online and disseminate them to participants in a straightforward manner. Both online platforms are widely used by students when issuing questionnaires for the purposes of evaluating their practical outputs.

SurveyMonkey is free and allows you create 10 questions per questionnaire with 100 responses for each questionnaire. It also provides a premium plan with unlimited questions and responses per questionnaire. We currently have the premium plan for all of our research-related questionnaires, so it is really a matter of preference, size of questionnaire, and number of respondents in your project. *Google Forms* requires a *Google* account to use, and it provides unlimited access to design and disseminate questionnaires.

If you require the premium version of *SurveyMonkey*, you could check if your institution has a subscription.

Ease of use

SurveyMonkey and *Google Forms* are very straightforward to use. In *SurveyMonkey*, once you have logged into your account, you can click on the 'Create Survey' on the upper right-hand corner of the account page. You will then be provided with six options that include the following: (1) Copy a past survey; (2) Start from scratch; (3) Purchase a panel; (4) Import questions; (5) Start from template and (6) Build it for me. It is most likely that you will be creating a new survey to coincide with your research area. The tutorials are excellent and allow you to refine and edit a number of question types to construct your questionnaire. The limit of 10 questions and 100 responses is probably more than sufficient for most honours projects, but it is important to give some thought to the 10 questions you are going to ask.

Google Forms also allows you to get a basic questionnaire up and running. To begin the design of a survey using Google Forms, you click on a Start a New Form icon. When you have done this, a blank 'Untitled Form' page should open.

Templates and customising

Both online questionnaire software packages allow you to make your questionnaires more aesthetically appealing using templates. Templates can provide an engaging backdrop and colour scheme to your survey pages, making them appear less static to respondents. It is up to you what template you choose to incorporate into your survey design.

Choosing question types

You are provided with options to choose various question formats. It is important to remember that different layouts of questions can be used to generate different types of data to analyse. Unlike many qualitative approaches to research, questionnaires often present one primary opportunity to collect data, so it is important that you devote time getting your questionnaire design correct. Spending adequate time on this tool allows you to reflect upon the data you require, how you intend to analyse it, and address your research questions (Saunders, Lewis, and Thornhill, 2019). The principles of questionnaire design are addressed in more detail in Chapter 22. Your selection and choice of questions can be such that they include open-ended and closed questions. Open-ended questions allow you to obtain qualitative responses where you can conduct thematic analysis. Closed questions provide you with a contrast of quantitative responses where you can perform statistical analysis dependent upon question type.

Obtaining responses

It is very straightforward to acquire responses using both packages. For *SurveyMonkey*, you click the 'Collect Responses' tab, under 'Survey Collectors,' you will find a hyperlink stating something like 'Web Link 1'. If you click on that, then it opens the generated URL for your questionnaire that you can customise and copy to send out to respondents via e-mail.

To disseminate a questionnaire link in *Google Forms*, you open a form and click on the 'Send' button. Then if you click on the link icon, the URL for your questionnaire will be revealed, and you can copy and paste this link via an e-mail or send it to potential participants via another format.

Analysing responses

A useful feature of both online survey platforms is that they assist toward undertaking the analysis in a descriptive capacity through graphs and pie charts. An additional beneficial characteristic of both platforms is that you can export and download your results via Excel or CSV (comma separated values) format, which allows you to undertake statistical analysis using data analysis software, SPSS. For the purposes of writing up results, these elements allow a quick and relatively straightforward way to report their findings.

To initiate this feature with *SurveyMonkey*, you click on the 'Analyzing Results' tab. You will then be able to see the analysis of your questionnaire results as generated by *SurveyMonkey*. The way in which the results are presented will depend on the type of question being asked. To export your questionnaire results with *SurveyMonkey*, in the 'Analyzing Results' section, you click 'Save As' at the top of the page and then 'Export File'. After this step, you will be provided with three export types: 'All summary data', 'All responses data' and 'All individual responses'. Once you have chosen the data you want to export, you can choose your specific file format and then click 'Export'.

Like *SurveyMonkey*, *Google Forms* allows you to export results. If you switch to the 'results' tab on the right-hand side, you will notice a green cross symbol and an icon using three dots beside it, allowing you to view responses in sheets. In contrast, clicking on the icon provides you with the option to download responses in CSV format.

Summary

SurveyMonkey and *Google Forms* are popular choices for producing online questionnaires. What you use is a matter of individual preference.

We have outlined the main differences:

- *SurveyMonkey* allows you to create 10 questions with a 100–response rate limit and offers a premium package with unlimited responses, questions, and enhanced functionality, such as downloading directly to *SPSS*.
- *Google Forms* is an online questionnaire platform that you can use if you have a *Google* account, giving you access to *Google Editors suite*.

Regardless of the platform you use, we recommend that you put quite a bit of thought into what you are attempting to get from your questionnaire and design the questions well. Once a participant receives a URL in their inbox, you need to make sure that the questionnaire is interesting enough to sustain their engagement so they do not simply dismiss it or find it too tedious to complete and withdraw. **UT:** You probably only get one shot at getting a participant to fill out a questionnaire – so make it count.

Reference

Saunders, M.N.K., Lewis, P. and Thornhill, A. (2019) *Research Methods for Business Students*. 8th edn. Harlow, United Kingdom; New York: Pearson.

22 General Questionnaire Design

In this chapter, you will learn:

* What a questionnaire is.
* To consider who a questionnaire is aimed at.
* Basic questionnaire design.
* General questionnaire guidelines.

Questionnaire design requires thoroughly thinking about the objectives, sample, questions, and the data returned. Entire books have been written on this topic in various different contexts, including marketing, civil engineering, and psychology. In this book, we will introduce you to the speed version of the basics and demystify the process and issues, allowing you to think through the purpose of the questionnaire, where it can be used, who it is for, what data you intend to gather, and what types of questions you intend to use. It will also discuss general aspects of design, such as leading questions, bias, bad questions, and how to integrate aspects of academic rigour into a questionnaire to make it more credible. This chapter will allow you to appreciate the holistic steps from initial design, deployment, gathering data, and analysis of data to basic reporting.

What a questionnaire is

The terms *"questionnaire"* and *"survey"* are often used interchangeably and synonymously. The survey is the research methodology where the data is collected from a particular sample population and analysed to interpret their subjective opinions, and the questionnaire is the data collection method that asks the participant a pre-defined set of questions. Questionnaires can really be quantitative and quantitative, depending on questions asked and how they are analysed. A questionnaire/survey can be used in a dissertation for:

DOI: 10.4324/9781003054887-22

- Gathering preliminary empirical evidence to ascertain if there is a requirement or demand for something and the potential application, e.g., whether a game for teaching programming is acceptable, and to gather preliminary requirements.
- Gathering empirical data on opinions on a matter such as: customisability, inclusivity, diversification, and representation in games.
- UX or testing of a game/software to assess functional requirements and design issues.
- Evaluation of a game or piece of software to ascertain if it has performed its purpose, such as increasing immersion or effectively teaching a subject. Questionnaires can be part of the experimental design in that they can be pre-test/post-test questionnaires of different comparative groups, e.g., a control group learning through traditional methods or a game with a normal interface versus a VR interface.

Questionnaires are efficient data-gathering methods at this level, and using them in a dissertation timeframe (an academic year) is a popular option. It is important to ask: *"what is the questionnaire for?"* Specify what empirical data you want to gather and why. Firing a questionnaire out without thinking this process through just leads to poor design and weak evidence reported. Given that questionnaires are viewed as a weak methodology by some academics already – we want the data that we do gather to matter.

Who is the questionnaire aimed at?

You may wish to survey a representative sample of the population to get an opinion on a relevant issue or piece of software/game to gauge acceptability and gather preliminary requirements. Depending on the nature of your research, what group is best? University students, industry stakeholders, game players, teachers, employers, or vulnerable groups such as the elderly? These are questions that have to be considered as part of any institutional ethical-approval process, which is well worth the effort!

Basic design

Whether paper-based, online, or within a software application (at the end of a game), it is important to construct a structured questionnaire.

Having different sections/pages with a description of what these are for is good practice. A proposed structure is displayed in Table 22.1 for an example questionnaire to ascertain if computer games could be used for learning in HE.

Table 22.1 Example questionnaire

Title	Description
Page 1: Description/ Informed Consent	• a research description. • your name, details, institution. • questionnaire purpose. • ethical approval requirements by informing the participant that they can withdraw at any time and asking for consent via a yes/no selection box. • how long the questionnaire will take to complete.
Page 2: Demographic Information	Collecting demographic data such as: • gender (remembering inclusivity). • age. • position. • hours playing computer games a week. • preferences for single or multiplayer. • preferred video game genre.
Page 3: Motivations for playing Computer Games in Leisure	Collecting data on motivations for playing computer games utilising Malone and Lepper's (1987) framework of intrinsic motivation to add academic rigour including: • Individual factors: (challenge, competition, cooperation, recognition) • Interpersonal factors: (control, fantasy, curiosity)
Page 4: Motivations for playing Computer Games in Education	Collecting information on motivations for playing computer games in education. This page utilises the question from the previous page, which is slightly altered to ask about the potential new context demonstrating consistency and allows comparison of contexts.
Page 5: Attitudes and skills	Collecting information about attitudes toward computer games and perceived skills that could be acquired through playing them utilising recognised soft skills.
Page 6: Technical requirements, format	Collecting information on what particular aspects of a game for teaching would be more important such as: graphics, story, narrative, control structure, sound and what particular delivery format such as PC, console, mobile phone, tablet, etc.

(Continued)

Table 22.1 (Continued)

Title	Description
Page 7: Thank you for submission page	This page simply delivers a message of thanks for completing the survey and assures the participant that their data will be confidential and anonymous. It provides contact details of the investigator if the participant has questions.

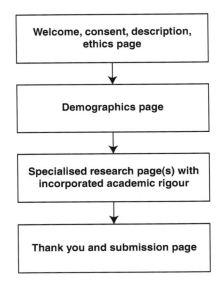

Figure 22.1 Basic questionnaire structure.

Questionnaires have been specially tailored, and we show a basic structure in Figure 22.1.

General tips for questionnaires

Tip 1: Try some online survey tools to see which one you prefer in terms of functionality.

Tip 2: Send your draft questionnaire to some colleagues, lecturers, and peers for feedback.

Tip 3: Do not make the questionnaire too long.

Tip 4: Do not use complicated language, technical jargon, or acronyms.

Tip 5: Vocabulary, language and grammar should be targeted at the population being surveyed.

Tip 6: Use the language of the organisation/context/discipline targeted.

Tip 7: Avoid unnecessary abbreviations.

Tip 8: Questions should be relevant to the research problem.

Tip 9: Avoid ambiguity and vagueness.

Tip 10: Avoid prestige bias where a response is linked to a prestigious person or group.

Tip 11: Avoid double-barrelled questions.

Tip 12: Questions should be as simple as possible.

Tip 13: Avoid false premises.

Tip 14: Questions about future intentions should be avoided.

Tip 15: Negatives and double negatives should be avoided.

Tip 16: Beware of response biases such as: The Halo Effect and The Pitchfork Effect.

Deployment

The two main ways to deploy your questionnaire are:

- **Paper-based** – where you distributed it by hand and allow the participants to fill it out and return it to you.
- **Online questionnaires** – where you use an online survey distribution mechanism.

If doing an exploratory survey questionnaire, you need to decide when is the best time to run it and for how long. If, for example, you are sending a questionnaire out to students, then a busy assessment time or during a vacation is not a good choice. In terms of the duration, we generally recommend approximately two weeks for an online questionnaire.

Types of questions

There are a large variety of question types, and online survey software provides interesting alternatives for variety with the main types being:

- Open-ended questions
- Close-ended questions

- Contingency questions
- Scaled responses
- Matrix questions

Open-ended questions

Open-ended questions do not provide any answers to select. For example: *"What is your favourite kind of food?"* Table 22.2 displays the advantages and disadvantages of open-ended questions.

Table 22.2 Overview of open-ended questions

Advantages	Disadvantages
• Respondents get the opportunity to clarify their response, and it is possible to follow their mental processes. • Respondents can supply unlimited answers. • Respondents are more likely to produce unanticipated responses.	• Requires more time and effort over the question. • Answers gathered may be completely irrelevant to the research problem. • The level of detail given in the answer differs from respondent to respondent. • Varying answers means analysing the data can be time consuming and tedious. • Forgetful or inarticulate respondents are at a disadvantage and may be intimidated. • If a respondent does not answer, the researcher cannot tell if it is due to belief or if the question has been overlooked.

Closed-ended questions

Closed-ended questions provide respondents with selected responses, and they simply select one or more. For example:

> "What do you like best about your car?"
>
> a   The colour
> b   The make
> c   The fuel consumption
> d   Other: (please specify)

The advantages and disadvantages of closed-ended questions are displayed in Table 22.3.

Table 22.3 Overview of closed-ended questions

Advantages	Disadvantages
• When all of the data is collected, then the answers are very easy to analyse in comparison with open-ended questions. • Data is easier to analyse using statistical software. • Respondents can answer the questions more efficiently. • As the responses are visible, then the questions become far clearer. • It is easier to replicate the study if an error is suspected.	• It is impossible to tell if the respondent has misinterpreted the question or whether the presence of answers has influenced the answer given. • Respondents may not have any opinion and proceed to answer anyway. • Some choices given may be confusing. • Detailed distinctions may be lost due to generalisation, and the fact that respondents are being forced into selecting more simplistic answers • Care has to be taken in the question design to avoid an overlapping response in the categories.

There are a number of different types of close-ended questions, including:

- **Dichotomous** where there are two alternative answers that the respondent can select. For example: *"Do you agree or disagree that the learning outcomes were properly met?"*
- **Multiple-choice** questions offering more than two choices for the respondent. For example: What illegal drug would you like to legalise? a) heroin b) cannabis c) cocaine d) LSD e) none f) don't know. In this case, it is important that questions are very carefully worded to ensure the choices represent all possible answers. In online questionnaire software, it is important to consider whether you are going to allow for multiple or single selection. Single selection is usually denoted as circles and multiple selection is usually denoted as squares. An example of multiple selection question may look like the following:

What skills do you believe can be obtained from playing computer games?
 ☐ Problem Solving
 ☐ Reflection
 ☐ Analysing/Classifying
 ☐ Critical Thinking

In this case, it makes sense to allow multiple selection.

- **Contingency questions** composed of a two- or more part question. The answer to the first part of the question will determine which of two alternative questions the respondent will answer next. Contingency questions are used to increase the efficiency of completion of the questionnaire. A contingency question may have the following format:

---

1   Have you ever played computer games?
     [] No (Please go to question 2)
     [] Yes
     If yes: How many hours a week do you play computer games.
     [] Less than one
     [] one
     [] 2 to 5 hours
     [] 6 to 10 hours
     [] 11 to 20 hours
     [] more than 20 hours
2   Have you ever used a computer?

Scaled responses

There are a variety of formats for scaled-response questions, and therefore, it is necessary to consider what format to use. In some cases, it is good to attempt to add variety to the questions in an online questionnaire and possibly alter the scales to ascertain if respondents are still engaged. There are a number of scales responses, including:

Likert Scale, developed by Rensis Likert (Likert, 1932) to further define the levels of measurement in social research; this scale uses standardised response categories. It generally has the following format:

Do you agree that the objectives of the course have been met?
     __Strongly Agree
     __Agree
     __Neutral
     __Disagree
     __Strongly Disagree

Rating Scale, where the respondents are asked to rate something, such as the usability of software. For example, a computer games magazine may be employed by a computer games company to perform research into the best input peripheral for a console. Respondents may be asked to list all of the peripherals they have used and then rate them from 1 (worst) to 10 (best):

Overall Control 1 2 3 4 5 6 7 8 9 10
Overall Feedback 1 2 3 4 5 6 7 8 9 10

When using this scale, it is generally acknowledged that an odd number of choices should be used, giving the respondent the ability to take a neutral standpoint. This is a preferred approach to having an even number of choices since a respondent with a neutral opinion may feel forced to select a more negative or positive side.

Matrix Questions are best employed to ask several different questions that have the same set of answer categories such as:

Please rate each statement with respect to how strongly you agree with it (Table 22.4):

Table 22.4 Example matrix question with same set answer categories

Statement	Strongly agree	Agree	Neutral	Disagree	Strongly disagree
Playing games is sociable.					
Playing games is interesting.					
Playing games is a waste of time.					

You may find that being adaptive with language is necessary to make sense. Table 22.5 shows some adaptations.

Matrix questions are easy to complete, and the format increases the comparability of responses. It is considered good practise to add a neutral-response category.

Table 22.5 Adaptations of matrix questions

Question	Answer range
Please rate the importance:	Very important, Important, Neutral, Unimportant, Very Un-important
To what extent do you agree?	To a very great extent, to a great extent, neutral, to a small extent, to a very small extent
How effective were the following?	Very effective, Effective, Neutral, Ineffective, Very Ineffective.
Please rate the suitability of the following:	Very suitable, Suitable, Neutral, Unsuitable, Very Unsuitable
Please rate how highly:	Very High, High, Neutral, Low, Very Low.

Reporting simple results

Only after running through the entire process of designing your first questionnaire, deploying it, collecting the results, analysing the results, and reporting will you be able to fully visualise the connection between what you ask and what appears on the page.

Reporting dichotomies

These are generally one or other responses manifesting in the questionnaire, along the lines of the following:

"Do you prefer single or multi-player games?"

- Single player
- Multiplayer

We have seen questions like this reported as a simple percentage, e.g., *58.2% of participants preferred single rather than multiplayer.* They can also be reported in graphical form such as a pie charts or bar graphs. One important tip to bear in mind is that if you get a small number of responses, it is important to be wary of having obvious graphical representations of data, e.g., a pie chart illustrating 100% or two segments of 50%. In inferential analysis, dichotomies can be used as grouping variables.

Reporting multiple-choice responses

Suppose the question is designed to be single selection, for example:

"What school are you in?"

- Computing
- Psychology
- Mathematics
- etc.

This can be reported using numbers and percentages and/or represented in a graph. Online survey software can generate these graphs for you, but true analysis really means getting your hands on the data, cleaning it, and performing it inferentially.

Alternatively, suppose the question has multiple selections, for example:

"What types of skills do you think can be obtained from computer games?"

- Problem solving
- Reflection
- Analysing/classifying
- Collaboration/teamwork
- etc.

These results can be reported either using percentages or graphically. The results can also be presented in a table (Table 22.6), for example:

Table 22.6 Example results

Types of skills	N	Percentage
Problem solving	771	93.1%
Reflection	294	35.5%
Analysing and classifying	417	50.3%

Reporting matrix questions

Here is an example of a matrix question and how it may be subsequently reported:

The matrix shows some possible motivations for playing computer games. Please rate each reason with respect to how important it is to you (Table 22.7):

Table 22.7 Example matrix question with motivations

Reasons	Very important	Important	Neutral	Un-important	Very un-important
Challenge					
Competition					
Cooperation					
Recognition					

These can be displayed using quantities and percentages, and this approach takes up some space; however, you can also quantify all of the rating categories by setting Very Important = 5, Important = 4, Neutral = 3, Un-Important = 2 and Very Un-Important = 1. You can then calculate the mean and standard deviation using a spreadsheet or statistical software.

Table 22.8 shows an example of a ranking the means of the attributes and Standard Deviation (SD):

Table 22.8 Reporting matrix data

Reasons	Rank	Mean	SD
Challenge	1st	3.93	0.77
Cooperation	2nd	3.03	0.95
Competition	3rd	2.74	0.96
Recognition	4th	2.30	0.81

It is also possible to give a description of the rankings, and we generally stick to describing the top three most important and the top three least important.

Reporting numerical related questions

You may have asked the participant what age or age range they are in years or how many years that they have engaged in an activity, such as playing games. If you have an open-ended question asking what age someone is and then clean up the data into numerical form, you can report the mean, standard deviation in the following manner:

> The mean age was 25.91 years (SD = 8.82) with a range from 17 to 77.

It is also possible to recode categorisations with averages and report the mean, SD, and range in this manner:

> To calculate the mean time spent playing games, the time bands used as responses were recoded with their mean value (e.g., 1–5 was recoded as 3, while less than 1 was coded as 1 and more than 25 was coded as 21). Using this recoded data, the average number of hours played per week was 7.46 hours (SD = 5.98) with a range of 1–21.

Reporting open-ended questions

This form can entail qualitative analysis, such as thematic analysis, by identifying a number of themes either reported directly or insinuated in the answers. We tend to take examples of the best, most interesting answers, and discuss them or place them in a table.

Academic rigour in questionnaires

Academic rigour can be integrated into a questionnaire by using relevant academic literature to formulate questions. This can involve using a recognised and validated taxonomy, framework, or model, using existing verified questionnaires, and using relevant research and materials uncovered in your literature review. Doing this enhances credibility and allows comparison with other previous studies, and we have constructed a number of questionnaires where we have integrated academic rigour into them using recognised research and here are some examples:

Using a motivational taxonomy

We have integrated Malone and Lepper's Taxonomy of Intrinsic Motivation (1987) into a number of questionnaires to ascertain what players' motivations are for playing computer games. Rather than making these motivations up, which is risky and exhausting, we used a credible existing source. Malone and Lepper's framework has four individual and three interpersonal factors that were integrated into a matrix-type question ranking from Very Important to Very Un-Important as follows:

The table below (Table 22.9) shows possible reasons for playing computer games. Please rate each reason with respect to how important it is to you.

Table 22.9 Example matrix question with importance scale

	Very important	Important	Neutral	Un-important	Very un-important	Don't know
Playing games provides me with a challenge						

Using Kolb's experiential learning cycle and learning models

We have also integrated the four learning styles of Kolb's experiential learning cycle (Kolb, 1984) into a questionnaire: Diverging, Assimilating, Converging, Accommodating, for example:

> What learning type best describes you?
>
> - Diverging (feeling and watching)
> - Assimilating (watching and thinking)
> - Converging (doing and thinking)
> - Accommodating (doing and feeling)

Due to the rather specific terminology, a description of each learning style was provided. It should also be noted that there are a number of questionnaires allowing the determination of learning styles based on Kolb's experiential learning styles, e.g., Honey and Mumford (2006) have developed a further formalised and tested questionnaire for determining learning style. We have seen examples of students analysing decision making based on personality types utilising Myers–Briggs personality types (Myers, 1980). There are many recognised learning theories and models, as well as motivational theories that can be used as a basis for the construction of a questionnaire, and here is a quick useful list at the Learning Theories and Models website: http://learningmodels.blogspot.com/p/learning-theories-and-models.html. **UT:** It is very worthwhile checking to see if others have developed a questionnaire surrounding your research interests to either utilise it or at least inform the academic rigour. Many validated questionnaires exist, such the Intrinsic Motivation Inventory from self-determination theory (https://selfdeterminationtheory.org/intrinsic-motivation-inventory/).

Using taxonomies and categorisations for general structuring of questions

Questions can be constructed from recognised taxonomies, such as game genres, formats, historical periods, organisational structures, educational frameworks, design principles, educational content, and recognised components of categorisations. Here are some examples:

- **Game genres:** What do you play most frequently? Strategy, RPG, Platformer, Fighting, Shooter, FPS, TPS, TBSG.
- **Formats:** What format do you believe would be most suitable for this game/software? PC, Tablet PC, Console, Mobile Phone ...

- **Historical periods:** What is your favourite musical period? Baroque, Classical, Romantic, 20th Century …
- **Organisational structures:** What faculty are you in? Business, Computing, Psychology, Science …
- **Educational frameworks:** What level of the SCQF is you highest qualification? 1, 2, 3, 4, 5, 6, 7, 8, 9, 10, 11, 12

Taxonomies can be used from your literature reviews and other studies with permission.

Summary

This chapter has provided an overview of general questionnaire design to allow you to contemplate what your questionnaire is for, who it is aimed at, and what kind of data you want to collect. We have produced a number of tips, as well as covered all of the basic available question formats that are open for your consideration. Questionnaire design is an art in itself and one where you only develop an appreciation of the whole process when you have designed, deployed, and reported your first questionnaire. We have also briefly described how to possibly report some of the data that you have gathered to add a professional touch to your dissertation questionnaire analysis.

References

Brace, I. (2010) *Questionnaire Design: How to Plan, Structure and Write Survey Material for Effective Market Research (Market Research in Practice).* 4th edn. KoganPage.

Honey, P. and Mumford, A. (2006) *The Learning Styles Questionnaire. 80-item version* (Revised edition, July 2006), Maidenhead: Peter Honey Publications Limited.

Kolb, D. A. (1984) *Experiential Learning: Experience as the Source of Learning and Development* (Vol. 1). Englewood Cliffs, NJ: Prentice-Hall.

Likert, R. (1932) 'A technique for the measurement of attitudes', *Archives of Psychology*, p. 7.

Malone, T. W. and Lepper, M. R. (1987) 'Making learning fun: A taxonomy of intrinsic motivations for learning', *Aptitude, Learning, and Instruction*, *3*, pp. 223–253.

Myers, I. B. and Myers P.B., (Original edition 1980; Reprint edition 1995), *Gifts Differing: Understanding Personality Type*, Davies-Black Publishing, 248 pages, ISBN 0-89106-074-X.

23 Basic Intervention Experimental Design

In this chapter, you will learn:

- What experimental design is.
- How to define variables and a hypothesis.
- About selecting a sampling strategy.
- Basic experimental design.
- Basic application reporting.

An appreciation of basic intervention experimental design is very beneficial, reasonably advanced for this level, and demonstrates excellent progress in tackling the next level in your educational journey. This chapter will give a brief overview of the basics of experimental design in a computer science and games context. It will discuss basic sampling, control groups, and experimental groups augmented by examples of experimental designs by experienced researchers. Computer science/games development evaluation, testing, and research – anything that involves human participants – touches on social science and psychology. This means that if you perform any research in these areas, then you have to learn a bit of this topic as well. Many people (including us – the authors) can find themselves drowning in a sea of terminology and research methods books, and this chapter will provide you with a brief introduction to the basics. All experimental designs and examples in this chapter are derived from ***Dissertation K.***

What experimental design is

A research design formulates a plan to collect the necessary, relevant data required, which can be qualitative, quantitative, or a mixed-method design. It can utilise focus groups, interviews, case studies, ethnography, or a meta-analysis. The general consensus is that making a prediction and

DOI: 10.4324/9781003054887-23

deliberately manipulating the IV to observe the consequential change in the DV with the experimental method is the only way to establish cause and effect unambiguously. Miller (1984, p. 5) defines an experiment as: "*a means of collecting evidence to show the effect of one variable upon another. In the ideal case the experimenter manipulates the IV, holds all other variables constant, and then observes the changes in the DV. In this hypothetical, perfect experiment any changes in the DV must be caused by the manipulation of the IV.*" An experiment must have at least one IV, and as a result of us only really being interested in that variable or those variables, then we must attempt to assert as much control as possible over irrelevant variables.

There are two types of irrelevant variable that can cause confusion or confound researchers during and experiment and these are situational variables and subject variables. Situational variables are associated with the circumstances and situation under which the experiment is conducted and include: the environment, context, potential interruptions, noise, instructions, and the tone of the experimenter's voice. Subject variables are associated with participants; they include motivation, intelligence, personality, and alertness. Situational variables are very difficult to control, but there is a hierarchy subject variable control mechanism:

- **Repeated measures** – The same subjects are in each group. If this is going to be used, then some consideration must be given to what group is performed first. If it affects the second group, then it may be an idea to randomly assign half the participants to the experimental or control group and have them sit the experiment and switch groups and run the experiment again to reduce bias. This is known as counter-balancing, where the treatment order is reversed, or the treatment is randomised ensuring that the order does not influence the results.
- **Match subjects** – This method mimics the repeated measures by attempting to find and use highly similar pairs of individuals, such as identical twins. This only happens in rare circumstances.
- **Independent groups** – This is where the groups are different and is probably the most popular mechanism due to practicalities. And, although you dream of involving the entire population and planet – you always get about a fraction of what you expect.

Defining your variables and a hypothesis

To develop a hypothesis, you have to identify the IV(s) and the DV(s) predict what the result will be when the IV is manipulated. Here are a few computer science and games development examples:

Example 1
Source: *Dissertation F*

Scenario: You would like to know if a game can help people revise for a programming test.
Research question: playing game relates to programming knowledge.
IV: The game
DV: Level of programming knowledge

Example 2
Scenario: You would like to know if an app can increase wellfullness.
Research question: App use relates to wellfullness.
IV: App
DV: Empathy

Example 3
Scenario: You would like to know if an immersive VR environment or an App is more preferrable for soft skill training.
Research question: VR or app for soft skills.
IV: VR or app
DV: Soft skill acquisition

Example 4
Scenario: You would like to know whether users prefer a normal user interface (traditional flat screen) or an immersive VR system interface.
Research question: Normal or VR interface.
IV: Normal interface or VR interface
DV: Levels of preference

Once the scenario, research question, IVs, and DVs are identified, it makes it easier to write an alternate and null hypothesis. What we tend to find is because our students are trying to fix problems, it is a simple question of the intervention having a positive result (alternate hypothesis) or a negative one or not working at all (null hypothesis). Here are examples based on the previous section:

Example 1
Null hypothesis: Playing a serious game for computer-programming revision will have no effect on programming knowledge acquisition.
Alternate hypothesis: Playing a serious game for computer-programming revision will result in an increase of programming knowledge acquisition.

Example 2
Null hypothesis: Playing an app does not alter levels of wellfullness.
Alternate hypothesis: Playing an App increases levels of well-fullness.

Example 3
Null hypothesis: An app or a VR environment is not effective for teaching soft skills.
Alternate hypothesis 1: A VR environment is effective at teaching soft skills.
Alternate hypothesis 2: An app is effective at teaching soft skills.
Alternate hypothesis 3: Both the VR environment and app are effective at teaching soft skills.

Example 4
Null hypothesis: The normal interface is more preferrable than the VR immersive interface.
Alternate hypothesis: The VR immersive interface is more preferrable than the normal interface.

Experiments are highly contextualised, and a good experimental research design has to take into account all the individual, special, unique considerations to collect data that is relevant.

Then you have to think about how you are going to manipulate the IV, measure the DV, and how you are going to reduce irrelevant variables. Generally, in these kinds of projects, what we find is that the IV is the game or the software or some part of the implementation of the game or software that you have added or developed. The DV tends to be things like level of knowledge, skill, user or player satisfaction, or preference.

Sampling strategy

Simply speaking, a sampling strategy should be considered when you are attempting to appropriately select the participants in your experiment,

Table 23.1 Sampling techniques

Probability sampling	Non-probability sampling
Simple random	Quota sampling
Stratified random	Snowball sampling
Cluster sampling	Judgment sampling
Systematic sampling	Convenience sampling
Multi-stage sampling	

evaluation, case study, or survey. In all honesty, very little consideration is given to it at this level and in these disciplines. Nevertheless, it is a very complex subject and is worthy of some consideration as there are several sampling strategies that can be used. It is very good at this level to even consider sampling, let alone make an objective selection of sampling method. Salkind (2010) defines sampling as examining *"a portion or sample of a larger group of potential participants and use the results to make statements that apply to this broader group or population."*

Taherdoost (2016) identifies a number of sampling techniques in Table 23.1 that can be considered and are split into:

- Probability sampling – where each item in the population has an equal chance of being included in the sample.
- Non-probability sampling – tending to focus on case study research with small samples and qualitative research.

We recommend that is you are considering a sampling technique then refer to Taherdoost (2016) for a comprehensive overview. Also investigate some of the techniques listed in Table 23.1 to acquire descriptions and select the most suitable approach.

Basic experimental design

The main purpose of performing any form of experiment is to contribute to knowledge and not necessarily trying to prove that an intervention works in a positive way. In reality, students approaching their first experimental research project feel pressurised that their game, software, or intervention should be a success. We would like to demystify this common misconception and tell you that UT: it is the process that is the most important part of running an experiment as well as the search for knowledge and truth. Leading to a very popular quote applicable to statistical analysis:

> *"An unsophisticated researcher uses statistics as a drunken man uses lamp-posts — for support rather than illumination." (Andrew Lang)*

Probably the simplest experimental design compares two conditions; however, even this can become complicated as there are several variations. To exacerbate the confusion, several terms are also thrown into the mix, which mean the same thing from various disciplines, including:

- **Measurements made within a group of people** – within-subjects design, repeated measures, matched pairs, related measures.
- **Measurements made between a group of people** – between-subjects design, independent measures, unrelated samples.

Within-subjects design

This condition is when a comparison can take place between a pre-test and a post-test using the same group of participants. There of course can be several groups whether these are additional experimental groups or control groups (comparing your intervention to a normal approach). If there are several groups, then this is a special case covered later. Figure 23.1 shows an experimental and control group design.

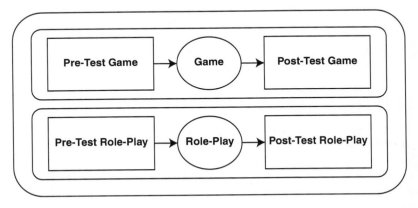

Figure 23.1 Comparing the pre-test and post-tests in the game group (experimental) and the role play group (control).

If the data fulfils the criteria for parametric tests, then a dependent t-test could be used, and if not, the non-parametric equivalent is a Wilcoxon matched pairs signed-rank test.

Between-subjects design

This is when a comparison can take place between a pre and pre-test result or a post and post-test result of two different groups. Figure 23.2 shows an experimental and control group design.

If the data fulfils the criteria for parametric tests, then an independent t-test could be used, and if not, then the non-parametric equivalent is a Mann-Whitney U test. It should be noted that it is possible to take one of these tests in isolation and use some grouping variable to split the groups into independent groups if there are sufficient participants. An example may be taking the pre-test game data and splitting the data using gender, online/offline participation, or single-player or multiplayer preference. Again, these independent groups can be analysed using independent t-tests for parametric criteria and Mann-Whitney U tests for non-parametric.

More than two groups

You may find yourself faced with the scenario of having more than one experimental group or more than one control group. This may, for example, include a game group (experimental group) and two control

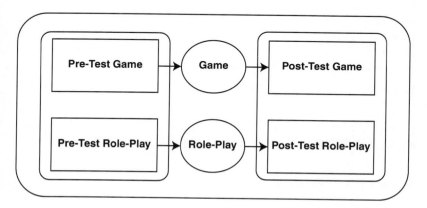

Figure 23.2 Comparing the pre and pre-tests and the post and post-tests of two independent groups.

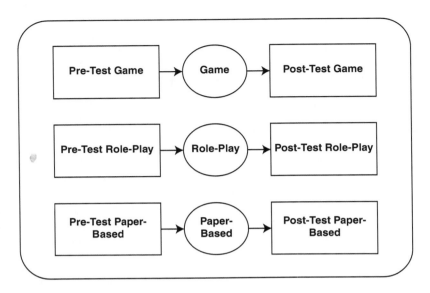

Figure 23.3 An experimental design with more than two groups.

groups (a role-play and a paper-based group) for teaching requirements collection as in Figure 23.3.

When there are more than two groups, the parametric test to potentially use is an ANOVA (analysis of variance), which is an omnibus test for equality in any number of populations means in a single F value. An ANOVA has greater power than a collection of t-tests and far less effort involved. It compares the variation (measured by items related to the variance) between the levels of the factor with the variation within the groups. The non-parametric equivalent of this test is a Kruskal-Wallis test.

Basic application reporting

This section will provide a very brief summary of tests that can be performed and examples of how to report them for all of the basic experimental designs we have discussed so far.

Parametric equivalent with two conditions

- A dependent sample *t-test* can be performed between and pre and a post-test of the same group (within groups).

- An independent sample *t-test* can be performed between tests of different groups (between groups).
- If p < 0.05, you can say that the data sets are significantly different. If p > 0.05, they are not. The lower the p-value, the higher your confidence that data sets are different.
- Example report of the test – t (306) = 7.01, p < 0.001).
- Males played games for significantly longer per week (10.11 hours; SD = 7.78) than females (4.78 hours; SD = 4.88), (t (306) = 7.01, p < 0.001).

Non-parametric equivalent with two conditions

- A Wilcoxon can be performed between and pre and a post-test of the same group (within groups).
- A Mann-Whitney *U* test can be performed between tests of different groups (between groups).
- Example report of the test – (Z = −9.803, p < 0.000).
- A Mann-Whitney *U* test also indicated that those who played online games played for significantly more hours per week (9.79 hours) that those who did not (6.04 hours), (Z −9.803, p < 0.000).

More than two conditions

- ANOVA (parametric test) reported like this: $F(2, 145) = 3.24$, $p = .04$.
- Kruskal-Wallis (non-parametric test) reported like this: ($\chi 2 = 0.021$, p < 0.884).
- An ANOVA test with a two-group pre-test/post-test data set returns the same result as an independent t-test.
- A Kruskal-Wallis test with a two-group pre-test/post-test data set returns the same result as a Mann-Whitney.

Summary

This chapter has briefly introduced experimental design to allow you to become familiar with the basics so you can reflect on how you will set up any intervention experiment. We have provided an introduction to experimental design and how to control situational variables. We have also provided examples of how to select IVs and DVs to formulate a hypothesis. The most basic experimental designs have also been discussed in terms of structure, analysis, and reporting in terms of real life examples.

References

Miller, S. (1984) *Experimental Design and Statistics (New Essential Psychology)*. 2nd edn. Routledge.

Salkind, N.J. (2010) *Encyclopaedia of Research Design* (Vols. 1-0). Thousand Oaks, CA: SAGE Publications, Inc. doi: 10.4135/9781412961288

Taherdoost, H. (2016) 'Sampling methods in research methodology; how to choose a sampling technique for research', *SSRN Electronic Journal*, 5(2), pp. 18–27. doi: 10.2139/ssrn.3205035

24 General Academic Writing Tips

In this chapter, you will learn:

- What academic writing is.
- How to write academically.
- Some academic writing tips.

Academic writing

Academic writing is a specific and unique approach toward writing that many students in these disciplines have not really encountered before because, up until now, design and technical specification documents have been the main concentration, coinciding with a practical output.

Many students are unaware that academic writing is a formal style of writing and is not opinion based, like a blog piece. It is a writing style that is not presented in a conversational manner. There should be no inappropriate colloquial speech used or slang of any kind. It involves careful sculpting, research, and referencing and is not just simply a case of typing the first idea that pops into your head.

Academic writing has a particular purpose. It is a style of writing that should be presented in a concise, clear, and logical way. Remember that you are writing to display and reinforce your knowledge on a specific subject area. The way in which you write and how you explain your research should be done in a way that anyone reading your dissertation should understand it. Academic writing is about how you express the points you are making and how you substantiate them. You cannot write your own personal views about things. You must provide evidence and specific information to validate the claims that you make. This is when you will be reliant upon the academic literature to assist you. A summary of what academic writing:

DOI: 10.4324/9781003054887-24

- Is formal in tone, avoiding an informal and conversational style.
- Uses correct grammar and punctuation within sentences and paragraphs.
- Substantiates points, with credible academic sources.
- Uses direct quotations from academic work sparingly to verify key points.
- Explains and offers clarity regarding specific terminology and defines key concepts.
- Is well-structured and presented logically.
- Provides the reader with references and appendices to follow up on sources.

How to write academically

Being able to write academically is a process that takes time. It is a different style of writing in terms of how you express the points you would like to make and how you would like to make them. This style of writing must be clear and concise for the reader, yet informative at the same time. When writing in this way, it is important that you establish the key facts and communicate them in an informative, substantiated way. There must be a sense of focus and purpose when you write. You must remember when engaging in it is that it adheres to a formal prose register when reporting and substantiating facts, authors' academic work, and findings from research studies.

Here is an example of the formal academic writing. This example will help you gain an overview of the academic style of writing and how it flows from one point to another. It also provides a good illustration of acknowledging academic authors and substantiating significant academic perspectives. This example focuses on the area of virtual reality use in higher education in the context of academic research.

Example of formal prose

In the context of VR use in higher education there are further research avenues and directions to explore. In addition to investigating the pedagogical applications of VR, it would be beneficial to determine whether VR technology is applicable towards most academic disciplines or whether it is specifically suited towards certain types. (Baxter and Hainey, 2019).

The example of formal prose gives you a good overview of the wording and style of prose when making points academically and substantiating perspectives from various academic authors. Reinforcing the rigour of an academic argument indicates that you have read around the subject area and that you understood the relevant points being made and can articulate them.

Here is another example using a direct quote to indicate the logic, thinking, and perspective of authors regarding their viewpoints:

Example of a direct quote

Source: *Dissertation I*
This thesis adopts the view of Collis and Hussey (2009, p. 82) *who consider a case study to be a methodology that "is used to explore a single phenomenon (the case) in a natural setting using a variety of methods to obtain in-depth knowledge." The definition provided by* Collis and Hussey (2009) *is associated with the principal aim of the case study methodology applied in this research study, which is to acquire specific knowledge about the case under investigation as opposed to forming generalisations.*

When writing academically, you can include direct quotations, but use them sparingly. Direct quotations are useful for defining terminology for the reader and when you want to reinforce a particular point that has been made by an author. They are also useful for capturing an original phrase or term expressed by an author where paraphrasing may lose the original context or meaning of the statement. Direct quotations should only be used where necessary, and it is not advisable to quote large chunks of work. You also need to be able to illustrate that can write about what you have read and that you have digested and understood it.

A further point to note about overusing direct quotations is that the more you use throughout your dissertation, the more it starts to become apparent that you have based most of your dissertation around direct quotes.

Academic phrases used in academic writing

Successful academic writing is in the formal tone of the writing. There is a certain way regarding how you can express your arguments, justify your research approach, articulate your results, and convey perspectives portrayed in the academic literature. Here are some examples:

- An important aim of this research is to investigate ...
- An important aim of this research is to assess whether the use of serious games can support organisational learning in the software project team environments of this case study.
- The choice in this dissertation was made to investigate the problem area of ...
- The research performed will focus on ...
- It has been noted in the academic literature that ...
- It has been acknowledged in the literature that ...
- Many researchers have noted that the term "case study" has different meanings to different people.
- It is acknowledged in the literature that case study research is sometimes criticised for its subjectivity.
- Though there remains a lack of agreement in the academic literature about how to define ...
- Though it has been stated by authors such as (*author x*) and (*author y*) ...
- According to *author x*, the principal benefits of undertaking case study research come from the methodology's particularistic, descriptive, and heuristic features.
- The empirical evidence provided will also contribute to knowledge in the research area of ...
- This dissertation provides empirical evidence of both the benefits and barriers as well as the use of serious games to facilitate ...
- The findings of this study will be applied to the creation of a serious game's implementation framework designed to provide recommendations on the steps to follow when introducing serious games into HE.

Academic writing tips

Writing in an academic fashion takes time to perfect and will not magically transpire overnight. Continuously working away at it in tandem with regular feedback from your supervisor can help you to get it right in the end. We have compiled a list of recommended tips adapted from

Bednar (n.d.) to help you. It should be noted that this list is not exhaustive:

Tip 1 Keep on topic and do not deviate

Try to stay focused on what you are writing and what you are trying to convey to the reader. Concentrate on the topic in hand and do not deviate from it. Try your best to succinctly summarise work you are referring to, authors' viewpoints and perspectives, and paraphrase concisely where necessary.

Tip 2 Writing tone is important

Keep your writing tone formal and avoid being conversational and informal. Do not use colloquialisms such as "doesn't" or "isn't." Use formal language and words such as "does not" or "is not." Try to adhere to the formal academic prose of your writing and not deviate from it.

Tip 3 Grammar and punctuation is important

Try your best to ensure that you make use of good grammar and punctuation. For example, use apostrophes where they should be, know when and where to include commas within sentences and when to use of colons and semi-colons. Using the correct grammar will aid the structure of your formal writing.

Tip 4 Avoid using ambiguous language

Try to use language or phrases that do not cause ambiguity. There needs to be clarity in your prose especially when you are communicating academic perspectives and viewpoints. If the readers views the argument you are making as being vague, then it will become difficult for them to interpret.

Tip 5 Use direct quotes in moderation

Do not overuse direct quotations in your writing. They should be used frugally when you are expressing points made in the original work of an author (Bednar, n.d.). You can also use direct quotes when citing definitions provided by authors to capture the meaning of what they have said. Avoid the inclusion of entire paragraphs of direct quotations.

Tip 6 Include signposting for the reader

Clearly include chapter titles to add structure and to signpost the reader to the various topics and sub-topics (Bednar, n.d.). In addition to the main table of contents, the use of section titles allows the reader to scan your dissertation quickly and focus on key segments that are of interest to them. Include meaningful titles such as: Introduction, Literature Review, Research Methodology, and Methods – titles where the reader will know what is contained within the various sections. It is important that you introduce each section to the reader so that they are aware of the context. For example, when introducing the structure, you could state the following: "The structure of this dissertation consists of a further ten chapters organised as follows … ".

Tip 7 Define a term or role for yourself

It is useful to define a label or term for yourself. It is useful that you specify what your role is (e.g., an observer or facilitator) and how you will be aiding the research and in what capacity. For example, as opposed to using the first-person pronoun I, you could call yourself "the researcher." You could state, "The initial role of the researcher in this case study will be that of an observer to assess … " Try to avoid using the first-person pronoun.

Tip 8 Be conscious of spelling mistakes

Be wary of spelling mistakes and homonyms (Bednar, n.d.), homophones, or homographs.

- **Homographs** – same spelling, different pronunciation, but different meaning, e.g., "book" as in a book to read or "book" as in reserve a place.
- **Homophones** – same pronunciation but different spelling and meaning, e.g., "write" as in to write a note or "right" as in being right or move to the right.
- **Homonyms** – same pronunciation and spelling but different meaning, e.g., "tear" as in shed a tear or "tear" as in tear a piece of paper.

These are easy often unintentional errors to make and a good list to clarify the point is located at the ESL website: https://7esl.com/homonyms/.

Tip 9 Refer to authors by surname

When mentioning a specific piece of work always refer to the author by their surname. This makes the writing more formal and coincides with the academic writing style. Ensure that you also spell the author names correctly as this allows the reader to follow up on the work by that author.

Tip 10 Making mention of texts

When referring to the name of a work or a particular text, such as the title of a journal paper, place the name of the work in double inverted commas, for example, "An investigation of employability skill sets required by graduates in Scotland's Creative Industries sector." Italics should be used for books, for example, *Writing Successful Undergraduate Dissertations in Games Development and Computer Science.*

Tip 11 Know your terms

If you use a term such as "anchored learning" in your dissertation, make absolutely certain you know what it means as you can be questioned later.

Tip 12 Do not waffle or use "in order to"

For example: I went to the shop in order to buy sugar in order to put in my tea can be more concisely written as: I went to the shop to buy sugar to put in my tea. It becomes obvious when you start to ramble to increase your word count.

Summary

In this chapter, we have included a summary of general academic writing tips for you to put a professional touch to your dissertation. Academic writing is a skill that takes years to master, and hopefully, this chapter will have given you a head start. We summarise with the following points:

- Writing academically can be challenging especially if you have never encountered writing in a style that uses formal prose before.
- UT: It takes time to be proficient at academic writing and the more academic books and journal papers you look at, the more

- familiar you will become with academic style, jargon, and the conventions.
- **UT:** It may sound slightly cliché, but practice does indeed make perfect.
- The key to successful academic writing is associated with the structure and the vocabulary used.
- Academic writing is not like writing an informal piece of prose such as a blog entry.
- The main thing to remember is that though you are expressing perspectives and opinions, they will be substantiated from credible academic sources.

Once you have become used to writing academically through substantial practice, you will find that it will become second nature to you.

References

Baxter, G. and Hainey, T. (2019) 'Student perceptions of virtual reality use in higher education', *Journal of Applied Research in Higher Education*, 12(3), pp. 413–424. doi: 10.1108/JARHE-06-2018-0106

Bednar, J.A. (n.d.) *Tips for academic writing and other formal writing*. Available at: https://people.utm.my/thoo/wp-content/blogs.dir/1795/files/2016/02/Tips-for-Academic-Writing-and-Other-Formal-Writing.pdf (Accessed: 10 February 2021).

Collis, J. and Hussey, R. (2009) *Business Research: A Practical Guide for Undergraduate & Postgraduate Students*. 3rd edn. Basingstoke: Palgrave Macmillan.

7ESL (n.d.) Available at: https://7esl.com/homonyms/ (Accessed: 26 April 2022).

25 Presenting Research

In this chapter, you will learn about:

- Tips to present your project.
- Planning your presentation.
- What to include in a presentation?
- Tips for delivering your presentation successfully.

Presenting – A student nightmare

You may have a presentation at some point to your project supervisor or other academics or peers. Presentations always fill students, and sometimes staff, with a sense of trepidation and dread. Standing in front of your peers or academics, presenting and answering questions, can make one uneasy. We want to assure you that presentations can be executed brilliantly and enjoyably whe viewed as a meeting of minds and not an interrogation or opportunity for criticism. Planning and preparation will make things run smoothly!

There are several contexts where you might be asked to present something at university, and this can even help in your personal life, e.g., a giving a best man's speech at a wedding. Table 25.1 summarises some presentation scenarios.

Doing the groundwork

There are several things you can reflect on in advance. Primarily, you need to understand what it is you are being asked to present and why. Fundamentally, what is the nature of the assignment you have been set? In addition, you also need to consider some of the factors in Table 25.2.

DOI: 10.4324/9781003054887-25

Table 25.1 Presentation scenarios

Type	Scenario
Poster	Conference, research event.
Individual	MSc or PhD Viva defence, Bachelor's project presentation.
Group	Team-based presentation.
Technical	Demonstrating software, an app, website, or a game.

Table 25.2 Factors before presenting

Factor	Recommended action
What are you being asked to do?	• Read the assessment guidelines carefully and ensure you understand what is required. • Seek clarity from your lecturer if uncertain.
How long has the presentation to be?	• Find out the presentation length and timeslot and rehearse to make sure yours fits. Usually this is 20 minutes or 10 minutes with 5 minutes for questions. • Perform several timed rehearsals. Time will fly by, and it is important to try and stick to time. Remember a number of presentations will probably be happening that day.
Date, time, and location of presentation.	• Either book a slot or make sure you have the time, date, and place memorised.
Location of presentation	• Ensure you have been there prior to the day on a practice run.
Room layout, software, and equipment	• Visit the room, familiarise yourself with the layout. • Ascertain where the best place for you to present to the audience is. • Check the equipment by either running your presentation, software on videos or bring your own. • Do you need to bring a HDMI cable?

You want to create a good impression from the offset and appear on time, ready and able to proceed. Try not to come unprepared, turn up late, and use up your time fruitlessly.

Figure 25.1 shows things you should consider prior to presenting.

Preparing for the presentation

You will be most likely be using presentation software to create your slides. These are all capable of animations and can make your presentation

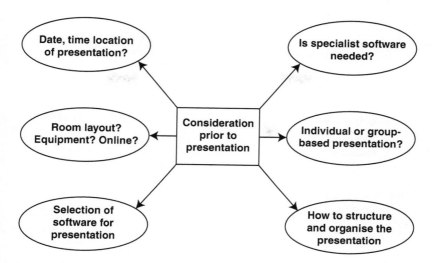

Figure 25.1 Considerations prior to a presentation.

look dynamic, interactive, and exciting. Table 25.3 shows some handy tips for content creation.

Figure 25.2 shows a diagram to help identifying the practicalities.

Table 25.3 Tips for creating content

Slide tips	*Points to consider*
Choice of slide template	• What colour will my slides be? • Avoid colours that will clash (e.g., orange background with red text). • Try to make colours easy on the eye and ask other people.
Slide template and transition design	• Choose a design template to go with your presentation. • Ensure that the transition design will not make the viewers feel dizzy or disorientated.
Content for the slides	• Devise a suitable structure with headings and sub-headings. • Ensure the structure of the presentation is logical and flows well. We will present a structure shortly. • Make your slides concise yet informative. • Include visuals where appropriate.
Rehearse, rehearse, rehearse	• Rehearse what you are going to say. • Time the length of your presentation. • Keep refining the presentation. • Check over your slides for layout, format, and content. • Ensure any media elements are working in case you must embed any interactive content (e.g., game or app demo).

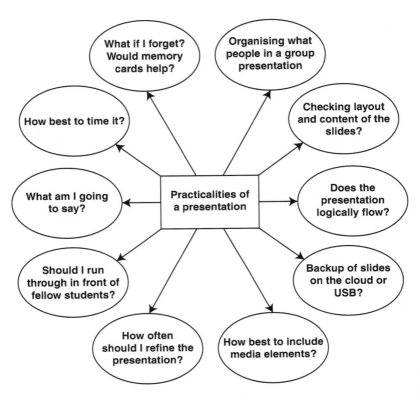

Figure 25.2 Practicalities of a presentation.

One ambiguous factor is the content and structure of the presentation. We present the following generic structure for games development and computer science to get you started. This should appear on your second slide to tell the audience what is coming:

PRESENTATION STRUCTURE

- **Introduction**
    - **Overview of Problem**
    - **Proposed Solution**

- **Literature Review**
- **Design**
- **Implementation**
- **Testing**
- **Evaluation**
- **Conclusion**
- **Future Work/Recommendations/Limitations**
- **Demonstration**
- **Questions**

First slide

The fist slide includes the following information:

- Name
- Identification number
- Title of dissertation
- Degree programme/course
- Lecture names/supervisors

Note that if you wish to be creative and have an image of something relevant, e.g., a picture of your game, software, or something triggering a point, then do so as it is highly unlikely that you will lose marks for creativity.

Second slide

In this slide, you would outline the structure as previously indicated.

Introduction slide

You would state what the nature of the research area or problem is and why you have chosen to investigate it. It is important that you justify the need for your research to be undertaken and why it is worth pursuing. So, for example, you could have chosen to focus on the connotations of video games and obesity and have developed a serious game to educate gamers about how to combine a balanced lifestyle. If undertaking a web and mobile degree, you could focus on the importance of website or app accessibility based on the principles of the World Wide Web Consortium (W3C). State the problem and your solution to address that problem because, in some respects, the presentation mimics the dissertation structure.

Literature review slides

The literature review section relates to the background research that informs your study. You can have one or more slide in this section of the presentation depending how detailed your literature review results are. This can include search terms, electronic databases searched, criteria, important papers, results, and a synthesis of findings.

Design slides

You can provide visuals of what you have developed or conceptual schematics (UML, EER) of what your design might look like. This would be useful for a game or app idea where you could include a level design typology layout or a wireframe for an app or website. Make it informative yet visual at the same time.

For any functional software, your slides can include visuals the GUI. Furthermore, you can also provide visuals on how you have used the software in terms of developing the output for your dissertation. When designing that layout for your presentation, it is useful to try and blend your slides with a mixture of text and visuals. You can also provide details of the GDLC or SDLC that you have selected.

Implementation slides

Here you can have screen shots of the actual implementation and talk about basic functionality and advanced functionality. You can discuss the interesting algorithms as well. This really mimics the structure of the dissertation proposed.

Testing slides

This is where you can specify your testing techniques and any interesting errors that you have overcome. Always remember that you are trying to keep the entire presentation interesting; highlight programming issues that are challenging and were overcome, which is very interesting to your audience.

Evaluation slides

This can be an overview of your procedure, participants, materials, and results. You can easily represent these using visuals such as tables, graphs, and descriptive or inferential statistics. This is of course dependent on whether there is an evaluation in your dissertation. It may be that your implementation has been successful or unsuccessful.

Conclusion slide

This is where you sum up the main points of the research and answer your research questions, if there are any, or conclude based on your title. We would recommend making this one slide with a maximum of four points.

Future work/recommendations/limitations slide

This slide should specify how you are going to proceed with the project. Recommendations that you care to make in terms of how your findings can be used and expanded. Also acknowledge limitations to demonstrate that you can think about your project objectively.

Demonstration

There may be a small live demonstration at the end of a presentation to showcase what you have developed. This of course depends on how confident you are in what you have developed running well on the day. For a dissertation project, this can be a quick subset demonstration, but in a showcasing event where you have decided to use your project application to gain employment, this is obviously a well-tested game or application that is used. Prior to the pandemic, supervisors would organise a room for presentation and allow students to select appointments for themselves, the supervisors, and other academics to attend. We recommend the following tips:

- Take your own laptop with the necessary software, if possible.
- Test the computer or presentation device in the room provided prior to the event, making sure all is well with software.
- Have a recording as a backup if the live demonstration fails.
- Have a backup presentation and demonstration on the cloud, USB, or emailed to you.

Presenting in the pandemic

The changing nature of educational delivery means that you might occasionally have to present remotely using online communication platforms such as Zoom or Microsoft Teams. Should this be the case, we propose the following useful tips:

• Ensure that you have Zoom or Microsoft Teams installed on your PC or laptop.
• Find a quiet place at home where you can present undisturbed and are free from background noise.
• Be familiar on how to use the various features of each platform (e.g., uploading your slides, sharing content or your screen, use of audio if playing a video).
• Make sure your audio is working on your machine and that you know how to mute and unmute your microphone.
• Test that your web cam portrays you clearly and that you are visible to the audience.
• Conduct some mock online presentations with friends to test the use of either platform.
• Continue to practice and rehearse.

Questions slide

Have a nice slide at the end saying, "Thank you for listening" and "Are there any questions?" Make sure this is a cheery slide and pre-empt the inevitable questions by asking for them.

Figure 25.3 shows things to consider including in your presentation.

During the presentation

Try to be prepared for the unexpected, such as:

• Changed room or venue.
• Equipment failure.
• People may not turn up.
• Problems running software demonstrations.
• You forget what to say.

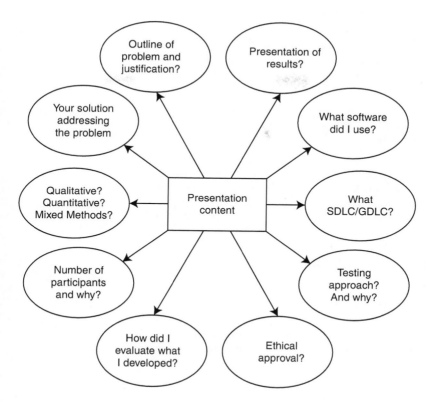

Figure 25.3 Considerations for presentation content.

UT: Try to remain calm – at the end of the day, it is only a presentation. Try to be confident in the work you have done and in your subject area. It is reasonable to have pointers written on little cards as memory triggers. Try not to produce an entire transcript on cards, and remember that you if you have prepared then you have nothing to worry about. Table 25.4 shows recommended actions at the presentation.

Figure 25.4 shows aspects to consider during the presentation.

Presentation questions

Once the presentation is finished, you can breathe a huge sigh of relief! Your presentation is over, but there is always a small number of marks

Table 25.4 Recommended actions

At the presentation	Recommended Action
Turn up on time	• Find the room in advance.
	• Check equipment.
	• Set three alarms.
Setting up	• Set up in good time.
	• Test and run media content.
	• Check it is the correct presentation version.
Starting the presentation	• Introduce yourself and the project.
	• Maintain eye contact throughout.
	• Provide a small overview.
During the presentation	• Speak clearly and calmy.
	• Being nervous is perfectly normal and observers are often sympathetic.
	• If you lose your concentration do not panic and try and follow your memory triggers.
	• Time the presentation.
	• Apologise for any technical issues and move on. People can see things later.
	• Thank those listening for their time.
	• Ask if there are any questions.

associated with how well you answer questions. You cannot anticipate the questions you might be asked, but the three most important rules are:

• Don't rush to an answer – take a moment to breathe and time to think.
• If you are unsure what is being asked, then ask for clarification.
• If you don't know the answer – simply say so and don't try to fabricate an answer.

Remember that your supervisor is on your side and the questions asked are to assess your progress and knowledge. Hopefully, you will also receive constructive feedback and guidance about what you still need to do. Your presentation might be a final showcase piece where you may be given feedback relating to future directions for your work. Overall, the main thing is to remain calm when answering questions, think about what you are being asked and then try to be as informative as you can

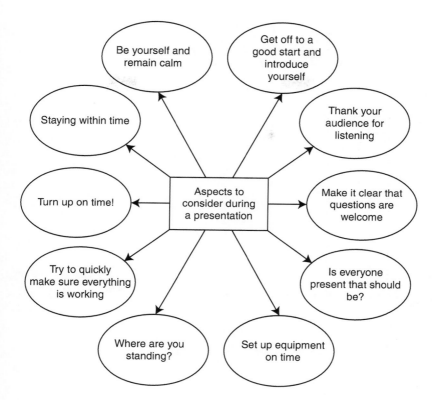

Figure 25.4 During a presentation.

with your answer. Once the question is answered try not to continuously babble. Table 25.5 provides some tips.

Figure 25.5 shows consideration when answering questions.

Table 25.5 Tips for answering questions

After the presentation	Recommended action
Audience questions	• Do not rush your answers.
	• Think about what is being asked and seek clarity if you are unsure.
	• Answer clearly and be as informative as you can but if you do not know the answer – say so.
Constructive criticism	• Do not take it personally.
	• Do not be overly defensive or aggressive.
	• Say thanks for any suggestions.
	• Act on advice given.

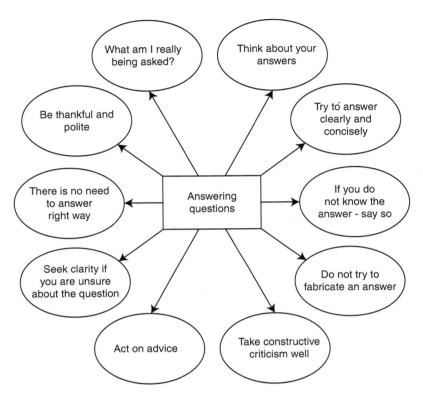

Figure 25.5 Answering questions.

Summary

Presentations can often be a bit nerve-wracking, but can be executed well if careful preparation has been undertaken. This chapter has provided useful tips to consider prior to the presentation, how to construct it, what to do during the presentation, and how to answer questions afterward, and, hopefully, it has provided all you need to succeed. Remember:

- Ensure that you have understood what is being asked of you.
- Planning and coordination make the process far less stressful.
- Pick a sensible slide template.
- Make the presentation content relevant and informative.
- Make backups.

- Rehearse as often as you can by actually speaking the presentation out loud – practice makes perfect!
- Time the presentation.
- Be adaptable and flexible toward changing circumstances on the day.
- Be yourself and be confident when presenting.
- Answer questions to the best of your ability.
- Take any constructive criticism given onboard.
- Breathe a sigh of relief when it is all over.
- Congratulate yourself on a job well done!
- At the end of the day, it is only a presentation and not the be all and end all. If things go awry – don't beat yourself up.

26 Defending Research

In this chapter, you will learn about:

- Defending and justifying your choices.
- Making best use of your supervisory meetings.
- Preparing for the oral defence of your dissertation.
- Reflecting on your research to help you defending it.

Defending and justifying

A good skill to is being able to defend your research. Quite often, this relates to justifying the choices that you make throughout projects. This is important for several reasons:

- You must justify choices and be able to objectively select courses of action from an academic and practical perspective.
- Justifying your decision-making process provides your supervisor insight into your thought process and why you are undertaking your dissertation in a particular manner.
- You may have to defend your research and development decisions during an assessed presentation.
- Engaging in a reflective process when undertaking your dissertation fosters an iterative outlook to address feedback constructively.

You will probably find yourself having to clarify various choices and your decision-making process in some of the following contexts:

DOI: 10.4324/9781003054887-26

- Choice of dissertation topic and the rationale behind researching it.
- Elaborating on and identifying key issues in the literature review.
- Choice of research design, methodology, and methods.
- Interpreting research findings in the wider context and accentuating the significance of your conclusions.
- Reflecting on the dissertation process and whether you might have done anything differently.

Table 26.1 provides some examples of practical development areas you might have to justify. Give all these aspects prior significant thought and during the completion and review of your honours project specification form. Having early discussions and receiving feedback from your supervisor will help alleviate any concerns or doubts you might have in the choices you have made.

Table 26.1 Development considerations to justify

Practical and theoretical considerations	Issues to reflect upon
Use of game engine	• Customisability of engine? • Which is best suited towards developing 2D, 2.5D or 3D games? • Which language? – C# or C++? • Built-in blueprint scripting system versus coding manually? • Ease of use of UI? • Ease of importing objects (e.g., Maya)?
Use of web development framework (e.g., Server-side vs Client-side)	• Server-side or client-side? • Server-side: e.g., Ruby on Rails, ExpressJS, Laravel, Django. • Client-side: e.g., ReactJS, Vue.js, Angular, Ember. • What web development languages am I most accomplished in using? (e.g., PHP, Python). • Which framework for prototyping and rapid development? • Is the development framework open source? • Security and protection features?
GDLC/SDLC	• Will software undergo iterative revisions? • Do you have a clear vision of what you want to develop? (i.e., less subject to change).

(*Continued*)

Table 26.1 (Continued)

Practical and theoretical considerations	Issues to reflect upon
Testing methodologies (e.g., Functional vs. Non-Functional testing)	• Will your development involve client interaction? • Is development going to be time consuming? • Will the project be complicated? • Consistent prototyping to minimise risk? • Performing software testing in conjunction with your development methodology? • How will you conduct acceptance testing? • Performance testing? (e.g., load testing, stress testing). • Security testing? For an app or website- (e.g., integrity, authentication, confidentiality). • Compatibility testing? • Showing test results? Functional testing? (e.g., via a test log).

Making best use of your supervisory meetings

Supervisory meetings could be as often as you require them, but we suggest weekly, fortnightly, or monthly to keep driving you forward. One of the first things you will have to defend to your supervisor is your area of research, your research topic, and to substantiate the reason for engaging in it. This also includes technical specifics of what you intend to implement, your chosen research design, such as SSDLC or GDLC.

The supervisory relationship

If you have a good relationship with your project supervisor, this will help. Maximise meetings with your supervisor and turn up with something to defend! This promotes discussion, growth, and progress. General discussion areas may include:

• Defining and pinpointing your research area.
• Progress related to your literature review.
• The ethical application review process.
• Software or game development implementation platform and issues.
• Selection of research methodology and methods.
• How to test and evaluate what you have developed.
• Presenting your results.

It is understandable at times that you might feel under pressure having to consistently deliver and to always have something to be reviewed by your supervisor, but this is good in terms of keeping the momentum and it is essential for your growth. Throughout your dissertation, it is normal for things to go awry. You may have to change software or deal with incompatibility issues. Predicaments can arise, but how you deal with them is important. Inform your supervisor and provide an honest appraisal of every situation. Your supervisor will use their personal appraisal of you to possibly provide a project management mark, so you want to appear hardworking, focused, honest, and professional. The supervisor will probably be one of the best people to give you a reference for a job as well – so bear this in mind.

Prepare for supervisory meetings

Answering questions, defending research, and being adaptive is all dependent on preparation and adaptability. Being communicative and transparent with your supervisor about progress is the way forward. Prior to a meeting, it is a good approach to send them work you have completed for discussion. This might be excerpts of your dissertation, such as the literature review. This can include software prototypes or game development recordings for demonstration. If it is a website, you can send a copy of the URL, or if a mobile app, you could even run through the app by way of demonstration at the meeting. It is very common for our students to showcase work on LinkedIn, and we follow them to comment on progress.

Addressing questions from your supervisor

Responding to questions from your supervisor can at times prove challenging, and this is perfectly normal as they are supposed to challenge you. It is a cognitive apprenticeship, a mentor–student relationship where they are attempting to make you better and make you more autonomous. Listen to and try to digest what you are being asked and analyse the advice. Sometimes a lot of the questions will primarily be for the purposes of clarity. Here are some useful tips regarding how to respond to questions from your project supervisor.

Tip 1: Take time to carefully listen to what you you supervisor is asking you and seek clarity if you do not understand a specific question.
Tip 2: Do not rush your answer but think carefully before responding to ensure you are providing the relevant information required.
Tip 3: Do not be defensive or aggressive in any way when responding to a question posed by your supervisor. Remember that you are being challenged academically and that your supervisor is there to help you.

Tip 4: If your mind goes blank on a particular question then do not panic! Your supervisor is there to jog your memory and assist you. You are not being interrogated, though it may seem like this at the time. Just confess that you do not know.

Tip 5: Try and be as informative as you can. The more information and detail that you can provide to your supervisor the more they will be able to assist you.

Tip 6: Remember you decide whether you wish to take your supervisors advise as it is your dissertation and project.

Reflection and defending your research

In the context of defending research and addressing questions, it is good practice to adhere to the process of reflection, which is a key graduate attribute. There are several definitions that relate to the concept of reflection. Kennison and Misselwitz (2002, p. 239) state that reflection can be described as: *"the purposeful contemplation of thoughts, feelings, and happenings that pertain to recent experiences."* This means that during your time at university, you should reflect on your own continued personal and professional development. This also relates to the academic journey undertaken throughout the honour's dissertation.

Defending your research entails being able to reflect upon it, adjust your approach toward problems, modify your behaviour, and act on what you have learned. For example, when developing a piece of software, such as an app, website, or game, you need to reflect on the tasks you have undertaken regarding the implementation.

Useful reflective tips

Here are some useful tips towards reflecting upon the progress of your research:

Tip 1: Reflect upon all possible options and choices. Act upon the decisions you have made and justify them in your dissertation and to your project supervisor.

Tip 2: Undertake the process of critical self-reflection and reflect upon tasks while you are performing them. Reflecting upon personal experience is useful to discuss with your supervisor.

Tip 3: A useful point to remember is to document your practical development from the commencement of the design and implementation of your software. This provides an audit trail that you can present.

Tip 4: Be able to demonstrate the knowledge you have gained toward problems or issues you have solved. You can show this to your project supervisor when you are having your meetings.

Tip 5: Undergoing the process of reflection from an early stage allows you to revaluate your experiences pertaining to actions you have undertaken during the dissertation process.

Summary

This chapter has provided an overview of the importance of being able to defend your research. There are certain times that you will have to do this during your dissertation. The main scenario will be when you are being asked questions by your supervisor about the work you have performed. Being able to justify the choices and decisions you have made throughout your dissertation process will help you improve your communication skills.

- One excellent skill you can hone during the dissertation is to be able to defend and justify your research.
- It is important that you can defend the decisions you have made and to illustrate that you have learnt from your experiences.
- The dissertation should be viewed as a reflective process whereby you are continuously forming opinions and judgments on the decisions you have made, their outcomes, and the best approaches on how to move your project forward.
- Dialogue with your supervisor is key to progress from the commencement of your dissertation towards the final submission process.
- The key to defending your research in your dissertation is to logically justify everything you do.

Reference

Kennison, M.M. and Misselwitz, S. (2002) 'Evaluating reflective writing for appropriateness, fairness, and consistency', *Nursing Education Perspectives*, 23(5), pp. 238–242.

27 Summary

This aim of this book is to provide an essential guide to writing a successful dissertation in games development and computer science-related disciplines, taking into account general dissertation writing but also the aspects that are discipline specific. We want to reaffirm that with dedication, hard work, and this book as a guide, this can be an enjoyable, rewarding process. We wrote this book to give you every advantage by providing the ultimate source of ideas, examples, and essential tips from real dissertations we have either supervised or written ourselves. A number of crucial tips are located throughout this book located in each chapter.

We now present a summation of the key points made in relation to:

- Getting started and thinking about your research topic.
- Time management, planning, and how to be organised.
- Balancing practical elements alongside the written part of your dissertation.
- Structuring and presenting your dissertation.
- General tips and advice about the dissertation process in general.

Getting started!

The key to success for any piece of university coursework is to start early, as soon as possible. Do your background research, identify a topic that you are interested in and passionate about, and start to think about how you study and apply it in a dissertation. Think about topics that have been addressed during your programme. Think also about employability. For example, you could choose a topic that currently has direct relevance to the games, web, and mobile or software industry. Discuss your ideas early with staff in your department. You might also want to undertake a research area affiliated with a staff member in your

DOI: 10.4324/9781003054887-27

department that might lead to further post-graduate study. Inquire about supervision as early as you can, bearing in mind that supervisors can fill up their allocation quickly.

Engage in the literature

You should engage with the literature at an early stage and throughout the process, ensuring that you can allocate, review, and interpret the relevant academic sources to inform your research design. This informs your research questions, research design, methodology, and methods. You will rely on the literature to write up the background section of your dissertation. Displaying your knowledge about your subject area and illustrating that you have understood the key academic arguments in your research area are central to producing a good literature review.

Completing your project specification/proposal

Try and get a proposal compiled and get your supervisor's feedback as soon as possible because, inevitably, your project will undergo several revisions and modifications before being approved. Give it due attention and try to present the project in a logical and comprehensible manner. Consider the feasibility and practicalities of what you want to do achieve in terms of time. So be conscious and realistic about what you can achieve during the academic year.

All things ethical

If your study involves dealing with human participants, you will need to apply for ethical approval through your school's ethics committee. It is worth doing this as soon as you have formulated a plan to evaluate any software or a game you develop. Completing an ethics form is a great step for consolidating your project.

Keep in touch with your supervisor

Establishing a firm mode of communication with your project supervisor is important. This process is central for keeping your dissertation on track and for receiving iterative feedback throughout the duration of the study. Updating your supervisor on progress, seeking clarification regarding matters you are unsure of, and sending drafts of work can ensure that your progress remains steady and on course.

Organisation, time management, and planning

Being organised and focused is fundamental to making the whole process easier. Forward planning, knowing what stage you are at, staying on top of what you still have to complete and when. Project management, in addition to the concept of version control, is core to helping with this process. Keeping your work accessible, up to date, and securely backed up so that you do not lose any valuable work is a sensible course of action.

Getting the balance right

Balancing your workload during your final year at university is challenging. We recommend giving each assessment the appropriate amount of proportionate time. The dissertation in our institution is worth double the marks over the entire year – so attempt to dedicate at least 8 to 10 hours on each module per week. At the very least, chip away at a little bit of each assessment or the dissertation per day.

Write in stages – Perseverance is key

We encourage you to never give up – keep going! Write up your dissertation in stages and at the times most suitable for you, when you are feeling most productive. This is not the year to be lax! Do not let your writing languish, and try to write the dissertation in sections. Procrastination will only have a detrimental affect on your overall dissertation. No matter how much you write per day, writing something is better than not doing anything at all.

Table 27.1 shows our final dissertation questions checklist to make sure you have not missed any details.

Draft, revise, and proofread

Writing a dissertation is an iterative process. Working regularly and constructively with your project supervisor will mean several that drafts of the dissertation will be required based on the constructive feedback you receive. Take time to address revisions and respect that the revision process takes some thought. Always try to start revisions as soon as possible, but try not to rush them. Revising and proofreading takes time, and you need to ensure that you are consistent with formatting and the layout. Examples of inconsistencies could include the font and size of your text, your use of headings and subheadings, your style for citations, references, and appendices. Consistency and layout are important in

Table 27.1 Final checklist

Task	TICK BOX
Do you have a subject that interests you?	
Do you have a supervisor and moderator?	
Have you written a project proposal/specification?	
Have you performed a feasibility study?	
Do you have a problem to address? Do you have a solution to address it?	
Have you formulated an overall project plan, such as a Gantt chart?	
Do you know what kind of researcher you are? What is your ontological, epistemological, and methodological stance? Are you a qualitative, quantitative, or mixed-methods researcher?	
Do you have research questions? What are is your methodology for answering them? What methods are you going to use?	
What kind of literature review are you going to perform? Have you contacted your subject librarian? Do you have access to electronic journals?	
Does you research involved participants? Have you applied for and gotten ethical approval?	
Do you have a SDLC or GDLC?	
What SML are you going to for designing you system/game?	
Have you produced a requirements specification, pseudocode? GDD?	
Have you considered an implementation language, games engine version control? Do you need a TDD?	
Have you documented the implementation in relation to basic and advanced functionality, screenshots, or a demonstration?	
What particular software or games testing technique are you going to use? Have you considered GUR/UX? Are you documenting play testing? Is it internal, external? Do you have a test plan or test log for functional testing?	

(*Continued*)

Table 27.1 (Continued)

Task	TICK BOX
Are you performing an evaluation? Is it formative, summative, or both? What is the procedure? Who are the participants, and what is the sampling strategy? What are the instruments? What are the results?	
Are you performing descriptive or inferential statistical analysis? Will it be parametric or non-parametric? What techniques are you using?	
Do you need a discussion chapter?	
What are your conclusions, recommendations, and future directions?	
Are all of your references present and in the correct format?	
Is the dissertation consistent in terms of font, structure, and presentation? Are there too many quotes? Do you have a cover, table of contents, mind map, and acknowledgments sections?	
Have you proofread the dissertation?	
Do you have any appendices and, if so, are they mentioned within the dissertation and can be mapped?	

terms of how your dissertation is presented. When reviewing your dissertation in years to come, or when showcasing it to a potential employer, you want to show off something you are proud of.

Autonomous learning

View this experiences as being a learning journey that promotes autonomous learning. It is also important to remember that undertaking it is both an individual process and a collaborative one with your project supervisor. Being able to make decisions using your own judgment about how your honours project should proceed is important. These skill sets will stand you in good stead in the future for employability or undertaking further study.

What happens if things go wrong?

If things start to go wrong, you fall behind, or life gets in the way, the single greatest piece of advice we can give is tell your supervisor. They can offer everything from a helpful ear, by listening to you vent about how pressured you are, to valuable life advice, by suggesting the best courses of action.

Final piece of advice

Appreciate the dissertation experience and enjoy it! No matter how hard it seems, it is nothing when entering the world of work! Regardless of whatever ups and downs you might have, the main thing is to enjoy what you are researching, developing, and evaluating. We thoroughly believe that if you remain focused, plan, and keep the pressure on the wound, that it will be a transformational, experiential, learning process, giving birth to a fully autonomous individual who can accomplish anything they set their mind to accomplishing. We have written this book to help guide you through the process, and we wish you the absolute best of luck.

Index

Note: Page numbers in **Bold** refer to tables; and page numbers in *italics* refer to figures